TALES
OF
TRAILS

Finding Game After the Shot

TIM L. LEWIS

PAGE PUBLISHING, INC.
Conneaut Lake, PA

First originally published by Page Publishing 2020

ISBN 978-1-64701-113-0 (pbk)
ISBN 978-1-64701-114-7 (digital)

Printed in the United States of America

To Mack Mosier—a thorough sportsman,
a true friend, and a noble human being.

CONTENTS

INTRODUCTION

BLOOD, TYPICALLY, IS NOT CONSIDERED pretty. In fact, maybe only a hunter searching for stricken game can see beauty in a thick, red trail, but to us, it is indeed an agreeable sight for it signifies a great chance we will find the animal and also that its death was fast. In this case, however, there was no heavy trail, but after all the effort and travail invested, even the tiny crimson droplet gleaming on a grass blade looked indescribably beautiful for it gave indisputable proof that the deer had passed this way. Mosquitoes kept me company as I bent low and played the flashlight beam ahead.

The mosquitoes had been persistent with their attentiveness earlier in the evening when the doe approached. My stand was not ten feet above the ground, and movement to whisk them away would definitely have alerted her as she sniffed for acorns. Sometimes fate or luck seems to bedevil a hunter. For weeks, no deer had ventured into bow range, and now a doe had been around me for forty minutes as near as eight yards and as distant as thirty yet never offered a shot opportunity with which I felt confident. The angle was wrong, or grapevines, palmetto fronds, or oak trunks interfered. The insect horde whined (and dined) enthusiastically as I tried to remain statuesque. Light began to dwindle beneath the forest canopy, and she fed southward.

When she was forty or more yards off, three trunks of massive live oaks lined up, and it seemed if I could climb from the stand undetected, the big trees would offer me cover for a stalk. There was no wind, so silence would be necessary. Rain in the form of a sprinkle had earlier moistened the ground. Hopefully, the damp earth would allow quiet footing. Her steps led her behind the furthest oak. I slipped down and wiggled forward in a low squat toward the big roots of the closest forest giant. Each movement along the swampwood floor sent up reinforcing clouds of mosquitoes. These insects were plaguing the doe as well and she was continually jerking her head up, shaking it and her ears, and scratching with her hooves. I had almost, but not quite, reached the cover of the oak when the ground became crunchy. The dense foliage of the live oak had protected the under-lying dead and dried leaves from the light rain, and in the prevail-ing stillness, the sound seemed terribly loud. The doe immediately looked toward me. I froze in the open. The tree trunk and its shel-tering shadows were so near. Two small steps or three at most were all I lacked. She resumed scratching and feeding. Slowly sliding my foot under the leaves, I endeavored to get behind the trunk, but this latest rustle aroused more concern from the doe. After a sharp stare, she strode northwestward. Her action actually brought her closer to me although, no doubt, she was attempting to get downwind. When she was broadside at twenty yards, I drew my longbow, Simplicity, as slowly and surreptitiously as possible, held the tight string until the shot felt right, and let the arrow drive forth. She jumped, but whether it was with the sound of the bow or the striking of the arrow I could not tell. If it was early, the arrow could have struck anywhere. She looped away and then fell twenty yards from where she had been and rolled about, issuing a *rabble-rabble-rabble-rabble* noise.

I rejoiced at having no trail to sort out but barely had the thought registered when she was up and running east out into more open terrain. The canopy of the swampwoods blocks light even at midday, so with evening's arrival, it was dusky and dim. Brushing mosquitoes from my face, arms, and back, I strode to the place she rolled about, but saw no blood either from lack of it or lack of light. I hurried to where it appeared she left the woods, not much over forty-five yards away. Here it was brighter. There was a green sward covered with grasses about fourteen inches high, glistening with the earlier rain, that extended from a shallow pond. Bent stems indicated something had crossed to the east. Was it the doe? Or only a hog? Or a cow? Away from the pond, the earth was firm and the grass thick enough to obscure tracks. Bent grasses showed up at intervals to the east, and one was slowly springing back upright. It must be the doe's trail. No blood was visible. The grasses were shorter on this higher ground that held scattered myrtle as well, and there were no obvious indications of her passage. I checked the pond's edge for tracks in the surrounding mud or bubbles or splashes in the water without success. Going back to the last bent grass, I investigated the fence line and the dirt road beyond it for tracks imprinted after the rain. There were none. Daylight was fading. Returning to my pack, left in the stand, I pulled out a flashlight and checked the area again where she had rolled around, hoping to get an idea of the nature of the wound. The only sign was scattered leaves; no blood, no arrow. Where she busted out of the woods, a sapling displayed a smear of blood. I once again followed the grasses bent from her, and now my, passage. Where the taller grass ended, no clue to her trail could be discerned. I had ruled out the pond and the road, so she must have turned north or south. The last of the bent stems hinted at the northerly choice, and so I searched and scanned. Finally, the gleaming spot of blood confirmed the trail, and then, scant yards ahead was an incongruously large area eighteen inches long and ten inches wide where every blade of grass shimmered with water diluted blood. After finding so little it was peculiar to see so much, but perhaps she had stood there a while. This was sixty yards from the last bent stems.

The trouble was now the pasture was more overgrown with myrtle and briars, and ramifying pathways laced through them in all directions and many times the paths interconnected. A half an hour's exploration down all the channels continuing to any degree north uncovered no corroborating sign. For some reason, I explored one trail that led west back toward the creek bottom woods for over fifty yards despite no encouraging indications. Once in the woods, spots of blood gave evidence she had run this way, and after eight yards, the blood sign blossomed into the ideal trail for which I had earlier yearned, one that could be followed by flashlight with ease at a normal, upright walk.

It is very puzzling how a trail metamorphoses from nearly unde-cipherable to prominent in a matter of yards. Questions reverberated in my head. Had the wet grass so thoroughly erased the trail? Had the doe's pace slowed dramatically to allow more blood to escape? Had something jostled or moved the arrow? Had the wound been blocked and suddenly burst open?

She lay, nearly black with mosquitoes (although I'm unsure how much blood they can drain from expired animals, they are certainly not at all restrained in their efforts), about eighty yards from where she reentered the woods. The arrow went through her chest, the nock end had broken at the fletchings, and the break was just inside her right shoulder. The broadhead, a two blade, protruded more than a foot on the opposite side. Relief flooded over me for only minutes before it seemed there was little to no hope of finding her. Between the hours spent, the persistent mosquitoes, and the dearth of sign, I had almost given up and had investigated the westward course more from psychological compulsion than from any belief or hope.

This account of a trail was included in the introduction because it has many factors into which this book delves: abrupt turns, changes of pace, poor tracking terrain, changes in blood flow, rain and much more. Over my many decades of bowhunting, between game I've arrowed and animals my friends and acquaintances have shot, I've participated in over 1,400 blood trails. The relatively few cited here were chosen to illustrate certain tendencies, terrains, or difficulties discussed herein. One point should be brought to the forefront concerning these trails. Out of the total number, almost all the game fell within sight or at the end of a prominent and easy blood trail with the animal living only a few seconds. However, the trails hunters may desire more information about are not these simple ones but, rather, the exceptional ones where the animal traveled further or survived longer. Therefore, a disproportional number of the examples are of that nature, so a reader not recognizing this fact may mistakenly conclude that hunting routinely results in something other than a speedy death. Also keep in mind, that hunters would not seek my help on straightforward trails. There are easily scores and scores of simple trails for every puzzling one I am asked to lend assistance. Hence, quick, clean kills outnumber the ones that color the pages of this book by an incredible margin.

Finding wounded game is important for many reasons. First and foremost, nobody wishes an animal to suffer nor for it to go to waste. Universally, hunters seem to naturally shoulder the task of doing their utmost to recover any game they have shot. The animal deserves that effort, and in truth, the hunter deserves it as well, for the loss of targeted game weighs heavily upon one and is not easily forgotten.

Howard Hill coined the term "hunting the hard way" to describe hunting with archery gear, and it is very apt because of the multiple aspects a bow hunter must master to be successful consistently. Firstly, proficiency with the gear itself is required. This not only means accurate delivery of the arrow to the target but also being able to draw undetected and from sometimes awkward positions. Secondly, immense knowledge of the game animal and its habits and habitat is necessary to stalk or ambush the prey from the short distances that bows are lethal. Lastly, since arrows seldom drop game in its tracks, the bow hunter must be able to find the stricken animal. This book gives insight into this third aspect.

As an archer, I think in bow hunting terms, but rifle, pistol, and shotgun hunters benefit from expertise in tracking as well. Often, when game doesn't go down with the shot, a bullet may produce a scanty and difficult trail.

It is my hope that instead of just a "How to" book, the inclusion in this volume of actual accounts of hunts and blood trails will arm hunters with more information regarding tracking and, at the same time, provide some interesting reading. With that in mind, let me slip one more trail into this introduction. I'll call it "The Mystery Trail":

My first bowhunting trip to Colorado came in 1992 and western hunting instantly took hold of my heart and, I believe, the hearts of my companions and friends. The reader can imagine we were true novices when he or she learns we hailed from a spot where a place with an elevation thirty-five feet above sea level earned the name High Point! I was struck with the clear, clean, cool air; the vast spaciousness between mountains and ridges; the ridges themselves with the green, gold, and white of aspens; the green, rust, and garnet of oaks; the pale shades of sage; and the tones of rugged earth and rock. It filled one's soul with a sense of both beauty and awe. Our days were spent roaming freely among the ridge fingers, breathing in the scent of sage and mountain freshness, and our evenings gave time for sharing adventures and sharpening broadheads in a log cabin more than a hundred years old. The mountains abounded with game, and each day we saw mule deer and elk, jackrabbits and cottontails, porcupines, grouse, ducks, squirrels, and chipmunks. A few times we saw coyotes, beaver, weasels, snowshoe hare, magpies, raccoons, and mountain lions. The wildlife was abundant and the vision unimpeded!

Our very first morning, with no scouting and little knowledge, we elected to hunt the mountain ridges that were east of the little roadway that ran to the old cabin. My friends dropped me a good bit to the north, the downhill portion of the main ridge, to allow me to venture uphill into the wind. They planned to start south of the ranch house and work east, swinging north as the thermals reversed. Before the sun was visible, its light probed the mountainsides. The strange (to me) chirps of elk, more birdlike than what I expected from big mammals, echoed and answered each other through the canyons. These, combined with the loud and mysterious ringing of bugling bulls, the sharp fragrance of sage, the partially risen sun illuminating the sheer side of Thornberg in a way that revealed its colorful layers and yet left its cracks and fissures dark, unknown shadows, served to inspire me with a sense of the wildness of this land, little changed from when Thornberg himself was beset by the Utes. I moved gradually southward, seeing cow elk and mule deer does, chirping with a diaphragm call I picked up in Steamboat Springs and happy to have a chance to hear and mimic them. I managed to spook a few mule deer does despite my intentions, and again my greenness will be exposed by my delight at the way the mule deer sprang away, totally unlike the long, fast, graceful leaps of a whitetail. The stotting of these deer struck me (who had never before witnessed it) like deer bouncing off with pogo sticks, and I almost wanted to say "Boing, boing, boing!" as they bounced along. By the time lunch hour approached, I had seen three groups of elk and countless mule deer and passed up close shots at both cows and does.

Since my buddies had planned to wend their way in my direction, when I stumbled across a blood trail twenty minutes before our rendezvous time, I decided to follow it with the thought that I would find them at the end or that they would be surprised mightily to find me when they caught up! How exciting! One of them had arrowed something our very first morning! It was easy to determine the direction of travel from the splatters of blood. The trail was long yet decipherable without travail on the arid and rocky surfaces. It certainly wasn't very old. It led down, after maybe four hundred yards, to a damper area with grass over head high which must have grown from a pond during wetter times. The blood sign became much harder to find and harder to read. I heard a vehicle and pushed out of the tall grass to see our truck up on the roadway. I beckoned to them and yelled that their game was down this way, but they responded by looking perplexed so I trudged up to the vehicle and learned they had launched no arrows. Nonetheless, my friends were as curious as me, and we clambered back down and resumed the trail. It only continued another forty yards to a fallen mule deer doe. We were staying on a friend's ranch and asked the ranch manager to report the doe to the game warden, who felt a hunter in the national forest must have killed it. We never heard if they found the hunter who lost it, but the mystery trail was our introduction to Colorado, and twenty years later, blood trailing on the exact same slope, I found a perfect stone arrowhead—proof of people pursuing game in the region with bow and arrow more than a century before!

CHAPTER 1

How Wounds Kill

BEFORE TACKLING TRAILING TECHNIQUES, IT may be best to cover how wounds kill as an understanding of this information affects the time when trailing should commence and also the type of trail to expect. In the end, death is brought about by brain damage caused by either direct physical injury to the brain or cerebral hypoxia, a diminution in oxygen reaching the brain tissue to the point the brain cannot function or survive. This reduction or cessation of oxygen delivery to the brain in turn is caused by loss of blood, loss of available blood, inability of the lungs to oxygenate the blood, or loss of blood pressure. Most often, more than one these four factors are involved. Even with gutshots, death itself can be traced to diminished oxygen reaching the brain.

A bullet or broadhead to the brain is an instantaneous, painless death that necessitates no trailing. The disadvantage to the shot is that the brain is small in comparison to the total head size, and a shot that misses the brain will likely not bring about a fast death nor result in recovered game for it is unlikely to cause enough hemorrhage to prove fatal. The largest portion of the head in game animals is devoted to the eating apparatus and damage to the jaw, jaw muscles, or tongue can render eating difficult or impossible and starvation is a possible sequela. Most sportsmen are so keenly aware of this terrible possibility that the shot is seldom taken unless it is point blank. The skull is hard too and designed to protect the brain. Shots not exactly perpendicular to the bone can ricochet. I've heard of a case with a human when a bullet careened off the frontal bone of the forehead and yet was entrapped by the scalp so it continued around to the back of the head before exiting, looking as though it passed completely through the brain but actually never penetrating the skull. One example of the short trail that ensues when a shot does reach the brain is a boar hog I arrowed from a few feet that dropped on the spot without a flinch or even a kick of his legs. I could not pull the two bladed broadhead from his head, so even today, it rattles around when someone picks up the cleaned skull from my shelf.

Most shots, from firearms or bows, are intended for the chest area. This area, medically termed the mediastinum, is the cavity enclosed by the ribs and bordered toward the abdomen by the diaphragm. The contents are the lungs, the heart, portions of the esophagus and trachea, the pulmonary arteries and veins, the vena cava, the aortic arch, and portions of the aorta, jugular vein, subclavian veins and arteries, and carotid arteries. The names of the blood vessels are less important than the fact that they convey great volumes of blood and convey blood to critical places.

A wound through both lungs results in substantial blood loss and a reduction in the lungs' ability to supply oxygen to the blood. The blood on a trail would be bright and frothy. How much blood escapes the body to be found by a tracker depends on the entrance and exit wounds. Is there an exit wound? How high on the body are the wounds? (The higher they are, the more blood may pool in the chest cavity rather than decorate the trail.) Are the wounds patent or obstructed by the arrow, skin, or other tissue? Holes through the chest walls compromise the diaphragm's ability to suck air into the trachea to inflate the lungs. The bigger and wider open the wound channels, the more of the diaphragm's efforts to ventilate the lungs will be in vain.

Animals are not invariably broadside when a hunter chooses to shoot. At quartering away or quartering to angles, there is a high probability that the diaphragm will be damaged as well as one or both lungs. The damage to a single lung will cause significant hemorrhage and diminished oxygenation of the blood but may or may not prove fatal. The diaphragm provides the majority by far of the ventilation of the lungs and significant damage to it will drastically reduce the intake of air into the lungs. In cases when only one lung is struck, the amount of trauma to the diaphragm may determine how quickly death ensues.

The lungs are designed for maximum gas exchange between the blood and the inhaled air. Basically, they are composed of miniature balloon-like structures walled entirely by tiny, nearly transparent blood vessels. This creates an astronomical amount of surface area for gas exchange. The presence of anything other than air spaces and thin-walled blood vessels would only interfere with and diminish the exchange of gases, so there is nothing else. The interesting outcome of this absolute specialization of lung tissue is that it allows no room for nervous tissue. There are no nerves in the lungs. Obviously, the skin and muscles around the chest do have nerves, but the lungs themselves cannot feel pain. Many hunters have witnessed deer hit only through the lungs that seemed but little fazed. I've marveled at it many times but will restrict examples included here to three classic incidences each with a correspondingly short blood trail.

Mack was bowhunting with his mother in a stand next to him operating a video camera. The footage is fascinating: Mack's arrow zips through a buck at very close range with the only obvious result a little side hop. "I think you missed him," Cecile's voice whispers. (Her view was limited by the camera's viewfinder.) The buck wanders forward maybe seven steps, and then a smacking sound is heard, like a loud kiss on the back of a hand. Blood had been draining out before, but coinciding with the noise, blood floods straight down. The buck, which had showed no signs of distress up to this point, falls, thrashes momentarily, and is dead. The nonchalant behavior of the deer up until his brain responded to the lack of oxygen leaves no doubt that he was not in pain or even alarmed.

Hunting from a stand in a low oak while a squirrel barked at me from a yard or two off, I was amazed to see a doe and button buck approach unconcernedly and begin nosing for acorns. I drew my bow Deer Bane. The arrow flew and slipped through the doe's chest. She jumped a few yards and stood over a shallow creek and looked about.

Nocking another arrow, I considered a second shot since she seemed perfectly natural and unwounded, but then I noticed water rippling out in tiny circles below her from rapidly draining blood. After a moment or two, she walked a yard toward me to the ground beyond the water's edge and sank into a bedded position. Her death seemed peaceful and painless. Right at the end, her legs thrashed a little, but by then, her eyes were already hazy and unfocused. The button buck noticed nothing unusual in her behavior and continued to feed.

Below two beaver ponds, a draw emptied into a thin part of a canyon, and amid a smattering of aspens, I waited with my old longbow Simplicity. An elk cow and calf had walked by at eight yards traversing the draw without noting my still form. My back rested against the smooth bole of an aspen, and the white trunks of others with their vivid marks of black and grey contrasted strangely with the lush green of the canyon sides. A bull with good spread and massive brow tines appeared and quietly made his way down the canyon bottom, a course, if he maintained it, that would bring him past me at less than fifteen yards. His plans were different however, and he climbed the opposite slope and began browsing sixty yards distant. With my heart thumping, I stole from trunk to trunk and closed the distance to a reasonable bowshot and drew Simplicity. With an older, slow longbow and very weighty arrows, the trajectory was exaggerated and drawn out, almost as if happening in slow motion. I watched with happy amazement as the arrow that initially looked way too high dropped down and drove deeply into the bull's chest exactly where I had envisioned. The big elk took two hops down the canyon, actually toward me, and turned about to look quizzically back at the place he had been. I began to pull another arrow from my quiver because he was very close now, and also elk can be tough, strong, and incredibly tenacious. He looked calmly at the slope for a few seconds, but before I could draw, his breathing became labored and he tried to leap. His fore hooves barely lifted off the ground, and he collapsed on the spot. I approached with Simplicity ready, but there was no breathing, no movement. He was dead. Maybe twenty-five or thirty-five seconds had passed since the twang of my bow.

Other than his first reaction, he betrayed no sign of pain or even of distress until his breathing failed in the last few seconds.

I've witnessed many more instances that manifested the lack of nervous tissue in the lungs, but these three should suffice as examples. A bow hunter once told me of something I have not ever witnessed. After he double-lunged a doe, she resumed feeding before simply sinking to the ground. This seemed surprising to me, but I had never been misled by this man, and I, myself, over the years have seen a few things that would have aroused my skepticism if someone else related them to me.

A wound through the heart or the great blood vessels that join it will damage the lungs as well. The blood pressure in these vessels can be so great that, providing the wound channel remains patent, blood will spurt mightily from these injuries. The blood is bright but not frothy, although some lung blood may easily be seen on the trail as well. A chest wound that evidences an instantaneous and pronounced jet of blood confirms this type of hit and promises the likelihood of a simple trail. The explosion of blood corresponding with the hit is so fast it almost seems like a red ricochet. An archer, straining to see the arrow's hit, may even be startled by the jet of blood suddenly shooting back his way. Injuries of this kind result in a loss of blood volume, a loss of blood pressure (since either the damaged heart cannot pump well or the damaged vessels cannot contain the pressure), and likely a decrease in the lung's ability to oxygenate the blood. Death ensues quickly. Unlike the lungs, the heart is heavily innervated, so any damage to the heart causes both pain and tremendous adrenaline release. Many times, heart-struck deer run much further than lung only struck deer for this reason. Even though the animal likely survives a shorter time, it is compelled to greater speed and exertion. As a young hunter, I was astonished when a friend cleaned a deer he had tracked over two hundred yards. His 30.06 had ruptured the heart, and to me, it seemed mind-boggling that the buck could have run a tenth that distance! I mentioned deer in this regard because hogs are different. Maybe it is because hogs cannot achieve anywhere near the speed of a deer, but usually heart-shot hogs fall quite close at hand. Although I've taken ten elk with a bow, it is nowhere near a high enough number to truly compare how far heart shot elk run compared to lung only elk. My guess is that it is similar to whitetails. I would expect the same from bear as they can be pretty fast and from reading *Alaska Bear Tales*. Denis Lyell hunted in Africa before World War I and in his writings made mention of heart-struck elephant running further than double lunged elephant: "When hit in the heart, I have seen an elephant fall immediately, though the usual action is a rush forward for any distance up to a mile according to the section of the heart struck." He goes on to describe lung wounds, "With a shot in one lung he may get clean away and lost, but when he has got the bullet through both lungs he will usually stop and die within half a mile."

Whitetail hunter and writer Archibald Rutledge remarked many times about the distance heart struck deer can run. Here is one quote: "I must add that when the stag was dressed we found that one of the three buckshots that struck him had passed straight through his heart. Yet he had run nearly a quarter of a mile at top speed without a hesitation or blunder. The vitality of wild game is a thing almost incredible."

An account of a whitetail struck in the heart by an arrow demonstrates the impetus imparted by heart damage: My hopes for a buck were high so when a doe presented eating acorns, I merely clicked exposures on my camera. After feeding several minutes under the oaks, she turned and headed west under my stand. Deer were moving, and her presence should quell any suspicions bucks might harbor, but now, with a couple more steps, she would be both downwind of me and on my approach trail. Her alarm would have just the opposite effect, so I set the camera down and picked up Mellifluwood, my longbow. It drew silkily, and its limbs sprang forward eagerly issuing the arrow on its way! It happened quietly, the minute twang of the bow and string, a *slepp* as the missile slipped through her chest, and the incredibly rapid but noiseless race she made to the northwest. Nothing could have been disturbed, and she ran downwind. The arrow, driven into the ground, was brightly red. She ran and ran. I expected her to topple any second. By now, only glimpses of her were visible through the gallberries. I picked a couple of landmarks. Despite the remarkable rapidity of her flight, binoculars revealed good blood on the grass stems.

Against my hopes, no bucks (or any other deer at all) presented. The coyotes howled prettily about fifty minutes before dark. A little later, I climbed down and made my way to where I had last seen her, hoping to intercept the trail there. The grass was thigh high and the gallberries taller. I found no blood. The light slowly faded. I tried a flashlight with no better result. My attempt to save time had backfired, so I set my pack, bow, and stand down in the grass and trudged back to the stand site. The blood trail was good, but I always find trailing in grass tricky and even more so after dark. The trail proved not too difficult, but it was a slow process and even puzzling in a few spots. Eventually, I ended up at my pack! The trail went within one and a half feet of where I had deposited it, yet I had failed to notice any blood earlier. Unbelievably, that was only the halfway point. The shot was perfect; through the middle of the chest on her left and out the low portion of her chest on the right side due to my elevated position and her nearness. Even so, she managed to travel at least 180 yards. I don't believe she lived any longer than a normal deer shot through the chest but rather that she was just running that much faster. She had raced with a speed I've only witnessed a few times in whitetails, and whitetails are all fast!

The drag was a long and strenuous one even though she weighed only 88 lbs. When I cleaned her, I discovered the broadhead had sliced the ventricle of the heart. The cut was over two inches in length but did not extend through the heart wall. Because of the heavy supply of nerves to the heart, she was stimulated drastically into action, but in this case, the heart was not terribly structurally impaired, and the long trail resulted.

The following example gives more insight into heart shots and typical post-shot behavior and also demonstrates a non-heart shot, half-circle-style death run that is common and will be discussed later. One morning on the second to last weekend of deer season, I elected to sit deep in the swamp near some wild sweet orange trees. It had rained the night before and was now cloudy and cool, and the ground and its carpet of fallen leaves were wet enough to offer quiet footing. Even the eight hogs that passed by in the dimness of first light made almost no sound other than splashes in the creek and the occasional swish of a frond being pushed aside. This morning, I carried no spears, only my bow. With just a handful of hunts over the last two weekends of the season and two unfilled doe tags and a daughter who wanted a lot more jerky and some good backstrap steak, my goal was to harvest at least one deer. The hogs were tempting, but it was early, and I felt the chances for a deer were not slim. Sure enough, the hogs were only forty or so yards off and still in sight when the first doe stepped daintily and silently from below the cabbage palm fronds. Two more does joined her, and they sniffed under the orange trees for fallen fruit. I watched them, thankful I had passed on the hogs. Doubtless, a hit or miss would have spooked the hogs enough to spook the nearby deer.

All three deer were different in size with the largest at the back of the group but still quick to assert her dominance under each orange tree. Two fallen oranges were in sight under the tree nearest me, and probably more lay hidden beneath the palmetto fronds. One of them must have been tainted or rotten for the midsize mature doe, and young deer reached the tree first and sniffed the southernmost orange but did not eat it. The large doe stepped up brusquely and likewise sniffed it and showed no more interest. She cast about, found the other orange, and devoured it immediately. A shot presented with the large doe quartering away with her head low. I drew Bane Too and let loose an arrow which, despite the distance being only six or seven yards, flew over her back and struck the swamp earth loudly enough to cause all three deer to jump a few steps and look about anxiously. The largest doe made her jump at a diagonal to me and thereby ended up no further distant. She was still quartering away, and a cabbage palm frond drooped over her head and neck so she could not see me and also any sound of the release would be at least partially baffled. This time, I savored the strength of the limbs as I drew and focused without conscious effort on a small part of her hide. The arrow flew true. The doe leapt forward, ran a half circle with slow, weak bounds, and fell no more than thirty yards from the stand. The arrow, whole and straight, protruded skyward from the exit wound with only the nock end still in her. Even the fletchings were visible.

Happy with my good fortune—a second shot, a late season, rifle hunted doe taken with a bow, and the comfort of no worries about finding her, I decided to enjoy the swampwoods for a while. As everything that had transpired rewound through my mind, a doe approached from the northwest. With the possibility she may have been one of the other two deer that had vanished to the northeast, I grunted with my mouth softly. She stopped, turned, and ambled to an orange tree twenty yards west-northwest of my stand, and she began sniffing through the fronds below it. Again, with no conscious awareness of aiming, just a narrow and intense focus on the chest, I bent Bane Too deeply, panning with the walking deer, and the arrow darted forward on its deadly course. The doe bucked and took off, bucking twice more in the first twenty yards. She disappeared at top speed. Silence returned, and there was no doubt she was now dead. Every time I had seen that classic buck, my arrow had struck the heart or the great vessels attached to the heart.

I had filled my two tags plus Florida law allows only two deer in a day, turkey season had closed a week or two ago, and I had no desire to clean a hog in addition to the two deer already down, so I packed my camera and left the stand. The loud sounds of my second doe's death run would enable me to go directly to the creek finger's edge and cast for the trail there, but I was in no hurry and wanted to follow the trail from the beginning to maximize what I could learn from it, maybe to apply later if the trail fizzled or maybe to learn something that could be helpful on future trails. This trail started with great splashes of blood with each bound she had taken and soon became fairly continuous despite the saturated condition of the ground and leaf litter from the night long rain. Where palmettos grew in great patches, she pushed through and over the thickest with no attempt to take more open passages even when some were within a few feet to one side or the other. When the trail left the swampwoods and fringe, it remained easily followable even in the grassy patches between myrtles in the pasture. Some of the red swathes in the wet grass were two by three feet. The trail ran basically north, curving gradually to the east. With so much blood, it seemed I should find her any second, but a hundred and thirty yards passed before I reached her fallen form.

I would be able to get my truck quite close to her by driving west and crossing the creek strand at a narrow spot and then paralleling the creek back east. The other doe was a different proposition for even though she had fallen closer, getting her out would be more work. Readers of my other works know how I fashion backpacks from deer by skinning their legs and tying the opposite sides with opposite ends. It is a good way and the best if the hunter has a long ways to tote a deer, but it takes a bit of time. In this instance, I utilized Larry Koller's method. With my knife, I cut two eight-inch lengths from a cabbage palm frond stem and also cut slits like would be made to insert a gambrel through the skin of all four legs. The front hooves were then inserted into the slits of the rear legs, and I slipped the stem pieces into the slits in the front legs, thereby locking them in place. It was a very fast prep, and with a front leg on each of my shoulders, I carried the doe to the woods' edge. She weighed 97 lbs., and my arrow had double lunged her. With the bucking jumps and the long death race, it seemed likely the heart was hit on the second doe, and sure enough, the aorta and pulmonary arteries were sliced right at their mergence with the heart. She weighed 78 lbs.

Here is another heart shot trail: This particular year, the oak brush held lots of acorns, and on the last afternoon of our Colorado hunt, I slipped along the edges of some oak strands and clumps. Movement caught my eye, and binoculars revealed it was the flicker of a bedded deer's ear. With careful and quiet steps, I slowly closed the distance, thirty yards, twenty-five, twenty. Glassing during pauses between steps revealed at least three mule deer, all does. At fifteen yards, I had to squeeze between some sage clumps with a multitude of dead limbs extending from the base of each trunk and my foot dragged against one lightly. Despite how little noise it created, six eyes were instantly directed my way. The living part of the sage screened me. A long standoff did not diminish their vigilance in the least, so I began making soft eating noises and smacking my lips. The largest doe rose to her feet. She was broadside, and I stealthily drew Elanever and eased skyward a bit behind the sage. With my focus on a part of her chest and the broadhead touching my left forefinger, I released. The longbow's limbs sprang forward with nearly no sound, and just as quickly, the arrow zipped through her rib cage. The other deer departed without me glimpsing them, apparently rocketing directly from their beds under all the oak brush, but she raced downhill, the way she was facing when struck, her tail down and her body blurred with speed, looking more like a streaming bird skimming the ground than an animal coursing along it. She vanished over the next drop off of the ridge, probably ninety yards from me. My arrow was coated and dripping with blood, and I assumed she fell just over the ridge. This was not the case. The sage I worked down through held some blood sign, but below where she disappeared, I could find no more. My spirits were not daunted at all for I was positive she was nearby and the cover here was not terribly thick. Somehow, my eye was attracted to a brownish boulder another two hundred or more yards down the ridge near a tiny creek. It looked smooth and peculiar, so I paused to glass it and was astonished to discover the "boulder" was the doe. If I hadn't had the fortune to spot her by luck, I may never had found her for the idea of extending the search that far with a pass through double lung shot would never have occurred to me. I cleaned and quartered her and toted the meat to where I felt a truck could reach. The broadhead had passed through the heart explaining her speed and the distance covered. The same speed spread the blood thinly, making the trail less obvious than expected. By the way, my intention was to take any legal deer with this being our last evening. I encountered her within the first half hour of the hunt, and even after tracking and cleaning her, plenty of daylight remained, so I moseyed on along the ridge with an elk tag still in my pack. Within two hundred yards, I spied a very nice mule deer buck that allowed me a close approach so I shot it several times with my camera!

Damage to the spinal cord causes paralysis of the portions of the body more distant from the brain than the site of impact. The phrenic nerve, the nerve to the diaphragm, leaves the spinal cord in the cervical (neck) portion of the backbone so damage there could stop the breathing process and result in cerebral hypoxia and death.

Otherwise, a wound to the spinal cord may anchor an animal but is not fatal. The animal will be totally or partially immobilized, but unless there is also damage to a large blood vessel or lungs, it will not expire quickly and will need to be dispatched. Typically spinal shots make for no trail or a drag trail that can be readily followed.

Years ago, a friend shot a nice buck with his rifle as he was climbing his ladder stand. The buck, with a major hole through its chest fell right there, and my friend tied it to a tree and continued hunting for the next few hours of the morning. Back at camp, I saw the ideal chest shot and asked him why he tied it to a tree. He answered that he invariably tied dead deer because he had once dropped a buck with a shot through its body only to have it get up and lunge away after several minutes. African hunting literature abounds with similar cases where people have actually posed for pictures with "dead" game only to return later to find the animal gone! These are animals like elephant, rhino, hippo, and buffalo—too large and heavy to have been dragged away without a trail. Severe shock to the brain or spinal cord is the explanation. This results in a concussion of the nervous tissue, be it brain or spinal cord. If the skull is drastically jarred, the animal is basically "knocked out" and can regain consciousness. The body shot that drops game but only temporarily seems more mystifying but is still the consequence of the same phenomenon. A bullet smashes a vertebral fin or part of the body of the vertebra with enough force to jar the spinal cord but not enough to sever it and a temporary paralysis ensues. Arrows impacting vertebrae can likewise cause permanent or temporary paralysis.

Deer dropping from an arrow to the backbone is not an unusual thing, but twice I've witnessed an arrow cause paralysis of the hindquarters not from the blow of the initial hit but from subsequent movement of the arrow that wedged the vertebrae asunder. Once, an exceptionally nervous doe scatted around so fast at the sound of my bow that the arrow aimed at her right shoulder from about twenty yards caught her high on the left flank. As she leapt away, she tangled with a barbwire fence about ten yards from where she had been standing and, in the struggle, twisted the arrow enough to bring about the paralysis. I hastened over and secured her with a second arrow. The other occasion was a doe also. She ran unimpaired until she bounded into a thicket laced with greenbrier vines forty yards distant. Then she collapsed and could only flop. Again, I had to run to her and finish her with another arrow. The whole thing was very puzzling for she was less than nine yards off when my arrow drilled her, and it looked like a perfect chest shot other than there was an unusual lack of penetration. Careful dissection revealed what had actually occurred. For some reason, the arrow striking the broadside shoulder turned back toward the hip and expended its force in that direction and, rather than driving into the chest, angled back parallel to the backbone and above the lateral processes of the vertebrae. The tip stopped at the interface between two vertebrae. Either the movement of her shoulder (through which the arrow had passed) or the tugging of the vines on the protruding fletching end of the arrow pried the vertebrae apart and put pressure on the spinal cord. By the way, although both of these does died very quickly after a second arrow penetrated their chests, I don't believe either original wound would have been lethal if not for the damage to the spine from their efforts to flee.

Wounds that do not involve the chest cavity, the brain, or the spinal cord can only be quickly fatal if they happen to cut a major blood vessel such as the carotid or jugular in the neck, the brachial in the foreleg, the abdominal aorta, portal vein, or hepatic artery in the abdomen, or one of the femoral arteries in the hindquarters. All these vessels are thin targets, and hitting them is more or less a matter of luck. I know of no hunters who would deliberately target them. However, the trails of deer struck in the abdominal aorta or femoral arteries are typically very short. Blood spurting from the abdominal portion of the aorta though is often contained within that cavity, and in such a case, even a short trail may not be easy.

If the shot does not strike the chest cavity, brain, or spinal cord and also does not cut a fairly large-sized blood vessel, it will not result in a fast kill without a follow-up shot. These wounds can broadly be divided into flesh wounds (that may or may not also involve bone) and abdominal wounds (most often termed gutshots). These two categories need to be addressed fully, but first, a phenomenon called shock requires some explanation. Shock is predominately associated with bullet wounds, but it occurs to some extent with nearly all injuries. The small blood vessels in tissues that are damaged or bruised open spaces between the cells that comprise the vessels' walls, allowing the liquid component of the blood, serum, to escape into the site. This same mechanism explains the swelling around a sprained ankle. The heavier the "shocking power," the more tissue is affected. This loss of fluid even without hemorrhage (bleeding) decreases blood volume and, therefore, produces reduced blood pressure. If it is dramatic enough, the brain will be deprived of oxygen and succumb. If not that severe, it can still cause the animal to reduce activity and be susceptible to quiet tracking. Broken bones, besides inducing shock, can also limit an animal's mobility. (By the way, shock is often the cause of death in wildlife struck by vehicles. Even in the absence of bleeding, so much tissue is subjected to fluid infiltration that blood volume and blood pressure drops precipitously.)

Flesh wounds devoid of significant shock will result in a wound that can heal unless serious infection ensues. Broadheads cut cleanly and are less likely to cause infections. Bullets, at times, push hair and dirt into the flesh and have the potential for more tissue damage. The wound may be ragged and traumatized, especially at the exit site. This raw and enlarged area can easily become contaminated with dirt, debris, and insects and, thereby, has a higher incidence of infection. Infection, whether from an arrow or bullet wound, can be survivable or lethal depending upon the severity of the infection and the virulence of the microbes. The mechanism by which an infection causes death is, of course, cerebral hypoxia and will be explained more fully in the section on gutshots. Wild animals have an incredible vitality and ability to hang on to life, and many survive these "flesh" wounds. The ones that do not are problematic to the tracker because the wounds typically provide poor trails, the animal may go far, and death may be very delayed.

Some tribes of Native Americans deliberately contaminated the arrowheads of their war arrows (not hunting arrows) with fecal material, spit, rotten meat, or a combination of these to increase the rate of infection so even relatively minor hits could prove fatal. I employ the exact opposite tactic by endeavoring to keep my broadheads clean and nearly sterile so that shots that are not quickly lethal are less likely to induce infection. With modern equipment, most bowhunters use replaceable blade or mechanical heads that are clean right from the package, but for those of us who still favor sturdy, re-sharpenable broadheads that have been driven into animals or dirt on previous shots, it is worthwhile to bear in mind that by keeping them clean, we may save an animal some suffering if a shot goes astray.

Many flesh wounds do heal. The problem for the tracker is the determination of whether the wound is relatively minor and not worth pursuing or a lethal one that happens to be difficult to trail for one reason or another. Again, there are no hard and fast rules, but experience helps the tracker form an opinion. Flesh wounds, even at the onset, spurt or spray very little or no blood. The blood is not frothy or bubbly, and while it is red, it is not bright red. On the trail, the blood shows up as drips or smears where it is rubbed on vegetation. The drips gradually become less and less frequent as clotting begins to occur. The hunter's description of the hit should be considered as well. This sounds fairly cut and dry, and no one wants to waste time tracking game that will never be found, but personally, blood sign has fooled me into believing a wound could not be fatal (you will read of Don's buck soon) only to discover the game in the end often enough that I try to follow all trails as far as I am able. If nothing else, I learn from the trail about the game and may improve my tracking skills as well. (With a tracking dog, a decision has to be made at some point for the dog could follow an animal with a wound of little consequence indefinitely.)

A projectile that punctures the body cavity behind the diaphragm is called an abdominal hit or "gutshot." As mentioned earlier, on occasion, major blood vessels are cut (notably the aorta or liver vessels) or major shock ensues, but typically this is not a wound that kills quickly and therefore one that sportsmen abhor. The liver is comprised of a multitude of blood vessels and a wound to it may cause fatal blood loss even without the major blood vessels being cut, but it is not likely to occur quickly. Wounds to the liver are very painful, and the afflicted game animal most often beds at no great distance if not pushed.

The digestive tract of an animal fills the majority of the abdominal cavity. This tract teems with bacteria, so when it is ruptured or punctured, the bacteria are introduced into the body cavity. As they reproduce in the gut cavity (normally doubling their population every twenty minutes) the resulting infection is termed peritonitis. This progresses to a bacteremia and sepsis, bacteria reproducing in the bloodstream with the result that the bacteria and their toxic products are pumped throughout the body. Septic shock sets in with its attending drop in arterial blood pressure, organ failure, and ultimately death as the brain fails to receive enough oxygen. Peritonitis is uncomfortable and characterized by restlessness. The animal often changes positions without going far. Bacteremia brings about lassitude and lethargy, and the animal will move less and exhibit diminished alertness. Game animals disturbed in the throes of peritonitis are not dramatically hampered physically. They are capable of normal flight and can quickly put large distances between themselves and the perceived threat rendering them more difficult to find. Once the malady has progressed to sepsis an animal struggles to flee, doing so at a slower pace and for shorter distances. The exact schedule depends on the extent bacteria have been released in the peritoneal cavity and bloodstream, the virulence of the microbes, the constitution of the animal, and environmental conditions, such as temperature and humidity. Also hemorrhage associated with the wound could contribute to a faster drop in blood pressure. Complicating things further, some wounds do involve the abdomen but also puncture lung tissue and the diaphragm. As you can see, putting a definite timeline on gutshot game with all these variables is not possible. I have helped track gutshot game animals that were still alive after forty hours and others that were already dead when we found them after seven hours. Many trackers allow at least six hours for sepsis to begin but keep in mind that not only does each case vary, but the change from peritonitis to sepsis is not an abrupt change but rather a gradual transition. Another factor with gutshot game is the influx of bacteria into the bloodstream routes these germs to the muscles as well, so meat can quickly become less palatable or even spoil. All these parameters as well as weather and tracking conditions affect how soon after a gutshot the trail should be followed as is considered in more detail later in this book.

Out west, in the nineties, a bear approached an elk hunting friend of mine. It saw him from about forty yards but continued on its course. He shouted and raised his arms, one of which held his compound bow, over his head, and waved them around. This seemed to have the desired effect for the bear stopped and stared, turned, and retreated ten yards. Then it turned again and resumed its approach. Billy shouted again, and when this did not deter the bear, he put an arrow on the string. When the bear was less than twenty yards off and still ambling toward him, Billy drew, aimed for the front of its chest, and released. The bear rushed right at him in a heartbeat, and he had only time to yell. It was a good yell as I can attest. I was over a thousand yards distant, and elk near me responded with a chorus of bugles! Apparently, the bear only wanted to use the trail as it passed within a foot or two of Billy and kept going. Other than nearly frightening the life from him, it harmed him not at all.

Billy admitted being unsure of his wavering aim and of the exact hit with everything happening so fast and unexpectedly. There was little left of the day, and he felt it best to track it the next day. We all agreed to a short elk hunt in the morning, and then, when the light was bright, to meet up and search for the bear. I arrived first and from his description found where Billy had stood, and a little blood on some brush on the trail testified that he had not exaggerated how closely the bear had passed by him. Beyond that, I could find no blood or any evidence of where the bear had been hit. My other friends, the ranch manager, and his two border collies arrived, yet none of us could extend the trail any further. It was evident the bear had run down the canyon, so we split up and searched for sign. After a couple hours without a speck of blood or a conclusive bear track, we were discouraged. Then, pushing into a side draw really not more than six hundred yards from where Billy had stood, I saw the bear. He was flat on the ground but alert, looking directly at me from no more than twenty yards. I nocked an arrow onto Daddy's string

("Daddy" is a Ron LaClair Super Shrew longbow). The bear's body was tight against the ground and his head angled toward me. He was slightly uphill, so his body was a very compressed target, but he was watching me keenly, and I was afraid if I tried to position myself for a better shot or yelled to attract my friends, he would be gone. Since his head was angled downward toward me, it seemed logical that his chest would be just below and slightly to the right of his nose. I drew Daddy and aimed deliberately. The arrow hissed to its target, and the bear was off and down the draw in an instant. There was a new but disappointingly sparse blood trail. It petered out quickly but gave evidence that the bear had at least started across the canyon. The two dogs were put on the fresh blood but gave no sign of any interest. (They may have been exceptionally sagacious dogs!) By midafternoon, our party gave up. I felt personally involved now and also did not want the animal to suffer longer nor to have an unsuspecting hunter stumble upon a wounded bear, so I continued to search until dark. It was a wee bit spine tingling to examine thickets that restricted the view to a few feet armed only with a longbow without even an arrow on the string, but although I had no bear hunting experience, my guess was that a wounded one would seek thick cover. Overnight, I mulled my shot over. The dismally scant amount of blood baffled me, and I concluded that I must have aimed too low and gutshot the bear. Although I was completely wrong about my shot, the reasoning proved fortuitous as, although we did not know it yet, Billy's shot was a gut wound. With the assumption that it was a gutshot, I reasoned the animal would seek water. From where he had laid up that morning, there were only two water sources within fifteen hundred yards, both beaver ponds. The closest was small, eight by sixteen yards, and its far bank was nearly vertical for ten feet or more. The other pond was larger, but further, so the following morning, I first checked the little pond. I had approached quietly with an arrow on the string, but the water was still and the pond looked empty. Then at the far corner I noticed a dark bump that could be a nearly submerged bear head. Sure enough, binocular magnification proved it to be the eyes and nose of a bear. There was no movement of the head nor even rippling of the water. I approached from the low end of the pond and at the water's edge, despite my belief the bear had died in the pond, I bent over to pick up a rock to toss toward the inert form. As I started to bend, before I could reach a stone, the bear, now less than ten yards away, exploded out of the water and raced to the right. With the little longbow, I took a running shot that drove through his chest. He reached the steep bank and turned around and raced back to the north. I sent another arrow that appeared to drive through his chest again except this time from his left side. The steep mountainside was vegetated with oak brush and serviceberries, so I lost sight of him but thought I heard him pile up. A quick scoot down the slope confirmed that he had not made it sixty yards and some of that was probably sliding downward after his death. My first chest shot had double lunged him. The second, which had looked so good to me, had entered behind his shoulder and exited his neck without entering the rib cage at all. Billy's arrow had entered behind the left shoulder and pierced the guts and slid along the inside of his left hind leg. It turned out when I found him the morning before, he was lying with his back toward me and his head was looking over his back. So the arrow planned to drive into his chest was stopped short by his backbone and barely penetrated at all, making the nearly nonexistent blood trail understandable. This strong animal survived thirty-eight hours after the initial hit and may have lived longer if I hadn't found him.

A preponderance of gutshot animals die. I used to believe 100 percent did, but I have revised that number although, no doubt, it is very close to the truth. The exception I learned of was not a game animal but a man. In April of 1867, George Reynolds of Texas, in a conflict with Indians (the tribe was not specified in the accounts I read), was shot with an arrow that entered his abdomen just above the navel. He pulled the shaft out, but the head was left in his body where it remained sixteen years, three months, and sixteen days, finally working its way through his back and was removed by a doctor without anesthesia. The steel head was two inches long and quite rusted. The remarkable thing, of course, is that he survived the gutshot, and although he had a great deal of pain, he did not develop any serious infection. He received no medical care and obviously no antibiotics. In fact, he underwent a strenuous ordeal to reach his home. If a man can live through such a wound without surgery or antibiotics, as vital as game animals are, it must be extrapolated that with the exactly right wound, an animal might survive as well. No doubt it is extremely infrequent.

In summary, other than direct injury to the brain, wounds kill by reducing or eliminating the availability of oxygen to the brain. With reduced oxygen, the brain functions less and the animal goes through a period of diminished awareness and responsiveness. During this time, whether it is milliseconds or prolonged, the animal does not feel pain. I can offer an example of this extreme lack of responsiveness:

A cold front brought cold temperatures (for Florida) and my thoughts turned to some sweet orange trees in the depths of the swampwoods. A few weeks before, a scouting foray revealed some buck sign in the vicinity but no evidence of anything feeding on the oranges. In fact, the ground was littered with fallen ones, some already rotting. The cold snap should have sweetened them and heightened their desirability to wildlife. On a Thursday afternoon after a short day of work, I slipped among the trees and placed a climbing stand on a palm, noting with satisfaction that only a couple freshly dropped oranges were visible beneath the trees nearby. The understory was dense and blocked any easy approach, so I was forced to walk under an orange tree to reach my stand site. It was twenty-five yards south and was the one least in line with the other orange trees and, in prior years, was only visited by deer after the main group of trees had been investigated. The wind was strong and from the northwest, ideal for my position. A myrtle skirted my cabbage palm and hid me somewhat. A bay tree and a couple of myrtles interfered with spear throws to the north and northeast, so I cut them before climbing and stacked the cut portions at my palm's base. I climbed up even with the myrtle's top, ten feet from the ground. By the time I was hunting, it was 4:00 p.m., and the light would fade early in the swampwoods, probably not much later than 6:00 p.m. I began updating my journal, but almost immediately, a doe strode briskly out making for, of all places, the southernmost orange tree! Her course kept her twenty-five yards or less from me but well out of spear range. I could only hope my scent trail wouldn't spook her too badly or else maybe spook her toward me. Another doe emerged and, with hurried steps, joined her. They were both mature. A third doe slipped out from under the orange tree west of me and headed directly toward me. She had a huge, long head. A fourth deer bounded out from further back and raced in my direction, but a look at the bigheaded doe's posture brought her up short, and she followed meekly in the rear.

Six yards out, the doe halted abruptly and became nervous. The wind was fine, so her behavior bewildered me. My enthusiasm for the prospect of a pending spear chance metamorphosed into bafflement at this sudden change in demeanor. A glance at the first two deer explained everything. They had encountered my residual scent and manifested their nervousness. The bigheaded doe had noted their alertness and followed suit. As their ease returned, she resumed her approach yet was still cautious and sniffed about after each step. When she was a yard from my cabbage palm, she stretched her neck out to sniff again and, fearing she might catch my scent at the tree's base or on the cut shrubs even with the wind behind her, I decided to throw. My spear was headed with a fifteen-inch double-edged blade. A heavy posthole digger handle served as a shaft. It was very windy, and the movement of the myrtle branches below me worked in my favor as deer easily catch sight or sound of a thrown spear and can side step it. My hopes soared as she did not react, but then at the last instant, she glimpsed it and twisted to wheel away. She was too late to escape entirely, and the huge blade, aimed for her chest, tore through her neck and blood sprayed wildly. She ran forty yards west. The deer that followed her earlier joined her, and they walked slowly southeast, disappearing from view. The other does had initially frozen nervously and then headed southeast as well but by a different route and did not join up with the bigheaded doe.

Blood was sprayed about below me, and even from the stand, I could see a crimson path to the west. I climbed down immediately. The sanguine trail was unmistakable and could be deciphered at a fast walk even where the black earth of the swamp was exposed. After a short distance, I stopped for she was standing in front of me with her head down, facing directly away. My thoughts were jumbled and conflicting. "She must be on her last legs." "You don't want to spook her." "Sneak around and get broadside." "Don't take a chance. Shoot her as she stands."

The decision was not easy, but I felt that I had to act fast. I did not want to prolong her death. Also, she was only a few yards in front of me, and if she turned and discovered my presence, she might flee. I nocked an arrow on Mellifluwood's string, drew, and sent the shaft straight into her body perfectly centered. The arrow drove in to the fletchings. It was instantaneously obvious that the shot was not necessary for she did not move or respond in any way. I stood wondering what to do next, but then she swayed, sank down, and rolled onto her side.

The spear had cleaved deeply into the neck and cut the skin and tissue all the way down the neck bones. Her left carotid artery was severed and the brain, deprived of oxygen, had shut down. She was not aware of anything by the time I reached her and must have been beyond pain as well for how else could her complete lack of response to an arrow driven through the hams, abdomen, and into the chest be explained? By the way, her teeth, worn down to the gums, indicated she was eight and a half years old.

Before closing this chapter on wounds, something called the "dead space" should be considered and perhaps the best course is to include excerpts from an article I wrote for *Deer and Deer Hunting* magazine several years ago. While it does reiterate some of what has been covered, it makes the most sense to include it fairly whole:

The Dead Space

> Almost all bow hunters have heard accounts of shots high in the chest and under the spine resulting in unrecovered deer. The term "dead space" has been applied to this zone and quite experienced and knowledgeable hunters aver its existence.

Maybe thirty years ago (more now, by the way, as the article was written years ago), I went to north Florida for a special archery hunt and camped with a large group of hunters of all ages, some with three decades worth of bow hunting stories even back then. One evening around the campfire, someone mentioned a void in a deer's chest below the backbone and above the lungs. Several hunters asserted their knowledge of it, and no one voiced the least disbelief. With my understanding of anatomy, such a spot was hard to fathom, but when older hunters spoke, I listened carefully. Since then, it seems no season goes by without mention of the mysterious "space" either in conversation or in magazine articles. Investigating the possibilities in depth may help archers understand the likely effects of any arrow driven into a deer's chest.

Breathing, the physical act of sucking air through the mouth and nostrils into the lungs and expelling it from the lungs, is accomplished by changing the size of the chest cavity between the throat and the diaphragm, a region known as the mediastinum. This change in size is effectuated in three ways. The diaphragm itself; the thin layer of muscle that separates the heart and lungs from the abdomen, contracts and relaxes. Abdominal muscles can augment this action and, lastly, muscles between the ribs (intercostal muscles) contribute to it as well. An old fashion hand bellows offers a pretty good analogy.

The lungs and heart and the airways and blood vessels that supply them fill the mediastinum completely. There can be a space between the lungs and the chest walls of a deer when a hunter examines the chest, but this is an artifact resulting from the less inflated status of the lungs and the introduction of air through the fatal wound or the incision through the chest wall or both. In life, except for the intervening thin membranes and lubricant, the lungs are against the chest's interior. Obviously, a noticeably spacious vacuum could not exist because it would collapse more readily than force air from the lungs during exhalation. Likewise, the presence of an air space between the lungs and chest walls can be ruled out by the experiences of air travelers and SCUBA divers. Such an air space would change size with changes in pressure like air bladders in fish. The very fact that this does not occur proves the nonexistence of such an air space. Therefore, two of the common descriptions of the "dead space," a vacuum or an air space cannot be present between the lungs and the chest walls.

In the foremost (anterior) portion of a deer's chest, a cross-section view (a view like a slice of salami) would be somewhat oval or egg shaped with the lowest portion of the backbone at the top of the oval. However, only a small bit of the chest displays this configuration and immediately behind (posterior to) this area, the bottom projection of the vertebras extend down lower than the highest portions of the chest walls. A cross-section anywhere throughout this, the major, portion of the chest would look more like a long, slender valentine-style heart with a blunt point. The chest walls and the lungs that conform to them rise *above* the level of the bottom of the backbone. This anatomy makes it obvious that an arrow cannot pass under the backbone in this region of the chest and not penetrate lung tissue.

These facts seem so cut and dry, but why then is there such a persistence of the belief in the "dead space," and as mentioned, not just by novices but by knowledgeable and able hunters? Before discussing the possible explanations, it is worthwhile to consider the effects of an arrow wound to the chest of a deer.

Cross section of a whitetail's chest. Note that the backbone (midline) extends lower than the upper reaches of the cavity the lungs fill to the right and left.

Another view of the chest cavity. Not only does this illustrate that the bottom portion of the backbone protrudes down into the chest cavity, it also shows just how high the upper vertebral fins extend above the cavity. A deer's back would be above the top of the fin so the chest cavity is well below the top of the back. Worth noting as well is how the ribs project from the backbone almost horizontally for their first five inches. The resulting flat shelf can deflect an arrow.

The lungs are constituted primarily of blood and air. The air is in little, thin-walled, balloon-like sacs called alveoli. The blood courses through tiny vessels that are also very thinly walled and gases (oxygen, carbon dioxide, and others) within the blood are exchanged for gases in the air in the alveoli. With blood being such a major component of the lungs, obviously a lung wound causes substantial hemorrhage so one of the sequela of a broadhead piercing the lungs is a diminution in blood volume. If enough blood is lost, not enough blood reaches the deer's brain and the animal dies. This can happen with extreme rapidity. Besides the lungs, the chest contains major blood vessels and the heart, and injuries to these cause dramatic bleeding as well. Blood loss is a drastically important aspect of any arrow wound, but lung wounds affect the ability of an animal to oxygenate the remaining blood in three other ways.

Another action of the hemorrhage is that blood leaks into air channels and thereby blocks the intake of air into undamaged portions of the lungs. This renders some areas not struck by the broadhead unable to exchange gases.

Anyone who has blown up a balloon by mouth realizes that it requires a greater effort initially, but once the balloon has surpassed a critical diameter, the inflation proceeds much more easily. This holds true with alveoli as well and most of us can think back to occasions when the "wind" was knocked out of us. The difficulty in getting our first full breath was the process of inflating the alveoli to a point beyond their critical diameter. When a projectile strikes a deer's lungs, some alveoli are collapsed and therefore cannot contribute to gas exchange.

The tube that connects the lungs with the mouth and nose is the trachea, and when the deer's chest is intact, expansion of the chest cavity draws air in through the trachea. It is easier to pull air through a short tube than a long one, and this can be demonstrated by trying to breathe through various lengths of garden hose. The shorter the piece, the less effort required. The significance of this is that air may be pulled in through the chest wound more readily than through the longer trachea. This air is not channeled to the alveoli and thereby provides no respiration. The chest expands, but the amount of air sucked into the trachea is diminished by however much air enters the chest perforation. This factor has the potential for a great impact on a deer's ability to oxygenate its blood, but exactly how much impact depends on the wound size, number of wounds (entry only or entry and exit), and degree of openness. Skin and tissue and even clotted blood can obturate the wound. In short, a lung wound reduces the volume of blood to carry oxygen to the brain and reduces the deer's capability to oxygenate the remaining blood.

Just recently, I arrowed a buck high and forward in the chest. The arrow broke off, but when I cleaned the buck, the remainder of the shaft was up as high in the chest cavity as possible where the roof of the cavity is convex. Nothing could be slipped between the shaft and the backbone without forcibly displacing the shaft downward. While this buck did flee, it did not make it far. Absolutely, no arrow could pass under the backbone any higher in the chest cavity, yet this wound was quickly lethal.

So what can explain the steadfastness of the "dead space" belief? Instead of one answer, there are five possibilities. By the way, because of the lack of sensation in the lungs, I have witnessed and heard of lung shot deer not fleeing and acting unconcerned many times. However, never has a case come to my attention of a hit in the "dead space" not resulting in the subsequent immediate flight of the deer. I mention this because such behavior would be in harmony with a few of the possibilities.

First, the fins extending upwards from the vertebrae are longer in the forward (anterior) portion of the chest, but the back appears fairly straight to the eye. The spine, however, drops lower as the fins elongate. In other words, the backbone is not level horizontally, but drops anteriorly. Therefore, an arrow that would have transfixed a deer below the backbone a little further back would pass non-lethally above the backbone when it strikes forward. Also, the ribs angle from the backbone at nearly ninety degrees, basically horizontally. An arrow striking them could be easily deflected up higher than the entrance site would appear to indicate.

Second, if the shot was slightly too far back and high, it could miss the lungs and yet not strike the paunch. The arrow would then not show signs of much blood nor have a "gutty" smell, and the resulting wound may not be mortal, or when mortal, may not supply much of a blood trail. Mortality from this type of hit is not usually from hemorrhage but from peritonitis that may persist for 12 to 36 hours before causing death.

Third, and this can be in conjunction with either of the first two possibilities or completely independent, arrows don't always strike where we think we see them. Videos have captured deer ducking as arrows speed toward them. Our eyes can record the image of the fletchings and nock rocketing straight toward the chest and may not be able to tell the deer moved before, rather than after, the arrow struck. My eyes have been fooled countless times over the years. Just last weekend, I was positive my arrow drove through a running boar hog's chest. The easy trail with blood sprayed high and far did nothing to dispel my confidence in the chest shot. Upon finding the downed hog, I was totally shocked to discover my arrow had slipped through the hog below the tail and yet somehow severed a femoral artery. Minutes earlier, I entertained absolutely no doubt of a double lung shot and would have sworn to it if I hadn't found the boar and saw the irrefutable evidence of the wound. I even checked the wound to verify it matched my broadhead shape. My arrow came within a couple of inches of a complete miss, and I did miss my intended target zone by nearly two and a half feet. The explanation may be that my eyes saw what they expected to see or it may be that my eyes caught the image of the flying arrow lined up toward the chest and failed to register the hog's forward progress after that moment. The bottom line is that if for some reason I hadn't recovered the boar, I would be convinced and would probably tell people of the big, tough boar I slammed through the lungs that ran off despite my good shot.

This episode does little credit to my powers of observation, but let me assure you that truly hundreds of my arrows have struck game precisely where I thought. Still a few have deviated phenomenally from what I was sure I witnessed including two long, difficult trails on bucks my eyes led me to believe were struck ideally. Also, I have helped friends find deer and elk whose wounds contrasted drastically from the description of shot by the hunter. I don't mean this possible explanation as a criticism or attack on the hunters who have reported the "dead space" hits but rather as an acknowledgement from personal experience that no matter how certain a hunter is of a hit, there is a chance the arrow struck elsewhere.

Fourth, the arrow may have penetrated the lungs and produced either little hemorrhage or an exiguous blood trail. The aorta, the major artery of the body, runs along the backbone so the "dead space" hit must not have cut the aorta, but perhaps the broadhead pierced the lungs but high enough up to provide the poor blood trail. Much of the bleeding could be retained in the chest itself. The lack of a blood trail could leave a hunter to conclude the lungs were not hit despite seeing the good shot. The following account, although it involves a very low shot, gives an example of the very situation, and as you will see, a hunter without a trailing dog would not likely have found the deer and, if he or she did, would have every reason to believe it was not severely injured and would survive.

I have a friend who has trailed many, many wounded deer with his beagle for hunters all around our hunting areas and with his exceptional amount of experience, I called him to tell him about this article as it was evolving and to get his opinion on the "dead space." He believes any deer pierced through the chest can be found with a good enough dog. He does admit some double-lunged deer do live longer than might be expected, but when jumped up, they cannot respire well enough to run far and each successive run gets shorter. As an example, he related a trailing adventure from just earlier that week. (I later examined the deer's chest and the entry and exit wounds.) One morning, he arrowed a buck and, satisfied that the hit was ideal, waited an hour and a half on the stand. The buck had appeared to succumb to the wound in a patch of myrtle not far from his tree. When he went to retrieve the deer, he discovered no deer in the myrtle copse. He retrieved his beagle instead, and she worked the scent track a good ways. Then her manner perked up, and it became obvious that the trail was much hotter and fresher, indicating they had pushed the deer up, and it was still alive, so my friend pulled the beagle from the pursuit and did not return to try again until late afternoon, ten hours after the shot. The beagle resumed the trail without difficulty and led her owner through pastures, waist-deep cypress heads, and thickets of briars, fennels, and myrtles. Even though his attention is on his dog during a trail, my friend typically notices blood along the way, but very little was evident along their course. They jumped the buck from close distances two or three times. It did not go far. On the last occasion, the buck ran only a short distance into a pasture and began walking in the open, apparently oblivious to its surroundings and even to my friend running up to it with his chest waders flapping and flopping. Another shot dispatched it. The initial arrow had gone through the chest cavity, but very low and barely skimming over the sternum. Somehow, the broadhead missed the heart. The lungs were cut, but the hemorrhage was minimal because the lobes of the lungs taper dramatically and are only between one-half and three-fourths of an inch thick at this low region. However, the ability of the deer to bring air into the lungs was hampered enough that the brain was not getting adequate oxygen, and each burst of flight expended more and more of the little oxygen the blood was carrying. By the end, the buck was in a daze with the brain barely functioning. Unfortunately, the second wound flooded the chest with blood, so there was no way to ascertain just how much hemorrhage resulted from his initial shot.

It should be noted that the buck covered a great distance during the course of the day and left almost no blood on the ground. He waded through deep water, and the trail would approach impossibility without a dog, so a hunter that failed on the trail or succeeded long enough to jump up the deer a couple hours after seeing what he or she thought was a perfect chest shot could easily be confounded and assume that the shot was not mortal. By the way, my friend described the arrow after the shot as being coated more with slime than with blood. Many of the "dead space" hits I've heard about included a very similar description of the condition of the arrow.

Lung wounds, of course, are almost always rapidly fatal, but this occurrence exemplifies that some lung-shot deer can survive for extended periods and make tracking difficult. No case of a double lung punctured deer surviving the wound has come to my attention, but *Deer and Deer Hunting* many years ago related two separate incidents of hunters finding foreign objects in the chest of harvested deer. One was a piece of arrow encapsulated in scar tissue. If my memory serves accurately, neither the orientation of the arrow fragment to the lungs nor the point of entry were described. My guess would be that the wound came from the front and only one lung or the lining of one lung was in contact with the piece. The other case involved a stick that definitely entered from the front and broke off. It either entered or drove along one lung. These incidents demonstrate the incredible vitality and recuperative powers of deer.

Fifth, nobody wants to believe he or she killed a deer and was not able to recover it. Believing that the deer did survive is comforting even though the arrow or the hunter's vision offered proof of a hit. I don't believe anyone purposely tries to deceive his or her self, but the "dead space" offers an explanation that doesn't contradict the accuracy of the shot and yet offers hope the animal survived.

In conclusion, because a deer's lungs fill virtually all the space in the chest not occupied by the heart, blood vessels, or airways, it is nigh to impossible for a broadhead to pass through the chest without cutting lung tissue. There is no void or "dead space." The reasons for the unrecovered deer that perpetuate the myth are several and probably vary with each case.

That concluded the Dead Space article, but the mention of deer surviving lung injuries reminded me of a passage from one of Russell Annabel's writings:

"Something I saw one autumn at the Big Bend of the Susitna convinced me once and for all of the enormous vitality of caribou. A Talkeetna Indian I was traveling with killed a bull for camp meat. While dressing the animal he gave a surprised grunt and held out an object he had taken from the animal's lungs. It was the end of a spruce limb, six inches long by an inch thick, covered with tough membrane.

"We looked the carcass over carefully and found an old scar between the forelegs where the limb had entered. The Indian's opinion was that wolves had stampeded the bull through a stand of dead timber, and that he had crashed head-on into a spruce snag, driving the limb deep into his lungs. Vitality? Such a wound would have killed most animals within a few minutes. But the caribou bull not only had survived, but actually had grown fat afterward."

This incident, like the two described above with whitetails, involved a foreign object encapsulated within an animal's lung. It should be pointed out that in all three cases only one lung was involved. Therefore, it must be assumed that at times, game can survive wounds to only one lung. The determining factors may be whether the diaphragm was compromised as well or whether the wound channel remained open enough to significantly reduce the volume of air pulled into the other lung.

CHAPTER 2

When an Animal Is
Hit/Tracking with Blood

WHEN GOOD BLOOD IS PRESENT, tracking is not difficult, but it may be best to discuss these trails before going into tracking with little or no blood. First, let's consider the moments right after the shot. Three locations are important to mark as precisely as possible when an animal is hit. In the excitement of the shot, this information can be forgotten or remembered incorrectly, but as the hunter gains experience, he or she will learn to pay particular attention to the exact place the animal was standing when struck, the very last place it was in view, and the location from where the last sounds of its flight emanated. For the first two, the more specific landmarks that can be chosen, the better. Sometimes a distinctive tree or clump can mark the sound as well, but if not, a compass bearing can be taken. It is best to firmly establish these three points before moving from the place the hunter was when the shot was taken whether that place was a stand or just a spot on the ground. In fact, if the hunter was on the ground, it is worthwhile to mark or memorize that location as well. Sometimes it can be useful to return there to revisualize what happened or to guide a friend to the last sound of the retreat. This routine is performed for every shot before the hunter even knows how good or poor a trail is waiting. It may not be of importance every time, but there will be occasions this habit will prove of great value.

Next, the site where the animal was at the time of the shot can be evaluated. Obviously, if the animal is in view or other animals are nearby that could take fright and thereby further spook the target animal, it is better to hold still and wait. The less distance an animal flees, the greater the ease of finding it. The impact site can reveal substantial information about the wound. Bullets and arrows both often cut hair, and the hair color, length, and amount, coupled with the hunter's observation of the shot, can give an idea of the wound's location. For instance, white hair for deer would indicate either an entrance or exit wound through the bottom of the chest, abdomen, the insides of the legs, or underside of the tail. The hair on the inside of the legs is shorter than that on the underside of the torso. The hair on the sides of the chest of deer is brown or grey and not very long. Lots of hair can actually be a bad sign for a grazing shot with a bullet or broadhead contacts the skin for a longer distance than a direct hit that punches through in one spot. As the projectile furrows along the skin hair is cut. For turkey, the feathers are great indicators. Wing feathers are obvious and tell one part of the wound. Breast feathers tell more—the more symmetrical the feather, the closer to midline the injury. So as an example, a cut left wing feather coupled with some right-side breast feathers gives clear evidence of the shot piercing through the turkey's body cavity.

A detailed knowledge of the anatomy and characteristics of the game animal, regardless of the species, will help the hunter interpret the sign at the impact site. Accounts of early hunters in Africa nearly all have a common aspect. These various hunters all studied and dissected the animals they killed, committing every minute detail of internal and external anatomy to memory. Many drew pictures and wrote notes to aid their learning. Bell's dissections and drawings are perhaps the most famous. Here is African hunter Lyell's advice: "Until the beginner knows the internal anatomy of the game thoroughly, he should make a practice of watching them being dismembered. A good plan is to leave the heart, lungs, and kidneys inside, and with an axe split the upper ribs of along the spinal ridge, allowing the vital organs to remain in their natural position, and then make a rough sketch of their relative positions. Of course these organs in an animal flat on its side will not assume exactly the position they would do when the beast is standing up." This precedent still holds value for us, the hunters of today.

Blood found at the site of impact also offers clues to the nature of the hit. However, blood is not always found at this location. For bowhunters, finding the arrow manifests a pass through and the amount and nature of the blood on the arrow helps confirm where the animal was hit. Is the blood on the arrow heavy or scant? Are there bubbles? Are there smears of meat or fat? Is there a green or brown coating on the arrow or a gutty smell?

A thorough but unsuccessful search for the arrow indicates it stayed in the animal. Possibly the arrow or part of it will fall out on the trail. An arrow that remains in the animal may or may not indicate a lack of an exit wound. Again, hunter observation as to the location of the hit and the degree of penetration should be considered in concert with the evidence at the site. Arrows protruding from wounds often slap tree trunks or vegetation and the hunter may have clues from the sounds of the retreat. Typical penetration varies from bow to bow and game animal to game animal, but a hunter should have an idea of what is normal for his or her set up. Less penetration than expected would indicate increased resistance. This could result from the angle of penetration or from the arrow encountering bone. With the appearance of a chest shot, resistance from bone could be from the shoulder which, unless the arrow was badly deflected, should still result in a quickly lethal wound for deer-sized game, but it could stem from the backbone, which could indicate the chest cavity was not reached. The second doe I chronicled earlier that became partially paralyzed by trying to flee is an example of this very thing. The shot looked ideal to me, but the lack of penetration was unlike my typical chest shots for even though the draw weight of my longbow Daddy is not exceptional, the arrows it propels are very heavy, weighing in over seven hundred grains and usually drive through deer and sometimes elk. Had the deer not fallen within sight, the drastically reduced penetration should have aroused my suspicion that the chest cavity had not been breached.

As mentioned, blood may be found at the impact site. If not, a few steps in the direction the animal was last seen may allow a hunter to find some. It is evaluated for quantity, bubbles or frothiness, and whether it is spraying, spurting, or dripping. As far as quantity is concerned, keep in mind the speed of the animal's flight. A little blood from a rapidly moving animal could indicate a higher rate of hemorrhage than a medium amount from one moving slowly. Bubbles and frothiness are not the same thing. Foamy, frothy blood is nearly always indicative of a lung hit. Bubbles, on the other hand, can be introduced by other means. Just this year, a friend sent me a picture of a good-sized pool of blood (he described as pie plate-sized) with a lot of bubbles clustered in the center that had been interpreted as evidence of a lung hit. Subsequently, it was discovered that the arrow stopped at the backbone above the chest cavity. The bubbles were caused by more blood leaking into the accumulating puddle. An illustration that many people have seen is when we urinate on the ground. The first bit causes no bubbles, but as the volume builds, bubbles form. Another demonstration would be to pour salad oil on the ground. Differing causes of air in the blood can confuse the tracker, but lung caused bubbles should be present even in small bits of the blood trail and the bubbles are very small. An opening to the chest cavity or airway can introduce bubbles into the blood. Even a small hole in the trachea or a slit between ribs would impart air to whatever blood leaked from the surrounding tissues.

At this time, the hunter needs to assimilate his or her best recollection of the impact, the way the animal acted as it departed, and the sign on the ground. The sum total of these observations will offer guidance on when to start tracking the animal and what to expect. Animals are individuals, and few if any statements about their behavior under certain circumstances will hold true always. However, the target's reaction to the hit may offer some insight about the wound. Quite often, deer, for instance, struck in the heart, do a sort of buck—the two forelegs kick out and the hind legs back before rapidly departing. I've witnessed this many times bowhunting, and my daughter's first deer, taken with a .22 Hornet rifle displayed the exact same reaction. At the same time, I've arrowed whitetails that simply ran off with no preliminary buck, yet upon dressing them, discovered broadhead damage to the heart. Hogs that react with anger vented on a nearby hog or tree are generally shot in the lungs (and may die even during their tirade) or suffered only a flesh wound. Personally, I've never seen the anger reaction from a heart shot or gutshot hog. The immediate hunch-up or the hunch-up that follows an initial flight is very typical of an abdominal hit for both deer and hogs. The forelegs and hind legs are held close together, and the back curves upward in the middle. Often the animal is stationary or moves with little steps and frequent pauses. Once again, the absence of this behavior cannot be construed as proof against a gutshot. Hits that impact a lung and the diaphragm as well as the guts often result in a more classic flight reaction. Also, deer that have seen or smelled the hunter before the shot are more likely to immediately flee and may hunch later.

This arrow passed through a deer and drove into the ground. Copious blood on the arrow leaves no doubt of a chest shot. Air bubbles are few and large suggesting an artery or the heart was struck as well.

Blood with bubbles and foam—convincing evidence of a lung hit.

A different buck was arrowed that raced off at great
speed. Despite the blood droplets being widely scattered,
the bubbles are still obvious and confirm lung damage.

Here the blood is as brightly red as the prior photos, but no bubbles or foam are visible. The arrow struck the deer in the aorta behind the mediastinum. The blood trail was thick and death remarkably fast. The lack of bubbles coupled with the bright color provides the tracker knowledge of an arterial hit.

People often associate a whitetail's position of the tail when fleeing as evidence of a hit or miss. My observations have shown a slightly greater incidence of fatally wounded deer keeping the tails low during their flight but not by a large enough margin that I set any store by that factor for I have witnessed many deer flag ostentatiously on their death race. Archibald Rutledge, who killed over three hundred bucks, had similar experiences: "I have seen many mortally wounded deer go off with tails as high and flaunting as ever. Perhaps a deer pulls down his flag only when he is hit in a certain place, but where that place may be, I do not know." In another article he says, "I have often heard it said that a buck will slap his tail down if he is badly hit. This I have not found to be true. Sometimes a deer will put his tail down for no reason of which we can be sure—perhaps the crack of the gun has suddenly decided him to be wary and less spectacular in showing all that topsail. On the other hand, I have repeatedly seen a buck, mortally wounded, go off with his tail high, even nonchalant and jaunty."

Rutledge hunted primarily with a shotgun loaded with buckshot. He staunchly believed a change of stride was indicative of a hit: "An experienced hunter can nearly always tell by the actions of a deer when he has made a successful shot. If the shot is followed by a blunder, a wild rush, or even a change in stride, the shot have found their target."

What a hunter believes he or she saw and what actually occurred with a shot is not always the same. Most of the time, our eyes do record things accurately, but now and then we can be tricked. My experience with the boar hog mentioned at the end of the preceding chapter is an example. It was a running animal, but it was also ridiculously close. My first introduction to this phenomenon was many, many years ago at St. Marks. One evening, a hunter described his hit of a doe that he couldn't find. He told us the arrow hit the front left shoulder of the deer as it quartered to him and the arrow drove into the chest. We pitched in to help trail her in the morning and eventually found her in the afternoon after a long and time-consuming trail because of both distance and lack of blood sign. The doe had been hit in the right ham, and the arrow proceeded into the abdomen. Whether she swapped ends before his arrow reached her or if she was looking at him over her back and he thought he hit the shoulder, he could not say. Another time, I was trailing a bull elk after dark. The archer had said his arrow had driven deep into the chest on the bull's left side. The frothy blood on the trail was in harmony with this description. At the crest of a ridge, a large block of rock stood, and below it and to its right was a big splash of blood. With the wound on the left side, this indicated the bull had gone over the crest, but despite careful scrutiny, no further sign could be discovered there. Finally, I returned to the last blood and checked to the left. The bull was not more than thirty yards in that direction. He had an arrow in his chest, but it hit his right side. Having been mistaken on hits myself, I understand how easily this happens. The impact occurs in a split second, the animal or hunter can be moving, and the excitement is intense; adrenaline is rushing and the heart thumping! The bottom line is that anyone who undertakes enough blood trails will eventually be on one where the hunter's (whether it is the tracker himself or someone else) recollection of the wound is at fault or at least imprecise. Recognizing this as a possibility keeps the tracker's mind open to other explanations for the sign encountered. On the bull elk trail, staunch conviction that the wound was on the left side would have negated ever checking his true course.

Some people initiate the tracking process where they last saw the game or even try to intercept the trail at the last sound. This can save time, and when pressed, there have been occasions I have done the same. Generally, though, I like to start the trail at the impact site to get a feel for the type of sign and how it shows on the terrain. Knowledge of the last spot the game was seen can help guide my efforts. Usually, by the time this site is reached, I have an idea of what to look for and at what intervals. On blatant trails, it definitely is not time efficient, but on tougher trails, it can save time. (Plus, piecing the trail out is interesting in itself. I'm enough of a blood-trailing nut to even follow the trail on game I've witnessed fall.)

On a trail with decent blood sign, there are a few trailing techniques that can be employed. Which one is best depends on the terrain, amount of sign, and the tracker's or trackers' ability and experience. Sometimes it is wise to mark the latest blood with toilet paper or ribbon. Besides providing a record of where blood or other sign was found, markers also offer a view of the animal's course of travel that may be extrapolated to give a searcher an idea where to expect more sign. (If something nonbiodegradable is used, it is worth the effort to remove it later to keep the environment natural.) Quite often, the tracker knows the locale so intimately that he or she can refind the last blood at will with no markers. When blood is found, it can be advantageous to look further along the anticipated trail or possible routes from that point to locate more blood or sign of travel. Surprisingly often, sign can be discerned without taking a step. Still without moving, the eyes can scour beyond that sign and even beyond any further sign discovered as far as vision allows. It is remarkable how far ahead the course can be traced in this manner and, at the same time, the chance of the tracker accidentally fouling the trail is avoided. Some types of trails, through dewed vegetation or wavy grasses for instance, are much easier to distinguish from the distant view than from up close.

An alternative to marking the trail when more than one tracker is present is for one person to continue the diligent search along possible routes while one remains at the last blood. The person acting as a marker need not be inert, for the area can be studied for prints or ruffled vegetation that indicate the direction or speed of travel, and the blood can be read to interpret information about the wound, and it too can demonstrate the direction and rate of travel as well as the time elapsed since the passage of the animal. The degree of coagulation and drying lets the tracker, depending on humidity, wind, and local factors, estimate the time it was deposited. When the blood is fresher than at previous sites, one should suspect that the animal has been jumped from a resting site and wounds reopened. Thick blood that does not run or splatter on the surface on which it falls is indicative of a wound that is clotting. Shade must be considered when evaluating blood sign for age. Blood falling in places protected from the sun will look much fresher than those in the open. Keep in mind, shade moves with the sun too. Blood in bright sunlight could have been in the shade earlier and vice versa. Splatters of blood yield evidence of the direction the blood was traveling as it contacted the substrate. A portion of its momentum can be attributed to a spurting wound, but most of it will be imparted by the movement of the fleeing animal and will point generally in the direction it was heading. A simple way of imagining it is that each bit of blood is like a thrown water balloon. There will be a wet spot where it hits, but the splashes extending from it will primarily follow the direction the balloon was heading. This not only supplies the tracker with the animal's direction but also sheds light on the speed the animal was traveling. By the way, if a larger spot or pool of blood is encountered, the likelihood of a pause or stop on the part of the target animal should be considered. If the animal is stationary, the falling blood may not splatter or the splatters may extend equally in all directions. Whenever animals pause, the course they take from the spot may differ substantially from the one held to before the hesitation. At any pool of blood, it is worthwhile to mull over the possibility of a change of direction.

While discussing blood sign, it is worth pointing out that how easily blood is discerned has to do not only with the blood and its freshness and quantity but also with where it lands. On absorbent surfaces, it becomes dull quickly, and dark mud can practically mask it.

With multiple trackers, sometimes the leapfrog approach is utilized. One or two trackers painstakingly follow the blood spoor while others range ahead in hopes of intercepting the trail to save time. Very frequently it does work. A disadvantage is that the people searching ahead are leaving their own sign that can camouflage, degrade, or destroy the true trail. This can be especially problematic if the trail deteriorates to a minimal level of blood. The trail from the doe at St. Mark's mentioned a few a pages ago is one where we employed leapfrogging, and while we were young and relatively inexperienced at the time (several of us still hunt together to this day), I feel sure we would not have found that deer without resorting to that tactic. There was pitifully meager blood, and the distance was extreme. Often, a leapfrogger found blood two hundred yards from the last sign. The terrain switched between knee-deep cypress ponds and dry, leaf-strewn scrub hills, and the doe's course meandered dramatically.

Blood droplets on frond with splatters distinctly pointing in the direction the game traveled—here to the picture's left.

Splatters show the fleeing animal's direction, once again to the left. When analyzing sign to estimate the time the animal passed, shade or lack of shade needs to be considered. Note the difference in the appearance of the blood exposed to the sun and of the blood pooled under the shade of part of the frond. The protected blood is still liquid and brightly red despite the photo being taken three and a half hours after the deer's flight.

Again, splatters on the same trail offer directional evidence (toward the top of the picture), but here it will be noted the animal's pace has slackened.

On absorbent surfaces, blood will look lusterless and
dull and is therefore more difficult to spot.

When a trail becomes unclear, whether blood is present or not, sometimes the tracker needs to investigate several possible routes stemming from the last sign. Tendencies exhibited up to that point influence which route should be tried first. If the animal has basically been progressing in a straight line, a continuation in that direction is warranted. If it is gradually hooking right, a pathway in harmony with that course should be examined. Each possibility is followed and scrutinized for a long enough distance to ascertain proof the animal did or did not travel that way. The distance required depends on the amount of sign being deposited and the type of terrain. It could be a few yards to fifty or sixty yards or more. Thick areas of vegetation pinching a trail could reveal smears of blood to confirm it, or a low, undisturbed spiderweb could rule out the passageway. Likewise, a prolonged area of mud or sand would manifest either prints or the lack of prints. This intense examination of possible routes is one of the most frequently used tools in the tracker's bag. Again, the tracker is depositing his or her own sign during this investigation so progressing very slowly and noting every detail carefully, even though it costs time exactly when time seems precious, is worthwhile. Hurriedly checking several possible courses is tempting and may speed up the process if sign is discovered, but if no sign is forthcoming, small details may have been obliterated and misleading sign deposited. Even trails that have so much blood that it seems the tracker should be able to follow by feel can end abruptly and one doesn't know beforehand when this will occur, so it is best to treat each trail as if it might dwindle suddenly and not risk destroying any small indication of the game's passage. Often, more possible routes ramify from each of the possible routes first encountered, and losing one bit of evidence may widen the search area exponentially. By the way, the advice to try the most likely course first is sound but doesn't need to be adhered to always. If some routes enter brush or terrain that would make determining if the wounded animal passed that way quick and easy, it might be very worthwhile to rule them out at the onset.

The trail included in the introduction demonstrated the value of following multiple possible passageways. Readers of *Bows, Swamps, Whitetails* will remember the following account that demonstrates both the puzzling termination of tremendous blood sign and the practice of trying all possible pathways. (In fact, a few of the trails mentioned in that book will be included here where they are ideal examples of techniques or tendencies being discussed.)

On a misty, mosquitoey morning deep in the swampwoods, I stood vigil in a stand on a cabbage palm. It was mid-November, but the temperature was still destined to reach into the nineties. The wind was predicted to be from the south (even though it proved to be light and variable), so I had entered the dark, pre-dawn woods hundreds of yards to the west and headed north and eventually looped back east and then south. Normally, I have little difficulty navigating the swamp because I pay attention to my compass, and my binoculars pick up enough light to allow me to recognize distinctive trees, stumps, or patterns of growth. This morning I was worried, however, since the heavy fog forbade recognition of anything more than ten yards distant, and I wanted desperately not to leave any more scent on the ground than the absolute minimum. With unbelievably good luck, my looping course with "dead reckoning" delivered me exactly to the palm I wished to climb. Squeals, grunts, and roars just south of me as I readied my climber indicated hogs accompanied by at least one decent boar close at hand, but I had no wish to spread my scent in that direction after all the work I had shouldered to avoid that very thing. Despite some areas that would allow unimpeded arrow flight, my palm was surrounded by many young, low cabbage palms with their umbrellas of heavy fronds. Unlike brush that can be partially seen through, these big plants completely blocked any view.

As the light increased, the swampwoods looked white from the thickness of the fog. A doe stepped out from under one such low tree, and I readied neither bow nor camera for I had only one doe tag left and the light was insufficient for a good photo. Soon, I sat down to read but half a page later was distracted by the arrival of a buck where the doe had been, no more than ten yards away, his approach screened by the fronds (or maybe by too much interest in my book). I videoed him, but soon saw while one antler sported only three points, the other held four. His spread and mass were both good, and one point must have been injured when he was in velvet and made two right angle turns, one inward and one back upward again, which gave the thick antlers a very interesting look. He was head first toward me and nearly below me by the time I readied Bane Too, and he could catch my scent momentarily. A quartering away angle would be better, but waiting would likely mean no shot, and this was by no means a low percentage shot. Everything happened fast—the light *thunk* of the recurve, the *ssshep* of the arrow whisking through the buck, a great, vivid spurt of blood erupting from his back! He crashed off. I picked a landmark for his course and another for the last place I saw him. It was close, of course, with the limited visibility. The last sound was of a frond just beyond where he disappeared because the swamp floor was damp and the fog hushed all noise.

The spurt indicated a great wound, probably piercing the aorta with the midline hit. I scanned the way he ran with binoculars and then scanned again, seeing no blood. Now doubts assailed me. Had the spurt only been a figment? It was hard to remain on the stand with all the thoughts swirling through my head. My shot, although it looked good, may have been further back than I thought. A gutshot deer would need time, and it would not be good to push him in the thick and tangled jungle to which he had fled. On the other hand, gutshot deer don't usually race away blindly, especially when they don't know where the danger originated. Typically, if they do jump or run, they slow quickly, hunch up, and stop or wander off slowly. All these conflicting ideas circled about in my brain, and I knew the wait would be tedious. My watch said 8:00 a.m. There was no hope of losing myself back into the book.

A spike diverted my attention. He had three-inch hard antlers and probably weighed eighty pounds, which for our area was big for a six-month-old deer and gave me hope that he might be a good buck someday. He encountered my scent trail and instantly fled ten yards or so, then steadied and surveyed the area. After sniffing a few ferns, he began feeding again. Soon he fed to within a few yards of my arrow that had passed through the buck. He became very uneasy and left.

I viewed the arrow again with binoculars, and I couldn't believe it! The lighting must have changed. The blood trail started right at the arrow and continued the eight yards where it vanished under the palm fronds, brightly splashing everything with red bubbly blood! I was elated. It was 9:15 a.m., and I climbed down. The arrow was red and the trail great, and I followed happily with no concerns and with the tree stand on my back since he ran toward one edge of the swamp and I was deep enough in that I had no wish to retrace my steps. I could drive the truck around to a different pasture much more easily than drag a big deer an extra five or six hundred yards through the swamp bottom with its cypress knees, crisscrossed fallen trees, and mud. Yet now, the tremendous trail ended abruptly with a giant splash of blood against a palm frond twenty yards from my tree. How could such a remarkably super trail disappear, not petering out but simply ending all at once? The trail had to be somewhere and I circled about and experimented with different possible routes for fifteen minutes or so. Then, depressed, I returned to the start, took the tree stand from my back and dug in for some meticulous tracking, my mind still reeling from the repeated soaring and sinking of my hopes.

To shorten a long story, three tiny specks of blood (ten to fifteen yards apart), a bent fern, a loose piece of soil on a leaf, in concert led me, an hour and a quarter later, seventy yards from the stand (and the first twenty of those were blatant). Once again, I resorted to following out twenty or more yards in each possible route, looking for anything that could indicate his passage beyond that point. One of these searches revealed him slightly to the south. He had fallen midleap and died upright, his front legs stretched forward and his back ones crouched and looking ready to spring. His head lay to the side, one antler partially embedded in the black swamp earth. He was beautiful.

My arrow had severed the aorta, and his total run was less than a hundred yards. The exit wound did open his belly area, and a wad of intestines the size of a big fist had somehow pushed through and sealed the wound completely. Retrieving the tree stand, I began the drag. Two hundred and fifty yards doesn't sound terribly bad, but most of it was through vegetation so thick it forced me to crawl so it was plenty strenuous with a tree stand on my back, a bow in one hand and a heavy buck dragging behind the other. Happily, the sweat, discomfort, and travail of the drag were, but memories once I attained the more open pasture outside the tree line while the elation of arrowing a regal buck remained. I left him in the pasture in the shade of a myrtle. I walked unburdened through a corner of the swamp to get to the truck and three quarters of an hour later loaded him into the bed. What a beauty! He weighed 152 pounds, but that was on a scale that hadn't dragged him out. I would have allocated him a much heavier number!

Here is another account as a further example: One December, the game was concentrated in the swamp and each hunt was a parade of deer, hogs, turkeys, raccoons, squirrels, otters, wood ducks, and more. The trouble was that while the action was nearly nonstop, the bucks were five points, six points, four points, spikes; not a single deer with antlers large enough to launch an arrow toward. This motivated me to hunt outside the swamp, and I spent a few days during which the total mammal sightings amounted to three raccoons and three does. This was a far cry from all the life and action in the swampwoods. Two and a half months earlier, in archery season, I had hunted an area of Tyson Creek twice. There were several good rubs, but both times I hunted it, the wind ruled out the spot that appeared to be best, so I had set up eighty yards off once and a hundred and twenty the other occasion. Even though I hadn't scouted it lately, the idea of giving it a try seemed irresistible, coupling buck sign and all that swamp activity with an uncontaminated area scent-wise. With the wind gusting from the northeast, I entered the swampwoods three or four hundred yards to the south. A creek channel came close to the edge there and bent westward as it progressed north, allowing me an approach to the area first in flowing water and then into the wind. Eighty or so yards south of the spot, an oak was raining down acorns continuously, and the swamp floor had been churned to black mud for ten yards in all directions from its trunk, and not a span of two inches existed in all that mud between hoof prints! I continued north, happy for the flowing creek water that was carrying away the greatest portion of my scent. Fifteen yards beyond was a stand of dozens of young bay trees that a few years ago a buck had utilized repeatedly for rubbing. In archery season, none bore fresh rubs, and now several were bared to the core. I retraced my steps and scanned for a climbable tree just west of the mud-haloed oak. The one that would serve best had a few heavy branches that would thwart my climbing stand, but there was a folding saw in my pack. I climbed, sawed, and sweated and climbed, sawed, and sweated, finally getting up about thirteen feet. Somehow, my binoculars bumped the seat portion of the stand during all this, and the right eyecup was dislodged. My impulse was to immediately look for it under the stand because binoculars are so helpful in so many ways, but the exertion of all the sawing had me drenched and parched. Going back down would mean even more sweating. I was vehemently opposed to increasing or spreading my scent any further. In addition, the work had left me very thirsty, and more effort would deepen that thirst. Plus, sounds indicated animals were afoot! The binoculars could be used as they were with careful bracing against my face, but the concern was that ordering a replacement could involve weeks, and this was no time of the year to be without them.

Hogs began to show up immediately. They came and went and were replaced by others, but one or more were with me as persistently as my thirst for the entire afternoon. Sunset was probably around 5:30 p.m., meaning legal hunting ended at 6:00 p.m. Rarely do I give up before the time limit has arrived, but at 5:40 p.m., I was ready to get down because of my strong thirst and my concern to find the eyecup amid the mud and ferns while there was still light. Standing to start my decent, I took a last sweeping glance and noticed a white thing bobbing up and down maybe sixty yards away. It disappeared and came back. The lopsided binoculars revealed it was a well-camouflaged eight-point buck vigorously making a rub. When he would turn to get both antlers on the trunk, his throat patch faced me, and that was the moving white blob that caught my attention. Ferns hid most of him, but nonetheless, it was amazing to witness how difficult it was to discern him whenever he stopped rubbing. There is no doubt, if he hadn't been rubbing, I would have detected no inkling of his nearness and spooked him as I climbed down. He stopped rubbing and walked quickly to the oak. He was broadside, and Bane Too pulled as smoothly as ever; the release was a muffled *thunk*, and the arrow flew true. The hit looked good, but the sound was hollow and "splooshy." The buck walked south, staying in the creek thirty or forty yards and then angling southwest. I lost sight of him behind a tree eighty yards away. The arrow lay on the mud where he had been, at right angles to the path it had flown. From the tree, it looked clean.

I clambered down immediately. Fortune smiled, and I found the eyecup with ease. The arrow proved to be soaked with blood but did carry the smell of stomach contents as well. Few plants extended above the flowing creek waters but each exposed leaf was coated with bright blood, and it was very obvious where he left the creek. However, just ten yards further, the trail became quite sparse. He had not hunched like a gutshot deer, but the smell on the arrow was worrisome. Something, probably another hog, crashed off north of me. Even though I had seen the deer south of where I now was trailing, I became fearful I might spook the buck and then my chances of finding him would plummet.

I eased out and returned the next morning. With the dampness of the swamp, the blood trail remained easily readable, but I still couldn't find a drop past where I had been stymied the night before.

Discouraged, I walked out possible trails, looking for any hoof print or speck of blood. On the third path he was laying thirty yards beyond the last drop. His rack was beautiful, full of fresh wood shavings and the rich color of tea with streaks of amber. The brow tines were long, and the third tines (G-3s) were longer than the seconds. The entry wound was close to ten inches in front of the rear edge of the ribs, and the exit hole was three inches forward of the back edge. The Wensel Woodsman had passed through both lungs yet somehow caught the paunch as well. Tissue had partially blocked the external wounds. The chest cavity itself was awash with blood.

The tactic of trying each and every possible route is used so commonly it will show up in many of the trails this book contains as examples. By the way, both of these trails started with a lot of blood and tapered off. The reasons differed a bit. In the first, the blood evidence ended abruptly when the exit wound was sealed completely with protruding intestines. As blood is lost, blood pressure falls so less blood is available to make the trail and less pressure is propelling it from the body. This, in combination with the partially obstructed wound channels, was the explanation for the second trail fizzling, and when it occurs, the animal is usually not too distant. Another possible reason for diminished blood on the trail is clotting. Clotting could indicate a non-lethal wound but not always, for one portion of the wound channel could clot while another is reducing blood volume or pressure without it leaving the body. A wound that does not enter the body cavity, and clots will most often not be fatal unless it becomes severely infected.

CHAPTER 3

Tracking without Blood

UNFORTUNATELY, NOT EVERY HIT ELICITS a trail glistening with blood. A poor hit could be the cause, but it may not be wise to jump to that conclusion for there are many possible explanations. With high wounds, blood may fill a lot of the body cavity before running from the wound itself. A failure to achieve an exit wound greatly restricts the volume of blood leaving the body. The buck a few pages back whose wound was sealed by intestines reminds us lethal wounds can be blocked. Shock and its attending drop in blood pressure should also be remembered. Skin is only loosely attached to the underlying muscle and bone. In fact, the reader can use a finger or two to slide the skin on the back of the opposite hand or the skin over the forearm to demonstrate how much it can move. When a game animal presents for a shot, be it from rifle or bow, the head may be turned or a leg outstretched in a way that pulls the skin over the chest. When more normal postures are readopted, the hole through the skin will no longer line up with the hole through the chest. This blocks or limits blood escaping the wound. When the expired game is found, the skin must be manipulated to make the two holes coincide. With all these examples, blood pressure and working blood volume drop precipitously with little or no blood spilling on the trail. On top of scanty blood leakage, dry terrain can soak in blood. Watery expanses and rain-covered ground and vegetation dilute blood. Plus, falling rain or snow can cover blood.

Let me return for a moment to the possibility of the hole through the skin not aligning with the hole through the ribs. This is not a freak occurrence. I've seen at least eighty such cases and probably several more. The same separation of holes that it would seem should correspond is also described by Jim Corbett in *The Man-Eaters of Kumaon*. As a writer, hunter, and outdoorsman, Jim Corbett has my utmost respect and appreciation, so it may be worthwhile to quote him: "The skin of animals is loose. When an animal that is standing still is hit in the body by a bullet and dashes away at full speed, the hole made in the skin does not coincide with the hole in the flesh, with the result that, as long as the animal is running at speed, little if any blood flows from the wound. When, however, the animal slows down and the holes come closer together, blood flows and continues to flow more freely the slower the animal goes."

Tracking when no or little blood is present is more difficult, but considering that unwounded animals (or people) can be tracked, it stands to reason that wounded ones can be as well. In fact, the term *blood trailing* is not ideal because it conveys the notion that the searcher is looking for blood when, in truth, the searcher is looking for any sign that reveals the animal's course. These indications are numberless and will vary with terrain, but we can examine several possibilities.

"Prints" are the depressions left in the substrate after an animal passes. They are registrations of the earth's reaction to the forces that balance or move an animal. Some substrates, for instance, mud, snow, or sand, react more obviously than others, say rock or heavily vegetated soil. All substrates react, but the ease with which it is discovered varies dramatically.

Animals maintaining the same rate of speed will have repeated stride lengths. With these repeated strides, the prints will register equidistantly. This fact makes a tracking stick incredibly helpful. A tracking stick can be fashioned from a branch, sapling, reed, or anything that is close at hand that is at least as long as the stride of the animal being tracked. Where tracks register clearly, the stick can be broken or marked to match the distance between tracks.

For anyone who tracks regularly, it is worthwhile to construct one. I like a sharpened peg, ten to twelve inches in length, fastened to the stick with a rope or heavy rubber band in such a way that the stick can pivot but does not slide up or down its length without deliberate pressure. The peg can be inserted in the ground on or adjacent to a track (adjacent is better to avoid disturbing any information the track may hold) and the stick adjusted forward or backward until its end coincides with the next track. After that, the peg is moved to the more advanced track, and the next track will be located on the arc the end of the stick can make. This drastically narrows the tracker's focus to an exact region and greatly improves the chance of discovering the subsequent track. The stick will remain accurate as long as the animal maintains its current pace. This fact is also helpful because it alerts the tracker of the change in speed and forewarns him or her of the quarry's altered behavior that could signal bedding or a shift in direction. Prints on formidable terrain are more likely to be descried with the tracking stick's way of fine-tuning the search. It is an invaluable tool in any tracker's bag. When tracking without one, even on superb substrate, changes in rate of travel are seldom recognized as early. The stick can be readjusted or marked to the new stride length.

One design that is simple, inexpensive, and light to carry is a length of three-fourths inch PVC tubing (length depending upon species tracked). Cut off ten inches. Cut this piece diagonally for about five inches from one end to sharpen the tip like a stake. With monofilament or twine or a strong rubber band, attach this piece at right angles to the main stick so that it can slide with difficulty along the stick's length and also so the main length can pivot on the stake portion. Typical stride lengths for various speeds and various species can be drawn with colored markers on the stick. This allows the tracker to compare the speed of the animal that is being tracked to known gaits. Also, for convenient carry, the main length can be shortened and made to house a narrower PVC or wooden dowel inside that slides out for increased length. Another design is simply a push broom handle with a few O-rings that fit tightly along its shaft that can be adjusted to mark stride lengths.

Although carrying a tracking stick may initially seem cumbersome, after enjoying the advantages it provides on trails, most trackers happily submit to the inconvenience. A tracker need not wait for a blood trail to gain experience with the stick for it can be employed anywhere a track is discovered. When the terrain changes so that the only sign is a bent grass blade or a dust free spot on a rock, knowing the exact distance to examine in detail is useful and time saving. Also, where an abundance of tracks from other animals of the same species confuse the trail, the stick helps keep the tracker on the correct sign.

The following account is of a trail that seemed too simple to require a tracking stick, but in retrospect, a tracking stick may have kept me from being misled:

In a large aspen grove in the White River National Forest, I happened upon a place where clear water trickled gently out of the side of a ravine, flowed as a tiny rivulet for maybe fifteen yards, and disappeared into a flat, muddy area that elk had converted into a wallow. Adjacent to the wallow, a large aspen had partially fallen, wedging between two others in a diagonal fashion. The angle was not very steep and allowed me to walk along it to one of the upright trees and there sit or stand comfortably almost directly over the wallow. The undergrowth that pervaded the surrounding woods was almost nonexistent around this little seep. Before finding the spot, I had gotten within fifteen yards of five different bulls without getting a single shot opportunity due to the thickness of the understory, so it seemed a perfect place to wait in ambush.

The next morning, I was there trading calls with big-voiced bull. He wouldn't leave the vicinity, but neither would he come to the seep. Suddenly, a 4 × 4 with pencilish antlers passed above my perch enticed by my cow calls. As soon as he dipped over the next little crest, I made a cow "chirp." He instantly reappeared, issuing low mewing sounds apparently trying to contact the cow but not wanting to let the belligerently vocal bull hear him. After the youngster had passed, the nearby bull went into a bugling tirade. None of my entreating calls, although each produced an immediate and vociferous response, would lure him back. Over the course of an hour or so, the big bull (based on voice) moved upward and east. Then a bull started bugling below me. He responded with alacrity to my cow calls. His rack was visible at thirty yards and looked good. The wind carried him enough of my scent that he retreated to about fifty yards and paced about trashing trees and shrieking out bugles but venturing no closer, and finally, after twenty minutes or more, he worked his way down the aspen-covered draws beyond hearing.

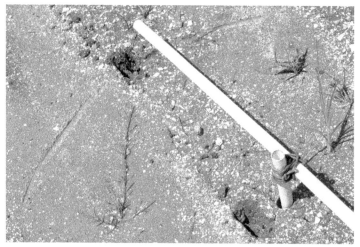

The stride length on the stick is adjusted and set where the tracks are obvious. The scraped sand to each side of the track highlights the arc upon which the next track should fall.

In this photo, the next track is slightly more difficult to
see, but the retained stride length is apparent.

Where the track falls on more vegetated areas, the tracking stick guides the tracker's eyes to the correct place to search.

Which track is from your animal? Where tracks from several animals converge, a tracking stick helps pinpoint the correct track.

The second morning, my first call enticed a spike to the wallow followed by a cow and calf. A big bugle rang through the aspens. Each time I called, his response came closer. A mature aspen forest with the thick, white boles starkly reaching skyward and the lushness of the undergrowth blending with the greenery of aspen tops from the trees growing out of the bottoms of deep, adjacent draws, accentuated here and there with clusters of bright red berries and flitting birds, is a beautiful and nearly magical place. Its spirit is a quiet one, and the way elk can ghost through it in silence seems in perfect harmony with the cathedral-like spell it casts. This bull however, changed the aura. His bugles raged like blasting screams and ended in coarse, harsh grunts and panting chuckles. Each roaring bugle conveyed vitality and an intense, primal force. They filled the air and echoed around and distance became hard to judge because of the heights of the crests and the depths of the ravines. One bugle shrieked out amazingly close and out stepped a massive 6 × 6 at twelve yards but south of where I had guessed his approach. Caught off guard and needing room to draw the bow, I shifted position on the slanted tree. The bull spooked. He ran upward thirty yards and, screened by limbs and brush, continued his roars and forceful squeals for a half an hour without returning. Eventually, his bugles faded with distance.

I was crestfallen. The excitement of the bull's shrieks and the power, force, and vigor they expressed had my heart pounding. He had not hidden his approach, yet still I hadn't been able to foresee where he would arrive. I didn't know if I could remain on the tree trunk looking at a spot of earth twelve yards away where a spectacular bull had been without me taking advantage of it. Mercifully, I did not have to ponder it long for as the giant relinquished the territory, another bull moved into it. He screamed readily to both my cow calls and bugles but from never closer than sixty yards as estimated by the sounds. By eleven o'clock, he would only bugle in response to my calls and sounded as if he were anchored to one spot.

It was obvious after all this time that he wasn't coming to the wallow, and even with my firsthand knowledge of the thickness of the surrounding cover, I elected to attempt a stalk. This involved first making my way downhill and downwind a little over a hundred yards and then easing southward sixty or seventy and then scrambling back up. At times, I used elk trails and quiet movement was not difficult with a little care, but most of the time, especially when venturing back up the densely vegetated draw, incredibly slow movement and great diligence were required. Even then, silence was not achievable, and when I reached within thirty or forty yards of where I estimated his last bugle had emanated, I felt further encroachment could not go unnoticed.

I bugled, and he went crazy. Maybe this was because of my nearness to him—I can't say for sure—but regardless, his bugles were combinations of vehement screams and roars, and all the time his antlers were bashing and tearing shrubs. His distance must have been no more than thirty yards, yet not a patch of brown nor a trace of movement could be seen through the densely woven brush. Despite this, sounds left no doubt he was approaching, squealing roars unbelievably loud and deep from their nearness and the breaking of branches as he lashed trees mercilessly with his antlers every couple yards. I looked frantically for a place I could stand upright. There were none. With no time left to move, I settled for a spot that might allow me to draw my bow. Branches cracked and walking legs could be seen at seventeen yards. He stopped and utterly destroyed a shrub. Then he was broadside at ten to twelve yards. I could see bits of his chest, but there was no avenue for an arrow to reach it. I drew awkwardly and panned with him, hoping for one gap, but soon he was hidden, and too soon he crashed off, obviously discovering my scent.

The next morning, I tried the wallow again. (Because of the thermals, evening hunts would only educate the elk.) The morning passed with no sounds or glimpses of elk, and I felt my repeated presence and scent had probably spooked them from the area. By nine o'clock, I felt I was about to burst and since I had given up on the wallow and felt I had already ruined the hunting there, took a leak right from the slanted aspen trunk. A peculiar thing happened. A mule deer doe from downwind walked quickly up and began sniffing. She shuffled back and forth, sampling the air, moving toward me until she was no more than three yards away. She milled about in states fluctuating from cautiousness to curiosity for several minutes and then left. I had planned to get down and cover some ground, but her lack of fear from the urine smell in concert with the lateness of the morning and the fact the book I was reading was good and suspenseful, convinced me to sit a while longer. The book was nearing its end, but it took me to 11:15 to complete it. Several times, I had been on the verge of leaving but each time allowed myself to be lured into reading just a little more. (Thank you, Tony Hillerman!) I took my sweater off in preparation of leaving, took a second leak, and was astounded to hear a crashing in the underbrush from downwind and below me. A 4 x 5 bull trotted to the wallow. He paused at seventeen or eighteen yards and turned broadside. I had Deer Bane in hand and drew. The arrow leapt from the string, slipping quietly and quickly through the bull's chest. The bull lunged off downhill with massive leaps, disappearing instantly. I took a compass bearing on the last sound of his retreat, fervently hoping it equated to his resting place. Quite possibly, though, it was only where the deep aspen woods and steep, earthy ravines swallowed the noise.

The part of my arrow not buried in the dirt was completely and thickly covered with blood, amazingly so for how fast it seemed to pass through. Not far from the arrow a little blood showed, but the running tracks with the splayed hooves and the fresh dirt sprayed about were so obvious I had no difficulty following them. Surprisingly, I found absolutely no more blood. After about 150 yards, the running trail became obscure. There were elk tracks everywhere in the soft, exposed earth on the trails. I tried to piece together the bull's further progress but became bewildered each time. Frustrated, even more so remembering all the close opportunities the last few days had offered, I turned to go back toward the running tracks. There above me, back near a vertical wall of earth, was my fallen bull. The shear drop-off was about twenty-five feet. Above him was a trail awash with blood. Apparently, another bull had been with him but had not yet emerged from the thick when I shot the 4 × 5. My bull's abrupt departure caused the other bull to race off as well, but it must have stopped when my bull fell. I had followed the wrong set of running tracks and been enticed away from the true and heavy blood trail. A tracking stick should have announced the change in strides and made me search for the correct track.

The following trail demonstrates how the distance remaining constant between tracks can help overcome confusion by additional tracks:

One early morning, I mounted a ladder stand in an oak scrub. Florida oak scrubs are very interesting habitats, actually remnants of old seashores from hundreds of thousands years ago when most of Florida was underwater. These areas are almost dessert-like with arid conditions and white sand as a soil that hosts specialized trees and shrubs and grasses. The oaks themselves are stunted-looking, and therefore, there are few suitable places for tree stands. My ladder stand was tied to the spindly topmost branch of a scrubby oak and guyed in several directions to keep it from toppling. Any motion caused it to sway unnervingly and shook the surrounding clump. I was barely up and still situating my stool, bow, and rattling antlers when a four-point walked out from the oak clump nearest mine. He fed about, oblivious to my form above him and the oscillating branches. The meager grey light of the new day prevented any photos. The view from the stand allowed distant vision in certain places but also could hide approaching game until it was nearly straight below.

Gradually, the day grew light and the mosquitoes grew less attentive, but only slightly less. It seemed marvelous that they could swarm here in this dry environment, but the creek bottom woods were probably only four hundred yards away. Another young buck walked by at thirty yards. I clicked a few exposures, but the light still wasn't all that adequate. Another deer was ninety yards to the north. The head was hidden, but the body looked impressive. When it stepped out of view to the east, another, smaller deer filled the same space. My first thought was that it must be a fawn following a doe, but binoculars revealed a young six-point.

I should have described the area better because it is unique and beautiful. The soil is white sugar sand sparsely vegetated. There are clumps of saw palmetto and matted sandweed here and there and islands of dark green and grey where the oaks form clumps and hedges and domes. A few places are carpeted with gopher apple, and the struggling grasses include silk grass with pretty yellow flowers. Scattered thinly are the narrow, wiry stems that hold the appealing blooms of sabatia. Under the stunted-looking oaks, the ground is brown with a brittle coating of dry leaves, but elsewhere, it is glaringly white, the contrast so great it challenges photography. Interestingly, people looking at wildlife photos from the scrub nearly all assume the background is snow.

The young buck followed the other deer and likewise was lost to sight, but I held my binoculars ready at the next place that should offer a view if they continued east. Minutes passed before a small buck walked through this opening. I concluded the bigger deer had already passed either while I was engaged brushing mosquitoes or looking elsewhere for deer. To the east, there were no more avenues to allow any view, so I thought maybe a grunt would lure the bigger deer back. As the sound came from my mouth, a buck stepped into the opening and looked squarely at me. He was a fully grown, mature buck with a great rack. He stared, then turned and followed the deer in front of him (which I assumed at that time had passed him, but as more bucks showed up, I realized there could still have been one behind him).

The grunt had not seemed to entice him, so after a minute, I picked up the antlers and bashed and rattled them. Setting them down on the dense oak branches at my feet, I readied Nightshade. Sometimes bucks react rapidly to the rattles, and twice I had lost incredible opportunities by not being ready quickly enough, but this time, minutes dragged on and then a small buck arrived. He was a four-point or maybe a six-point if he had brow tines. The bow in my hands precluded photos or binocular inspection. In time, he left and the scrub looked empty. Finally, I set the bow down and reached to pick up the antlers, only to have a big buck push through the oaks thirty yards to the north and walk directly toward me. Tine counting at moments like these doesn't occur to me, but I could see his neck was large, his body was large, and his rack was large! My assumption was he was a ten point and a very good one. By the time I could pick up the bow and turn toward him, he was twenty yards off and still heading straight at me. My movement to get ready shook the whole oak, and he stopped and stared at me, stamped twice, and scatted back ten yards. He half walked, half trotted in a prancey, nervous way west, slowed to a walk, and turned south, no doubt, to give his nose a chance to clear up the mystery. All this I could see through the thinner scrub like though a screen, but no arrow flight was possible. There was an opening west of me, and when he entered it, I released. Nightshade is not a quiet bow and with the sound, the buck lunged and I was aghast to see the arrow strike back! The buck ran west with cheetah-like speed, but he looked wrong, his rear end was low, and he seemed to be scrabbling. His pace never diminished even as he disappeared from view. Two bucks, one mature, the other racked but smaller, that had been north of my stand without my knowledge, now ran to where my buck had rocketed.

The evidence of the hit was conflicting and confusing. The buck was broadside when I released, and because of his leap forward, my arrow appeared to pierce the middle of his abdomen, the worst of all hits. Yet never had I witnessed a non-mortally struck deer plunge off that way, with phenomenal speed and no sign of a hunch. I elected to check my arrow and the area he had been when I shot for sign and then make a decision as to when to follow. The trouble was that a long period of searching discovered neither arrow nor blood. Nothing in the abdomen should have stopped one of my heavy arrows. The missing arrow heightened my suspicions that the wound was more dire than a gutshot alone.

The sugar sand prominently recorded his pounding tracks, the gouged sand a little greyer and moister than the surface sand because the morning sun hadn't heated and dried it yet. Now as the sun was ascending in the sky, the heat would quickly restore the blaring whiteness of the sand, so tracking sooner would be much easier than doing so later. His westward course would take him from the good tracking sand in less than a hundred yards. His strides were incredibly long, spacing the tracks much further than the length of any stick I could find near at hand, but I paced them off with my steps right away while the tracks were clear. They continued through more sand and leaf litter becoming more difficult to discern as I progressed and became even more complicated when the tracks of the other two bucks merged into the same general pathway. At this point, using my steps to mimic his stride length helped immensely as his leaps were dramatically longer. A comparison of the strides also gave an impression that his flight was more desperate and added a bit more weight to my growing conviction that my shot may have been quickly lethal. Sorting out the tracks and finding them in the leaves under the oaks was somewhat painstaking, and my progress was snail-like.

I looked up to see a buck peering my way over top of some palmettos from eleven yards. My first thought was that my buck was sorely hurt yet still standing so, remaining in my crouched position, I readied an arrow. Easing to my feet did not spook him. Oak branches obscured his antlers and much of his face, but his body looked large and mature. I hesitated, not wanting to shoot a second buck but definitely not wanting to pass a chance at getting a second arrow in mine if he was only gut wounded. The buck had been aware of me since I first saw him, but I guess the interfering oak branches rendered me indistinct enough that he wasn't sure what I was. He walked southeast and stepped into the open at fifteen yards. He was a mature eight point and alert enough to immediately bound away upon getting a clear view of me. I was glad I hadn't shot, but wished I had readied my camera instead of the bow. He may have been one of the deer that left the troublesome extra running tracks or may have been another buck altogether.

Bit by bit, I puzzled the trail out three hundred yards from my stand. Two drops of blood along the way confirmed I was on the correct trail. The rest of the way was gleaned from evidence of hoof prints, much harder to discover now that the ground was firmer and covered with grasses and other greenery. My measured steps were still effective at narrowing the search area, so the buck had obviously maintained his breakneck speed. Happily, the trail was nearly straight. In a half-hour's time, I managed to follow another fifty yards. Here I was stymied. He must have turned or changed his speed for no longer did my steps lead me to even the faintest bit of evidence. I searched along possible routes, which all seemed to lead to the fence line of a piece of private property. There were a few yellow signs posting it, and I walked south to read one in hopes a phone number would be listed that I could call for permission to access the property. Instead, I saw an antler on my side of the fence. He had fallen in a depression forty yards south, apparently turning from his westerly course when encountering the fence.

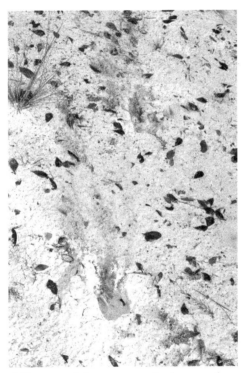

The color difference of the sugar sand when tracks are made in the early morning is easily noticeable. After the sun dries the moisture from the sand, the color becomes uniform again.

Blatant tracks in the scrub sand lead into leaf litter
where they are not so readily discerned.

He was a nine point, very big and heavy. Huffing and puffing and spitting out the mosquitoes sucked in with the air, I dragged him to where a truck could reach. Dressing him solved the mystery of the wound. With the sound of the shot, he lunged forward, south, and away, west. The forward part of the lunge caused my arrow, aimed for his chest, to strike in the abdomen just in front of the rear leg, but the away part of the lunge lined him up so that the arrow drove straight to the front of his chest. With a broadside target, having the arrow end up lengthwise in the animal seems unlikely, if not impossible, but the speed of his reactions effected that result. There was no exit wound, and the intestines sealed the hole around the shaft. For decades, I have heard archers say they like their arrows remaining in the animal to keep cutting. I have always preferred a pass through because I hold an exit wound in high esteem for improving the odds of a great trail. This buck, however, was an incredible example of repeated cutting. The inside of the ribs on the right side was cut so much it was nearly one giant abrasion resembling well ground meat, and the right lung was literally torn to pieces. Despite all the damage, he went 400 to 450 yards. Without blood and without a dog, I was very lucky to find him, and I would gladly have traded an exit wound for all the extra damage as he ran.

This episode illustrates several points. The shot was very far back, and normally, it would be prudent to wait at least twelve hours before taking up the trail. Knowledge and experience, however, contradicted what my eyes saw, the speed and urgency of his flight, the hoof tracks manifesting that he maintained his utmost speed even when well beyond a deer's "danger zone," and his path through brush and barriers rather than detouring a bit to go around them all pointed to a severe and quickly lethal wound. Measuring the stride length was important to keep me on the right tracks. A long tracking stick, if it had been available, would have been far easier than pacing out the stride length. Pacing can disturb sign.

A print alone can spell out a bit about its maker's course and speed. If a hoof or paw was pressed into a substrate and lifted clear perfectly vertically, the edges of the track would be of uniform height for the most part. On firm, impressible substrate, this tendency shows clearly. It can be disguised, however. Imagine placing your own bare foot in oozy mud. As your foot sinks in, some mud will run over the top of it. As the foot is lifted vertically, more mud will flow off the front portion than the heel area, so the edges of the track will be built up higher there. This exemplifies substrate induced inequalities in the print's edges, and this possibility must be kept in mind when interpreting tracks.

However, in compliance with the old physics law, "For every action there is an equal and opposite reaction," on normal substrate, inequalities in the track edges manifest where pressure was exerted. The further the edges have been pushed up, the greater the pressure, and therefore, the greater the force or speed with which the foot left the track. If the edge is pushed up too high for the particular substrate to sustain, it will break off or may actually be pushed away from the track proper. Evidence of the edges being raised to the point of breaking indicates more speed than just being raised, and in turn, more exaggerated and extreme breakage relates even greater speed. Raised or broken edges directly behind a track indicate movement straight ahead. If the raised area is behind and to the left of the track, the movement is forward and to the right. Likewise, movement forward and left would leave higher edges on the right rear portion of the track. Substrate raised or broken to the right or left of the track would be evidence of a sharp, right-angle turn. This information arms the tracker with an idea of both the direction and distance where the next track should be found. The signs of increased speed equates to the next track being located at a further distance. When deer or coyotes have really kicked into high gear, it is not uncommon to have dirt from the edge thrown back a couple feet or more. Stopping or slowing would raise the edge in front of the track.

Substrates vary considerably, so the exact heights that can be achieved and the speeds that cause the elevated portion to break apart, fissure, or spray will vary as well. For example, damp clay may display a very high ridge without crumbling that would denote a higher speed than a broken ridge in loose sand. The ridge in moist sand would break with less force than in clay but not as easily as dry sand. Also, drying of the substrate and wind can alter the appearance of the track between when it was formed and when the tracker reads it. Rain and dew and subsequent animal trails impact prints as well. The more time a tracker spends at the task, the better he or she will be at interpreting the story a track tells. Some of this story will foretell where to expect the next track, but other parts may reveal how desperate the flight is or maybe even if a particular leg is compromised. An injured limb would impart much less force to the soil than the healthy ones and may even display a drag mark. Also, the opposite side counterpart would of necessity bear more weight and leave a deeper track.

At certain gaits, many animals place their hind foot into the place their forefoot just vacated causing what is termed as "direct registered" print. Indications of the direction traveled for each limb will be present, but the second print may disturb the original and the first print changes the terrain upon which the second print is impressed. If the second print is placed on uneven ground or unevenly packed ground, the height of the displaced earth may not be as obvious. Even double registered prints may have some overlap and, thereby, some alteration of both prints. Most outdoorsmen encounter tracks across open ground with a good tracking surface occasionally. Time spent practicing on these tracks builds confidence and makes the chore simpler when it is time to decipher the tracks of a wounded animal.

This mountain lion track shows a fairly even height of mud pushed up around each toe and around the pad. The mud is slightly higher and more fractured to the right (far side of photograph), so the next track is likely barely to the left of straight ahead.

This bear track has pushed up earth behind it, indicating forward movement at a walking pace.

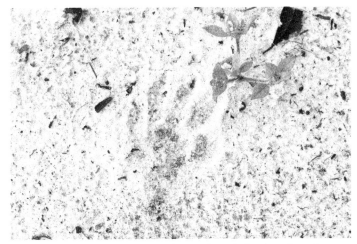

This raccoon track displays a hint of sand displaced to the rear and right, suggesting the beginning of a slight turn to the left.

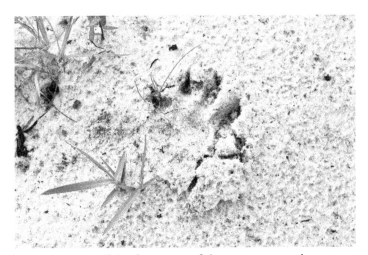

This registration of the front paw of the raccoon was the very next print after the above picture, and it shows a more pronounced turn to the left by the raised and broken sand to the right rear.

Following tracks on great terrain is fairly straightforward. The trouble is that seldom do wounded animals restrict their courses to great tracking terrain. Vegetation that grows in turf-like fashion, areas with inches of accumulated leaf litter, and rocky surfaces all make tracking more challenging. I was once drawn for a hunt on the cantonment area of Camp Blanding. Although woods had reclaimed the area, apparently there were once buildings present, and while no structures were still standing, old concrete slabs were scattered throughout the hunting zone. Deer could be tracked across these slabs because the concrete was less dull where their hooves were placed. To see this, the tracker would need to get very low to the slab and peer over the suspected track toward the sunny side. Also, little scrapes of hoof material would show on uneven parts where slabs had cracked. I've had no experience tracking on extensive rocky surfaces, but I expect they would require a similar technique. On turf-like terrain, prints may be limited to vague compressions, creased or bent leaves, or a minimal color change in the vegetation resulting from the pressure that had been applied. The pressure may have flattened it or squeezed moisture into or out of the plant fibers. Sometimes these barely noticeable changes are more readily spotted from a little distance to the side. Leaf litter may show fluffed up or disturbed leaves. These are also easier to pick out from a bit of distance. If not, there will be tracks there, but damp accumulations may render them very inconspicuous. The tracking stick helps because it limits the search. Carefully removing the top few leaves of a suspected track may reveal a fairly crisp imprint in the more broken-down matter below.

Our swamp bottoms harbor a very aggravating tracking surface. Water levels change continually. Wherever currents occur the bottom is washed of soft earth and what is left is a thick mat of tiny, interwoven roots that resemble huge expanses of soft, rubbery steel wool. It is soft enough to deaden the sounds of footsteps but so resilient that it springs back in minutes or less. I can lift my own foot out and see a distinct track that often even is partially filled with water, yet before my very eyes, it lifts back to normal and disappears. For a few minutes, close scrutiny will discern a different sheen or texture, but after that, try as I may, head low, head angled, I simply can find no remnant. It is a very perplexing local substrate, and no doubt, other locales are home to equally obstreperous surfaces.

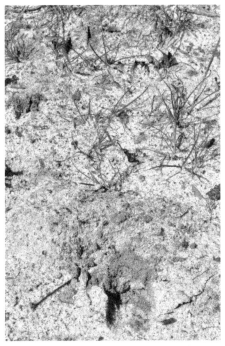

Here is an example of a substrate-induced artifact. A mole tunnel created uneven ground. The sand cracked to the right of the track as though the deer had turned abruptly left, but the next track (at the top of the picture) confirms it traveled forward. The raised edges and the crack were solely the result of the altered substrate.

This track is more complicated to read because the deer's rear hoof was placed into the position the front hoof had vacated. Even so, the sand on the left of the track (bottom of the picture) is more cracked and displaced than that on the right, indicating a minimal shift to the right for the next track.

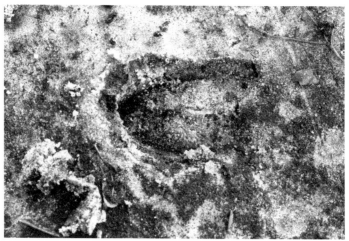

Another direct register track.

Even the greener regions around cypress domes have the same characteristic of rapidly disappearing tracks, although these do show creased and bent edges on the vegetation from deer and hog hooves. Bobcat and raccoon tracks vanish completely.

Blood and prints are the predominant signs upon which trackers rely. They are not the only ones, however. Many other signs occur only in specific terrains, and while this book will list some with which I've had experience, trackers in differing environments will assuredly know of others. Freshly broken twigs and sticks often indicate an animal's passage. The bigger the stick or branch, the more likely the animal was hurried, for at leisure, animals typically take the easiest way. Many brushy areas, cypress heads, and creek wood margins in our area include briars, greenbrier, and other vines. These plants seldom snap mid stem but are regularly pulled in the direction of travel. Many times, the obvious and attention-grabbing clues will be leaves turned wholly or partially wrong side up. Whenever the paler underside shows, it is worth studying the stem that often points toward the direction traveled.

The fallen leaves show some sign of disturbance.

When the fallen leaves from the above picture were
gently removed, a deer track became visible.

In this photograph, the disturbance of the leaf litter is minimal and, without guidance from the tracking stick, may have gone undiscovered.

However, once the leaves were removed, the deer track is readily seen.

Bubbles on the surface of water can evince the quarry's passage. Since water is ubiquitous in the swamps hereabouts, this book will address it more thoroughly in the section on special terrains. Dew is also common and, in open areas where it is present as the animal flees, can make tracking ridiculously easy. The trail an animal leaves by brushing or shaking the dew off wet grass, and vegetation will show up darker (or lighter depending on the vantage point). The tracker can often stand still and trace the route with his or her eyes for as far as vision permits. Usually, the trail appears lighter when the observer gazes in the direction the animal traveled and darker than the surrounding dew-wetted terrain when viewed backward on the trail. While dew heightens this effect, even unwetted grasses display the same phenomenon. The easiest way to demonstrate this appearance is to drive a vehicle across the grassy or brushy terrain and then back to the starting point in two parallel routes. When the trails are looked upon from the starting point, the trail heading away will appear silvery and light. The track used to approach the view point will be darker and greener. Of course, animals have slimmer legs and do not make continuous contact with the substrate, so their trails are not nearly as obvious but are nonetheless present and, once the tracker recognizes their appearance, can often be followed readily. It is amazing how long these simple trails can persist if not disturbed by other animals or excessive winds. The trails endure through rains if they are not torrential in nature.

If the trail is not apparent, sometimes putting oneself on the opposite side of the light source (sun for daytime tracking) can make it more noticeable. If that doesn't help, try a few steps toward the light. By the way, prints also show up most clearly when they are between the tracker's eye and the light source. The lower the light source, the more pronounced the effect. Therefore, for daylight tracking, the overhead light of high noon and the diffuse light of cloudy days can add difficulty to the search.

The exposed lighter underside of the blackberry leaves
indicate the passage of the deer I was trailing.

The gallberries were like a wall to screen the deer, but once again, the
white of upturned leaves gave evidence of where the deer entered.

At night, low flashlight beams from the opposite side can heighten the visibility of both trails through grass or dew and prints in general. For a single tracker, the flashlight is usually held in the hand, and its rays parallel the line of sight. Blood shows up quite well in this manner, but it actually renders subtle prints less visible. As an alternative, an extension that allows the beam to be played toward, but not directly at, the tracker can guide the light over the trail area. Depending upon vegetation, this can result in shadows interfering with vision so the angle and direction may need to be varied and adjusted as the trail progresses. By the way, a flashlight holding adapter can be added to a tracking stick diminishing the number of items a tracker needs to carry. Even holding the flashlight low and to one side by hand can enable the single tracker to pick out prints more readily. With two or more trackers, the flashlights can be angled from each side and alternately be turned on and off to allow each tracker a different view. Another trick that can be efficacious when tracking proves difficult is to change the height of the tracker's eyes. Getting lower to the ground changes the angle and, once again, with both prints and trails through wet vegetation, can highlight the sign. With all these techniques, it is worthwhile to try to preserve the original trail. It is easy to step or walk upon the quarry's path, and then the tracker's sign can obliterate the few traces the animal left behind.

Vehicle tracks exemplify the silvery appearance of the departing trail (*left*) with the darker look of the trail of the vehicle's approach (*right*).

This is a picture of the same two trails viewed from the opposite direction—the trail that was approaching is now departing (left trail). It was darker in the previous photo but is lighter and more silvery here. The right trail is now the one laid as the vehicle approached and is darker. An animal traveling through grass causes the same effect.

The day I took the last two photographs, I happened upon these trails and learned they had been made the afternoon before. The silvery trail was from a Jeep traveling away and the greener, darker trail was from its return. This photograph was taken seventeen hours later. If not disturbed by animals or vehicles or extreme winds, these trails can endure weeks. Often, rains do not erase them.

Animals leave similar trails. Their legs are more slender, and their feet are not in constant contact with the grass like vehicle tires, so they are a bit harder to discern. Here a deer walked a path first toward the left but, at the center of the frame, coursing to the right.

A deer's course is here manifested by the silvery look of
the grass and by the underside of a briar leaf.

A closer view of the upside-down leaf.

Here is the continuation of the trail. Note
the silky appearance of the grass.

When a trail ends and the game is nowhere in sight, some trackers employ a widening circle strategy. The tracker looks for sign along
a circular path that orbits the last sign. The diameter of the circle varies with terrain, but four, five, or six feet would be fairly typical. Since
the path is a circle, the tracker checks diligently for sign in all directions, behind, ahead, and at all angles of the compass. If no sign is
discovered, another circular path slightly wider is tried. If this search
comes up blank, an even larger circle is investigated. The process continues until blood or other sign is found, and then normal tracking
can resume. The advantage of this technique is it concentrates the
tracker's focus very close to the last sign, at least initially, which is
where the likelihood of more sign is the highest. The further one
ventures from the last sign, the less likely any one section of earth will
be where the animal passed. Another advantage is that the circular
pattern automatically checks for an animal reversing its course, a tendency that occurs much more frequently than may be expected. Of
course, the disadvantage is that the tracker disturbs and contaminates
a lot of terrain at the risk of degrading subtle evidences of the quarry.

This photo is of a coyote's track taken from behind it while the light source (the sun) is ahead of the track or, in other words, the track is between the sun and the photographer.

Here is the same track with the sun behind the photographer. Now the track looks flatter and less visible.

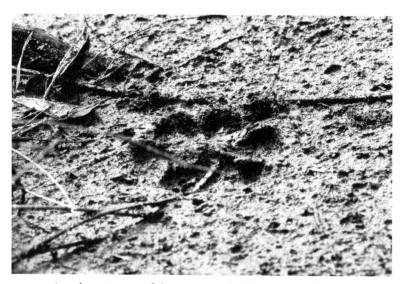

Another picture of the same track. This view is like the
first one except now the angle is lower and the track is even
more pronounced. The position of the light source and
the viewing angle both affect how visible tracks are.

With the morning sun behind the photographer, these coyote tracks are not exceptionally noticeable.

In this exposure, the photographer moved to allow the sunlight to be opposite the tracks, and they become much more apparent, even showing tracks from different directions. Note the little bit of grass that verifies that they are the same tracks.

Displaced rocks and stones and fresh crevices between a stone and its surrounding earth area all indications of a recent disturbance and can be useful clues to an animal's route. Feces are often evacuated by the fleeing animal and offer insight into both course and speed. Mud and other material can be carried by a creature's hooves, paws, or legs and spread along the path of retreat or rubbed on saplings, palm fronds, or other vegetation. After traversing water, the animal can splash some on the shoreline, trail, or surrounding vegetation, and more can drip or be shaken from its coat as the animal proceeds.

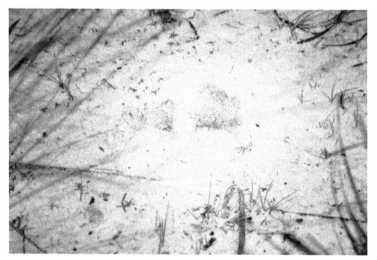

While blood shows up well in the beam of a flashlight projecting ahead of the tracker, prints do not. Here a hog track in easy tracking substrate is barely noticeable.

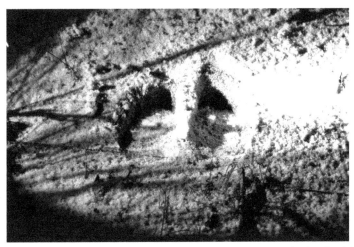

Here is another view of the same track, but this time with the flashlight beam aimed from the side, rendering the track more apparent.

A tracker can easily be lulled into looking for the next print or drop of blood and thereby restrict his or her focus to the ground level at fairly short distances. Ideally, when on a trail, one's awareness should be as broad as possible. (This includes sounds and odors as will be considered later.) Visually, this awareness should encompass all of the tracker's surroundings as clues may be anywhere and creatures' paths can be devious. Forward awareness and higher than ground level awareness deserve extra emphasis. Forward awareness can sometimes discern the continuation of a trail from the distance or maybe detect agitated vegetation or even the animal itself. Other times, the reaction of birds or other denizens of the wild sheds light on the quarry's location. Higher than ground level awareness should include heights a little above the pursued animal's height for the escape run may include leaps and jumps. This region is analyzed for pulled vines, broken limbs, disturbed spiderwebs, marks or hair on tree trunks, turned leaves, or anything out of the ordinary. Spiderwebs have seldom offered me conclusive proof of an animal's passage but many times provided concrete evidence that the trail had not been used.

On the subject of sign above ground level, I once trailed a doe that bled profusely. The trail was obvious and short, maybe sixty yards. However, the arrow was not in or near her even though I

111

had seen her run off with it. I retraced the path three times before I noticed it, three feet off the ground, imbedded in a tree that she had raced closely past. With the conspicuous and bountiful blood on the ground, tracking was not in the least taxing, and I had allowed my awareness to slacken. I have a similar account of lack of forward awareness or, more accurately, of a lack of careful consideration and interpretation of forward sign:

Splattered mud offers clues to a fleeing animal's course.

Again, bits of mud can indicate the trail.

On a Colorado elk hunt, two bulls, 5 × 5s, were within thirty yards when I bugled. A super large 4 × 4 came crashing down and chased them off and then paraded around me with glaring eyes and defiant posture. He paused, broadside at seven yards, but branches interfered with a shot. He strode back to where he had intimidated the 5 × 5s and thoroughly destroyed a small shrub. I swung low to keep the wind right as he walked off uphill and, when I had covered maybe eighty yards, bugled again. The bull came purposefully down but stopped at a serviceberry bush and wrestled and rasped its stubborn branches. This continued for nearly half an hour, time enough for me sneak up both sides of the bush from downwind and, frustratingly, still not find a single open path for an arrow to reach his vitals even though I was at times within nine yards. Anyone who has hunted those arid slopes where the serviceberry bushes nearly interlock can sympathize. At last, I elected to wait behind another serviceberry shrub about ten yards downhill and to the south. Finally, he finished his prolonged battle with the limbs and headed up and away, but a little squealing bugle brought him broadside at no more than seven yards. Bane Too was already fully bent, and the string seemed to strain with eagerness! The arrow drove squarely into his chest and lodged in the opposite shoulder.

After a short wait, I began to follow the trail, and as expected without an exit wound, blood sign was meager. My progress was slow, but at least it was steady, and I really hoped he hadn't made it far. Lifting my eyes, I was startled to see a 5 × 5 working over a small bush not more than fifteen yards above me. He was totally engaged with his mock battle and had no suspicion of my proximity. With my good shot on my bull, I had no interest in the smaller bull and watched his antics for a few minutes without even nocking an arrow. Sweat was running down my face, and the blood was drying by the second on the arid ground. I decided the best course was to continue the trail even if it meant spooking the small bull and I clambered upward on the scant sign. The bull, still engaged with the shrub, didn't notice me until I was nearly next to him. He bolted, and I felt like kicking myself for his demonstrations were directed at my sick bull, bedded five yards to the side, which managed to get to its feet and lurch off. In a flash, my trail went from nearly solved to one that took the rest of the day. I had many times seen whitetails attack or act tough around a fallen bigger buck but hadn't considered the smaller bull's bravado as a possible indication of my bull being near and my oversight came with the price of a long, difficult, and dragged-out trail (and a longer tote of meat).

I read a book by a tracker based in Africa who addressed forward awareness by asking his readers to divide the view in front of them into thirds, the near third, the middle third, and the most distant third. He then suggested scanning the closest part of each third from left to right and the further part of each third back from right to left. Thereby, before each step, the area ahead receives six examinations with the tracker's focus at different distances. This very methodical approach would definitely build good tracking habits.

A hundred and twenty or more years ago, Theodore S. Van Dyke discussed forward focus thus: "But remember to always try and see as far ahead as possible on the trail. Tracking does not, as some might suppose, consist in picking out each step by a separate search, but in a comprehensive view of the whole ground for several yards ahead. Sometimes it is necessary to grope one's way from step to step like a child in its primer, as where the trail gets very faint or turns much; but generally the experienced tracker reads several yards of the trail at a glance, just as the fluent reader does words in a book. The gaze is fixed as much on the surrounding ground, and the trail appears almost to stand out in relief."

Forward focus and the concept of following a trail as a whole rather than piecing it out aids all trackers. We can learn more from Van Dyke. In his book *The Still-Hunter*, he goes on to elaborate twelve classes of tracks:

1. Distinct impressions of the whole hoof.
2. Faint impressions of only the points of the hoof.
3. A slight rim of dirt or dust thrown up by the sharp edge of the hoof.

4. Slight scrapes upon hard ground, recognizable only by the change of color, being made by a faint grinding of the finest particles of the surface without any impression.

5. Mere touches or spots showing only a faint change in the shade of the color. There is scarcely any air so dry that the ground during the night will not absorb a trace of moisture. The least disturbance of the top particles of such soil, even without grinding them over each other, will be visible under some point of view though invisible from others, depending upon the direction of the light.

6. Crushing or grinding of the surface of friable rocks, and mere scrapes or scratches on harder rock or frozen ground.

7. Depressions in moss, grass, dead leaves, etc.

8. Dead leaves, sticks, etc., kicked or brushed aside or overturned, or broken or bent, etc.

9. A plain bending or separating of the spears of grass or weeds. This is generally caused by the feet treading down the stalks at the bottom and not as the next (Class 10) is.

10. A bending of the spears of grass or weeds, etc., by the legs of the passing animal. In this case, the bend itself of the spears is hardly noticeable except by the change in the shade of light cast by them. In such case, a faint streak of differently shaded color will be found running through the grass or weeds, visible only from some directions.

11. Change of color from brushing dew, raindrops, or frost from grass, weeds, etc.

12. Upturning of the under surfaces (generally moist) of stones, leaves, etc.

Tracking is an ageless pursuit, and Van Dyke's descriptions are as accurate and helpful now as when he first wrote them.

A quote from C. J. P. Ionides is also worth considering:

It always amused me to read those wonderful deductions of Sherlock Holmes. How he would notice mud on a client's boots and startle the gentleman by asking him if he had enjoyed his walk in the country. Adding, "Of course you are a free-mason who has lived in China."

"But h-how—" the client would stutter.

"How do I know? Why, that Masonic pin in your lapel tells me you are one of the secret brotherhood. And there is a small coin on your watch chain. It is Chinese."

The African tracker works on the same principle. He is not just somebody who is merely better at following foot prints than yourself; he is a sleuth constantly on the look out for clues. From long experience he can, at a glance, take in a section of bush or forest and pick out immediately the slightest interference in the natural pattern, from which he interprets and deduces with a skill that would command the respect of that prince of sleuths.

Ionides spent much of his life in Africa and therefore admires the African trackers. I have read of first-class outdoorsmen with equally as much admiration for Native American trackers. The point is that the more intimately familiar the tracker is with nature, the more readily he or she can discern aberrations an animal's passage causes. The more acquainted with the natural environment we are, the easier it becomes to develop tracking skills.

While much of this chapter has dwelt upon finding tracks, it is worth including something Paul Rezendes in his book, *Tracking and the Art of Seeing*, pointed out, "If you spend a half an hour finding the next track, you may have learned a lot about finding the next track, but not much about the animal. If you spend time learning about the animal and its ways, you may be able to find the next track without looking." Knowledge of the game animal is always of the utmost help.

Sounds impart information to the tracker as well. In Chapter 2, the importance of noting the location of the last sound was emphasized. In addition, sounds along the course of the retreat can be helpful. Crashing through palmettos or splashing through water or scrabbling down a rocky slope gives the tracker notice of where to expect sign. The protruding arrow slapping on saplings or against fronds would let the tracker know something about the penetration as well as the course. No sound could mean the game had fallen or was fleeing on quiet substrate, again steering the tracker toward the most likely place to find sign. Here is a case where the lack of noise aided me:

It was a peculiar morning in that it was exceptionally foggy, yet the sky was densely overcast and it had rained just before light. A light drizzle continued off and on. Typically, our heaviest fogs occur under clear skies and are pretty sure predictors of no rain. At 7:15 a.m., a buck appeared thirty-five yards away like a hazy apparition in shades of grey. Not surprisingly, the mosquitoes were a persistent annoyance. The buck worked gradually toward me, feeding on new sprouts emerging from soil exposed by hog rootings. He stepped behind a myrtle, and I readied Frilless, hopeful of my chances. With him still screened, I utilized the opportunity to brush mosquitoes from my face and continued to clear them until I realized, quite disconcertedly, that the buck was peering around the myrtle's edge directly at me! His body was sheltered by the thick shrub, so I could do nothing but wait statue-like while he stared. The mosquitoes did their part to assist him, but I endured the hours (that were probably only a minute or so), after which he resumed feeding. His suspicions were not totally allayed for he looked up at me several more times. He fed as deer often do, turning this way and that, leaving an observer unsure which way he would head next, although his overall course was bringing him even nearer. Myrtles obscured him much of the time, but it seemed likely he would drift further yet in my direction. Then he meandered south, and that course took him toward the route I walked to reach the stand no more than an hour before. I had chosen to travel over the open soil rooted by hogs to avoid touching vegetation and in hopes of soil bacteria degrading my scent, but I doubted he could miss smelling the trail in the moist, drizzly conditions especially since, with his search for new shoots, his nose was extremely close to the ground. Sure enough, his behavior displayed nervousness and he headed south, feeding no more. Myrtles hid him, but an open area offered a deer length window a few paces along, and as luck would have it, he paused there momentarily. I drew and released and for once Frilless seemed quiet in the heavy air. (Frilless is a wonderful and accurate longbow, but it is my loudest one.) Unfortunately, the buck stepped just as I let the arrow speed from the string, and the missile struck at the right height, but through the hindquarters. He went down and dragged himself in a semicircle but then regained his feet and crashed off to the north through briars and myrtle. I caught two glimpses of him, the furthest at fifty yards, and I could hear him run further.

It seemed prudent to wait before trailing, but then fifteen minutes later, the drizzle increased to a rain. The rooted soil showed where he had fallen and the running tracks to the north, but no blood. Beyond the rootings, the grass and low briars manifested no sign, so I continued north past my last glimpse of him and cast about there for some clue. Finally, I happened upon some broken briar stems, and later, a drop of blood confirmed the trail. From there on, it was regular trailing. I would try the way I guessed he had taken and either confirm it with blood or stop where I encountered a place thick enough that he should have smeared blood or pulled or broken briars. The briars here were thicker and higher and harbored distinct trails that zigged and intersected in all directions. A few spots held good-sized smears of blood despite the rain, but signs of spurting blood was sadly lacking. My arrow, minus the last six inches of the nock end stood upright on one section of trail among the blackberry bushes. Then a blood smear indicated he ran between two myrtles. From there, the trails branched in four directions. My gut instinct suggested one of those to the right, but the two to the left entered high briars immediately and therefore could be confirmed or ruled out quickly. The first of these proved untraveled. I reached the thick section of the second, only to hear and then see the buck struggling to get to his feet about four yards from me under thick briars. I had no arrow ready and wouldn't have been able to shoot through the briars even if I had. With him unable to get up, it seemed of no importance, but then he was fleeing again, instantly lost to view. His leaps through the briars were easily heard, but silence immediately followed. I marked the last sounds of his flight by the tips of two young maples protruding over the myrtle and briars. His course leapt through briars too formidable for me to penetrate, so I circumvented them and resumed the trail through less dense ones, their bent and broken stems clearly demarking his route. Nowhere was a drop of blood to be found even though his path was obvious. The briars gave way to an open grassy patch, and from there on, no sign was visible. Behind the two maples, a huge section of very dense briars stood. The briars looked undisturbed, but he could have jumped into them, and even from five feet or less there would be no way to see him. The rain started pouring down. I beat through the briars, their little claws jabbing with each step, my spirits tumbled low, haunted with the thought of how close I had been twenty minutes before. Now with the rain and no trail and no blood, discouragement assailed me. Returning to the grassy patch near the two maple saplings, I noticed a second grassy stretch extending west of them. An alternative explanation for the sounds of his retreat to stop at the maples would be if he busted through to them and made it to that open area. With no blood and lots of rain, there would be no trail, but it seemed worthwhile to investigate regardless. He was lying only twenty yards along the grassy channel. His head was up, and I feared he might charge off again. In this rain, any flight might be enough to make him impossible to find, so I dared not take even another step in his direction. I eased an arrow from the quiver. The grass sheltered his body from view. I drew Frilless again and aimed for his neck. With the strike, he jumped, fell, and died. I later discovered the broadhead used for the second shot (a two bladed model) bent into a kind of square U and did not penetrate or even cause bleeding. Luckily, the first arrow had caused a great deal of bleeding into the gut cavity, having narrowly nicked one of the femoral arteries, a tiny slice of less than one sixteenth of an inch. The sudden cessation of sound pointed to the end of his run or the continuance over quiet terrain, and that one clue helped me find this buck.

Two short accounts follow, both cases where getting a fix on the last sound of retreat were really the only means to locate the animal:

One evening, my dad arrowed a boar hog. He felt his shot was good but could not find any blood. When I met up with him, I was equally as stymied for our best efforts revealed absolutely no blood. The darkness made our search more difficult. Then my dad mentioned something about hearing the hog run through palmettos. He climbed back on his ladder stand, and I pushed through various palmetto clumps and called back to him until he shouted that I seemed to be about in the same place he last heard the boar. Within a handful of yards, I found the boar. My dad's shot was with the hog quartering away, and the punctured stomach pushed through the wound and sealed it so well that there was not even a drop of blood where it lay or around the part of the arrow that protruded. Fortunately, the hog didn't make it far, for tracking would have been ridiculously difficult.

A doe fed on browse not terribly distantly. Soon another deer joined her, and upon uniting, they discontinued feeding, instead ambling steadily up a nearly dry slough and passing about seventeen yards in front of me. I drew back, picked a spot, and pretended to let an arrow fly, but didn't actually do it because chances were not bad I could get a doe a lot closer to where a truck could drive. Dragging or carrying a deer through the Bull Creek bottom is effortful with the myriad fallen trees, waist high ferns that hide foot-catching, shin-splitting stumps, logs, and cypress knees, and mud that lets a boot slide one way one second and then grabs hold with no intention to release the next. Thirty yards from me, the pair began picking up acorns under an oak to the west. The smaller deer continued west slowly as it fed, but the larger one worked back toward me. Thoughts bounced through my mind. I really hadn't had many chances at does this season. There was all morning to tote her out. She was a nice doe. It is pretty obvious the way my mind was turning, and before long, the doe was broadside at eight yards. I drew Bent Medicine. The arrow struck home perfectly. She was facing north but about-faced to race to the south with her head and tail low. With a compass, I recorded the last sound of her flight. I found absolutely no blood. I followed my compass and climbed a fallen tree, peering from this slight vantage, and there she lay, a hundred yards from my stand. A bit of blood was smeared around the entrance wound. There was no exit wound, and even working backward, I found no blood on the trail. Her opposite shoulder was swollen and engorged with blood, more like a water balloon than a limb. She had bled profusely, but the blood had not escaped to the ground.

Books and magazine articles have made me aware of the death moans, bellows, and calls of animals like bear and Cape buffalo. I have once heard a whitetail utter a kind of long bleat as it expired. The sound was soft and low enough not to carry far, so it is possible it occurs at times yet remotely enough to escape detection. Nonetheless, large numbers of whitetails have died quite near at hand without making any utterance, so my assumption is that such a sound is untypical and rare in deer. Four times, deer have made a repeated "rabbling" sound upon being struck by my arrows, but this occurred at the strike and not upon death. Three of the four fell upon impact or directly after, but all regained their feet and ran off with good speed. With deer, the last gasp or labored breathing isn't typically heard either. This may be from the quietness of these breaths or that the animal runs as long as there is any breath left. The case is different with hogs. Not uncommonly, the hog will be prostrate, apparently dead, the eyes not blinking even when touched with a bow tip, yet suddenly it will gasp and let the air out in a low, wheezy burble. This may be repeated several times, widely spaced even though the animal is completely unresponsive. These breathing noises are loud enough to have alerted me to fallen hogs a few different times when they fell in thick cover.

The more intimate a tracker is with the environment that holds the trail, the more readily he or she will notice the sounds that convey something out of the ordinary. Even the lack of a sound can have meaning. Each region of the country and of the world will have its own denizens and sounds so my examples may not be applicable elsewhere but serve to highlight both the benefit of listening and of familiarity with the creatures and sounds in the tracker's region.

Whitetail deer snorts have many times led me to fallen deer. In the early eighties, some friends and I drove to Alabama to hunt whitetails. We scouted, and I found a beautiful spot with tall trees, gentle leaf strewn slopes, and many interlacing deer trails, where I set a stand. My friends found other promising locales almost a mile away, so they dropped me off the next morning with the agreement to pick me up at 11:00. Shortly after light, a doe traipsed directly to me and Deer Bane thumped. She ran a short circle and fell close to the stand. At the time (and maybe still today), the limit in Alabama was one deer per day. However, my friends wouldn't be back for a few hours, so I waited in the stand, updating my journal and enjoying woodlands that were quite distinctive from my Florida haunts. After a while, three does fed near the stand quite unconcernedly, but eventually, one caught sight of my prostrate doe. She stamped and blew repeatedly. Then the three left the vicinity, no longer feeding and showing their unease. That was my first recognition of the potential for a deer to announce where another deer had fallen, but over the years, I've witnessed this behavior many times.

Whenever I am tracking and hear a deer blow, I record its location by compass reading and the closest landmark. Sometimes I go directly to the spot to investigate, while other times I continue on the trail armed with information that could prove helpful if the trail becomes problematic. One evening, deep in the swampwoods, the trail of a doe proved difficult, and light was quickly diminishing. I disliked the idea of going all the way out to my truck to retrieve a flashlight, but it seemed inevitable. A deer suddenly snorted three or four times. The sounds came from the direction the trail led, upwind of me, so I walked in that direction, and the arrowed doe was lying dead, her white belly easily visible. The other deer happening along and reacting saved me a twenty-five-minute walk out, a twenty-five-minute walk back, and however long the tracking would have required. Readers of my earlier works will remember a few such cases. Let me include a more recent example here:

While I was glassing a distant buck, movement under my binoculars caught my attention. One of two does that a minute before had been feeding south of me walked by at four yards. The other followed. As soon as they passed, I grabbed my bow, nocked an arrow, and drew, but even though the largest was within fifteen yards, limbs from the oak I was in were about to screen her, and I had no desire to rush a shot. I glassed the woods again. The buck was nowhere to be seen. A group of three does were now following a course not greatly different from the first two does. I snapped a few photos and then readied Nightshade. When the largest doe was broadside at eleven yards, I let the arrow go. Almost immediately, boughs from my tree obscured her retreat, but I turned and leaned out and saw five deer rushing north-northeast. Where the extra deer came from will always be a mystery for one of the second group was still to the south looking at the commotion. I slipped down immediately as the weather service had predicted rain, and the angry, dark skies lent credibility to their forecast. The absence of blood was terribly disheartening for despite the lack of a perfect view after the shot, I felt the arrow had flown true. The crushing and crunching sounds of the brittle, hairy indigo stems had accompanied her flight, but with so many fleeing deer, it was not possible to tell which sounds came from the stricken doe's course. The sandy track from her first explosive leap gave me an idea of the direction further tracks should register, enabling me to piece out a sketchy trail of broken and bent hairy indigo stems. At length, a miniscule specklet of blood confirmed the trail and not too much further along lay the fletched portion of my arrow. A comparison with a whole arrow gave proof of good penetration. Soon, two more drops of blood assured me I was on the correct path but carried worries as well for now, forty yards from where she had been hit, I would have expected drastically more blood. Thirty-five more yards along the path of occasional broken stems, the creek woods started. No more blood was to be seen through the sparse and dead hairy indigo, but the lushness of the swamp should make the blood much more readily visible. Disappointingly, that was not the case, and even in its greenery, no blood was to be seen. It seemed unlikely a stricken deer could pierce through the creek woods and understory and leave no blood, so I was about to go back out and find where I had gone astray when a deer blew in front of me. I pushed through the thick growth, and not far ahead lay the doe. The arrow had shattered her shoulder, crossed her chest, burst through the far ribs, and formed a lump that protruded an inch and a half. If the skin had not trampolined out and stopped the arrow, there would have been an exit wound and a grand blood trail. Thankfully, one of the other deer had found her body either by accident or deliberately and snorted, for I had convinced myself she could not have taken the route she actually did.

Squirrel barks also have been instrumental in shedding light on the whereabouts of downed game several times. *Bows, Swamps, Whitetails* includes a description of one of my friends' hunt where he saw his arrow strike below a spike's chest. The spike departed, and since Ozzie was a hundred percent sure his shot had missed, he would never have looked for it. However, not too far away, some squirrels let loose with barks and screams and carried on for several minutes. Since the spike had fled that direction, Ozzie became suspicious and investigated. The spike had fallen dead below the alarmed squirrels. At the time of the shot, its head had been low in a feeding position, and the arrow, falling short of the chest, hit the bottom part of one of the front legs and ricocheted forward and cut a major blood vessel in the neck, probably the carotid. Ozzie also had squirrel barks lead him to another arrowed deer in September of 2006.

Spooked deer that flee often elicit squirrel barks, and when I'm hunting their sounds sometimes alert me to an opportunity lost to my scent or movement. The squirrels seem to regroup fairly quickly after such a disruption. Stricken and dying deer provoke a much more intense and prolonged period of distress for the squirrels. Their calls have guided me to perhaps a dozen deer and one turkey.

One September morning, I sat on a stand and saw no game except for a covey of quail. Like wood ducks and turkey, these birds have good eyesight and extreme concern for self-preservation, so only rarely do they allow me a shot, but this was one of the times, and Mellifluwood launched an arrow beautifully that punched into the bird. Noontime passed. With my small but tasty game, I started back toward camp. The dirt track traversed a narrow strand, and upon passing it, I noticed a group of jakes in the shade of an oak sixty yards south. I continued a couple hundred yards west until my truck was completely hidden by brush and then parked, ran north with my bow and a few arrows in hand. Once screened by dog fennel, I turned east and, hunched over, scrabbled along as fast as possible to the east, getting into the wooded strand and finally turning south toward the birds. Slowly and cautiously, I inched their way. Despite my efforts at stealth, the turkeys were no longer at the oak. Had they been spooked by my truck? Had they seen me hot foot through the pasture to the north? Or was my approach through the trees not as surreptitious as I hoped? Or had they been on the move earlier and only continued on their way?

If they ran, the chance of reconnecting with them was about nil. On the other hand, if they had been gently spooked or merely kept moving, they may not be far at all. I slipped down the strand further without seeing anything and came to a row of palmettos that paralleled the edge of the woods. I determined to take advantage of their shelter to run down to where they ended and peer about from that vantage. If no turkeys were in sight, it was time to get back to camp for a bite to eat. From the new spot, however, a red head was visible protruding from the lizard tail, and scratching sounds indicated more birds as well. Mellifluwood cast a broadheaded arrow toward the visible jake with nearly no noise. The flight looked good, and the hit sounded crisp and right. The turkey jetted through the woods and vanished from sight. Other jakes and a few hens raised their heads over the sea of lizard tail and must have seen me at the palmettos for they evacuated promptly.

My arrow was quite bloody, but the blood trail was elusive. The lush growth hid tracks, and the parts of tracks that showed may have been from any of the birds. I investigated four different routes without unearthing any clue, but then realized a squirrel that had barked at the commotion when the turkeys fled was still barking. I went to him. The squirrel was on a tree trunk, head down and tail up waving, facing directly at the fallen jake. The bird hadn't made it forty yards.

Speaking of turkeys, they mainly feed and travel in groups, and if not alarmed by the hunter's presence, when one has been targeted, the others quite often make a "pucking" noise at the fallen member of their flock as they cock their heads this way and that. In addition, jakes and toms often attack the dead bird, jumping on it with wings upstretched and this can be loud enough to manifest its whereabouts.

Both the "pucks" and the whooshing of their wings can give away the location of a hunter's bird.

Other birds are worth listening for as well. Out west, magpies flock to downed game and communicate loudly with one another. These interesting birds have led me to several carcasses either killed by predators or other hunters or caught in fences. Leg bones and carcasses hanging from fences are common sights in Colorado because of the prevalence of fences comprised of hog wire for the bottom two thirds and rows of barbed wire along the top. The hog fence prevents the animals ducking through the fence and if, as the animal jumps, a hoof goes between the strands of barbed wire, the strands twist and trap the leg, and the hapless animal is subjected to a terrible and prolonged death. It is usually the smaller and younger deer and elk that suffer. In Florida, with our strictly barbed-wire fences, I have never seen an animal tangled up this way. The magpies find freshly killed game as well, particularly if it falls in the open.

I was hunting for mule deer on a grassy area along Milk Creek where a little dry waterway meandered toward the creek. At midday, I practiced shooting the bow with just two fingers since my index finger was too swollen and painful to be of service. This changed my anchor point as well, but I felt with compensation for that, my arrows could be delivered adequately for short ranges. Does filtered through the open area early in the afternoon, and soon a buck approached. I wiggled down the waterway confident the taller grass it held would hide me. The extreme dryness of the grass, though, rendered my movement less quiet than ideal, and a doe close to me became nervous. She high stepped to the south, and the other does and the buck followed her lead. They didn't resume feeding for several hundred yards and even then were on alert. My plan had been to watch from a shady clump along the channel and then launch stalks wherever bucks fed near the waterway that extended eight hundred yards. The noisiness of the grass ruled that out, so now I picked a place where two sage-covered ridges pinched fairly close to the dry watercourse. The grass was only twenty inches tall at the spot, and there was no shade, but it worked reasonably well for shortly after I was in place a buck ambled past at ten yards. He was a 2 × 2, and I drew and practiced picking a spot on his chest but did not release. I resolved however, not to let any buck much bigger than him pass as with being halfway through a seven-day hunt, each afternoon or morning spent in the lowlands for deer was one less to spend pursuing bull elk among the ridges.

The thought had barely registered in my mind when brown movement revealed two bulls on a ridge west of Milk Creek proving the often-stated fact that game animals don't always restrict their presence to where hunters expect them. The idea of a stalk didn't seem feasible because between us were a thousand yards of open terrain with nothing to hide my approach, and also, elk cover ground so quickly that they could be a long ways off by the time I arrived even if I wasn't detected. Over the next forty-five minutes, they milled around the general area, sparring at intervals. Two more bulls joined them and likewise butted antlers mildly from time to time. Sometimes some of the bulls disappeared over the crest of the ridge for a while only to reappear again. From the distance, it seemed there were two 5 × 5s and two 4 × 4s, and they sparred accordingly. By staying in the waterway and subsequently in Milk Creek, I narrowed the distance down to four hundred yards, but no further cover was available. When all four were over the crest at once, I almost started to run across the open, but before I could even start, the bulls topped the ridge again.

Two mule deer, a decent 3 × 3 and a small 4 × 4, slipped along the watercourse behind me and I studied them, trying to decide if that stalk offered a better chance. There was cover, but noisy cover at that, and they really were not as close to it as I felt I could shoot. A glance to the ridge showed the bulls were gone. I started across the grassland but didn't manage fifty yards before they topped the crest once more. I could only freeze and sink to the ground. Whenever their attention seemed to be directed elsewhere, I inched and squirmed my way forward. All four went back across at the same time and I ran. If even one returned, my chance would vanish, but my luck held. Running provoked my cough, and between coughs and crunchy sounds as I worked up through rock and sage, it seemed unlikely they hadn't heard me, but the intervening ridge must have intercepted a lot of the sound for suddenly antlers showed at the top as if drifting along the ridge on their own. More cover would have been desirable, but the wind was right. I readied an arrow. Two bulls came up the steep slope opposite the crest further up the ridge but at twenty-five yards had enough view of me to send them lurching back down. Another bull, directly above me, came up to peer at whatever had gently spooked the other bulls. I could see his chest, although the crest hid his legs. He was close, fifteen or less yards. I drew Bane Too with two fingers, my index finger pointing parallel the shaft, pretending to shoot the ground below his chest since with the different anchor my arrows were flying high, and released. He was instantly gone, and with the sheerness of his side of the ridge, his disappearance was too fast to even see if the arrow hit, but the sound was the sound of a hit. The fourth bull ran up to the very crest itself and stood broadside even closer than the third one. Despite not seeing the arrow strike, I was sure enough of a hit that I had no temptation to nock another arrow, but the episode did postpone my scrambling up to the ridge top until he got nervous and whirled away. That wait prevented me from seeing my bull's escape route, the view of which would have been an invaluable aid in tracking. On top of that, there were four sets of running bull tracks to complicate things. I found no blood. Ozzie came and helped, but even with the extra eyes, no blood was to be found. With my weakness from the fever and chills, I decided to wait for morning.

It was an effort to get out of my fever-soaked bed, but I took up the trail at first light. The running tracks were soon lost on the sage- and rock-covered slopes, but the parts I could follow displayed no sign of blood. Two hours and forty minutes passed. I hadn't made an inch of progress. I did search around in all likely directions, hoping he had fallen fairly close. Weak and with little hope, I trod up to the next ridge to the west and was dismayed to see how densely the canyon beyond it was covered. Fifty elk could be piled together and I wouldn't be able to see them. I followed the crest with the thought that maybe blood sign could show if he crossed over, and I had to sit and rest a couple of times. My coughs were nearly continuous. Two does watched me, seemingly puzzled by this loud and apparently aimless creature, yet they alertly maintained sixty yards between us. I could hear magpies with their *wreet-wreet-wreet-wreet*, calls and I sat again and watched for them, hoping they had seen my bull. They flew about, but it looked as aimless as my wanderings, flying about and lingering nowhere long. With time, I realized their heading wasn't entirely random. Some were working down the canyon. With my binoculars, I studied the direction of their movement. Way down on Milk Creek, at least twenty or thirty magpies were congested on something that could be a branch or puddle or who knows what, but it could also be a dead elk hidden by brush. I plodded down, the does ambling ahead of me, but as my course now too closely coincided with theirs, they finally bounded away.

About halfway there, I topped a rise and, from this vantage, checked the magpie gathering. My binoculars revealed the bull! As the crow flies, it had run four hundred yards. Skinning and quartering it took an hour and a quarter and sapped what energy I had left. He fell where elk never fall for me—where I could get to in a vehicle! (It seems my average tote is measured in miles.) I decided to go to Craig to get a doctor to look at my bloated and useless finger, but first I needed water and then to hang the meat. The clinic couldn't help me in Craig, so I slept the rest of the day, this illness knocking me flatter than any I could remember. At Meeker the next day, a doctor did surgery on my hand and got me on antibiotics. The bull's rack was missing a brow tine on one side, making it an oddly symmetrical 4 × 5. The main importance of the story of the trail is the help the magpie communications offered, for I was searching nowhere near the fallen bull, and their guidance alone allowed me to find the bull.

Jim Corbett several times mentions magpies revealing the location where a tiger dragged its kill. Here is a quote from his writings where he doesn't mention magpies specifically but interestingly also includes blowflies (the presence of which, by the way, have on occasion alerted me to spots of blood or gut material or even the body of the animal I was tracking): "There are two generally accepted methods of tracking. One, following a trail on which there is blood, and the other, following a trail on which there is no blood. In addition to these two methods I have also at times been able to find a wounded animal by following blowflies, or by following meat-eating birds."

Our sense of smell, while dull compared to many animals, can still be an aid in finding game. Whitetails have an odor that is discernable, but I have never located a wounded one by its smell. From the stand, there have been times I've smelled bucks before they were in view. The smell of hogs, however, is strong enough that a few times my nose forewarned me that the dead hog was nearby. Also, smell can alert the tracker to urine or fecal material along the trail. Testing an arrow that has passed through game by sniffing it can reveal information sight alone does not. When copious blood hides the color of a gut wound, the smell invariably furnishes testimony.

When a trail is lost and examining possible routes, searching in widening circles, and all other means fail to relocate it, one technique to find the animal is to search in a grid pattern. The method is far from fail-proof because of the difficulty ascertaining the extent of the grid (how far could the animal's flight take it?) and limited vision because of vegetation or obstacles. The animal itself can add to the trouble. Turkeys often hide remarkably well, even going into gopher holes (in Florida, the term refers to gopher tortoise holes). Coyotes go underground. Hogs routinely and deer sometimes seek exceedingly dense cover. Here is an episode, while not involving a grid search, definitely illustrates a wounded hog's tendency:

One year, with a lot of season left, but without any deer tags remaining, I resolved to try for a fall turkey. I fabricated a blind in the shade of an oak in a strip of open pasture that was compressed to the east by a dense, marshy pond and to the west by a sprawling oak copse so any turkey passing between the two would be less than fifteen yards from the tree. The blind was a simple affair of palmetto fronds and dog fennels stabbed into the soil where the low boughs of the live oak hung within four feet of the ground. In the quiet grey of morning, as I made my way toward the tree, the back of a walking hog showed up over some of the marsh about 120 yards north where the vegetation was thinner. It was early, and the turkeys were not roosting anywhere near, so there was plenty of time for a stalk. The wind was right, and getting within twelve yards of the nearest hog was no problem. There were five boars, all impressive, rooting in the black muck of the marsh. The one closest to me was large and black, and I would be satisfied with him if need be, but beyond him was a brown one that easily outweighed the others. Their steady rooting left their heads partially immersed in the muck and vegetation and had allowed my undetected near approach but now disallowed any assessment of their teeth. The brown one was at about twenty-five yards, but vegetation hid his vitals. The close one was facing me. Usually hogs will turn as they root, so I waited. He was in no hurry to change positions, and I was thankful for the steady northwest wind and that the other hogs were nearly as stationary as he was. When at last his hindquarters were to me, I slipped north and a few steps to the east to permit a fifteen-yard broadside opportunity on the massive brown boar. Nightshade drew smoothly, and the arrow struck with a resounding *thwack*! In the scant second before his rapid northward scramble hid him in brush, both the hit and penetration looked good. Angry grunts rather than a surprised squeal accompanied his flight. Three other boars bulldozed through the same vegetation, but the nearest one stood, facing north, watching their retreat. After thirty or forty seconds, he half trotted, half walked after them.

As for blood, the trail was ridiculously exiguous. Bent grasses, broken shrubs, and splattered mud helped me work it out for maybe seventy yards over the next twenty minutes. Knowing that other hogs had rushed through the pond kept me uncertain much of the time, but a few smears of blood confirmed my guesses. At this point, the vegetation became so thick with shrubs, palmettos, and lots of briars that I was forced to worm forward on my belly to continue. After tunneling a short ways, the memory of the charging boar from the week before coupled with the knowledge that, with this one's size, I would not be able to hold him off made me decide to back out and wait a while before placing myself in so vulnerable a position where I would be unable to back up quickly nor rise to my feet.

I started again toward the blind only to see a flock heading in its direction from the south. In the open, with forty yards, before I could reach the cover of the oak, there seemed no possibility of not spooking birds with the phenomenal eyesight and total lack of curiosity of turkeys, so I just trudged to the tree with no effort at stealth. Miraculously, not one head was raised during the interval, and beyond belief or hope, I was ensconced in the blind undetected!

The turkeys were about 150 yards away but, in their back and forth way, were working in the direction of the oak. With time, the first nine drew near the blind ranging from fifteen to twenty-five yards. These were all jakes, although three hens lingered back about seventy yards. One jake was facing me with his head down and pecking. For the second time that day, I drew Nightshade. The arrow leapt forward and passed through the jake. He dropped on the spot. The other jakes milled around, puzzled, and afforded me several photographs. Then uneasily, they filed off to the south.

I retrieved the bird and sat a bit before returning to take up the trail of the boar. It turned out he had succumbed about eighteen yards from where I quit the trail. His mass thwarted all my efforts to move or turn him. His head was longer than the height of my eighteen-inch boots and it was very wide. His teeth were big and wide but not exceptionally long, although they did protrude beyond his lips. From left to right, his width, lying flat on the ground, was just less than my boot height so about seventeen inches. It would have been great to get him to a scale, but my truck couldn't reach him through the muck, and I couldn't drag him. I cleaned him on the spot. His shield was over one and a half inches thick. The arrow had passed through both lungs and the far ribs but stopped at the shield on the opposite side. The penetration was excellent for such a stout hog, but an exit wound would have made tracking simpler. The main point is that an animal, nearly double my size and weight, pushed through briars I had a difficult time wriggling through on my belly. So often have the trails of stricken hogs led into incredibly thick palmettos or briars that I'm convinced it is done purposefully rather than from blind flight. It may be embedded in the defensive strategy of hogs to retreat to thick areas. I should clarify that the mortally wounded hog may not be considering where he will be the safest but rather that habitual retreats to thick cover renders this the natural course. Deer display this tendency at times but more often when the wound is not quickly fatal. This may indicate that a deer's first response to danger is to put distance between itself and the threat rather than impenetrable cover and seek the cover only after the initial flight (if it is still alive).

To execute the grid search, boundaries are decided based upon the severity of the wound, the speed of the animal, and limitations imposed by the terrain. A north-south, east-west grid is easiest for reading the compass, but it does not necessarily have to be oriented that way. Landmarks, the more distant the better, are selected, and the searcher or searchers, armed with a compass, comb the area marching and investigating the cover in a direct line from boundary to boundary. After a linear march is completed, the searcher moves slightly over and marches back. This continues until the entire grid has been thoroughly searched. The distance between tracks (here track is used to denote the line the searcher follows) is dictated by the extent of vision—the more restricted the vision, the closer the tracks. If the field of operation is large and especially when multiple people are looking, making a map-like sketch and checking off each track that has been searched can be advantageous. Excessively thick areas can make it nearly impossible to see distant landmarks or even to walk a straight track. At times, it seems the land and plants are conspiring to push the tracker back on parts already covered rather than fresh terrain. That is why going east-west as well as north-south improves the odds of finding the game. Readers of *Bows, Swamps, Whitetails*, will remember a buck I searched for with a very methodical grid pattern in tall gallberries. After failing to locate the deer and having to traverse the same area later in the morning, I recognized that I was on one of my exact tracks from earlier. Rather than re-plod over the same ground, I scooted over a few yards, continued due north, and quite soon stumbled upon the buck. The gallberries restricted the view much more than I believed when I had set the grid pattern.

There are other available products for finding game, heat detectors, and lights and sprays that purport to make blood more visible. These may be beneficial, but I have no experience with them. I have a friend who, after wounding a buck, entreated his friend, a pilot and plane owner, to fly over the area, and they did succeed in locating it!

Of all tracking aids, a good dog is the ultimate, and tracking with dogs is discussed later in the book.

The absolutely best way to improve the chance of finding targeted game is to make a shot that is quickly lethal and creates a copious blood trail. I have opinions on how to effectuate the best blood trails pertaining to broadheads, arrows, and shot selection. They work for me with my longbows and recurves. Compared to today's compound bows, my weapons are slow and weak, so the concerns I've worked to overcome may not be of importance to archers with stronger faster bows and definitely will be of no consequence to rifle hunters. For bowhunters, an exit wound is a paramount prerequisite for a predictably great trail. Experiments, reason, and experience have all demonstrated that two bladed broadheads offer the most penetration. My belief in their penetrative excellence influenced me to use them for many, many years, and with them, I successfully took hundreds of animals including some as large as bull elk. Nonetheless, I have now come to believe wounds from two bladed heads close more often and leak less blood than those from three bladed models. It was earlier pointed out that the hole through the skin may not line up with the hole through the chest, and this seems a much more frequent occurrence when two bladed broadheads are used. I still favor them for hogs because they drive through the thick cartilaginous shields of the big boars the best, but for all other big game and turkeys, I now use Wensel Woodsman three blades. The taper allows good penetration, and the wound channel remains patent most of the time. I do modify the heads so the tip is not so thin and liable to bend by filing the very point at an angle about twice that of the head as a whole. In addition, I augment the penetration by using very heavy shafts and steel, rather than aluminum, inserts. My completed arrows weigh in over seven hundred grains. This arrangement deadens the sound of the bow, and the increased mass results in an arrow that carries a lot of striking energy. (If game larger than is found in North America were the focus, say Cape buffalo, my inclination would revert to the two-blade design for utmost penetration.)

The angle of the shot also influences the likelihood of an exit wound. The closer the arrow flight is to horizontal, the shorter the distance to the opposite side of the animal. Since my shots are at short range, when I use a stand, it is not set very high in the tree, twelve feet would typically be the highest and most often the stand is less than ten feet. A higher stand would be beneficial for diminishing the hunter's scent but would also cause the arrow to pierce the game at a steeper angle and require a greater length of penetration. The angle from front to back that the arrow enters the game similarly affects the distance the arrow must travel through the animal to reach the far side. Quartering away shots are very alluring because they allow the largest target area that steers an arrow into the vitals, but they do cause the broadhead to traverse much more tissue to create an exit wound. A perfectly broadside animal presents the least distance required for the arrow to penetrate the opposite side.

A whitetail standing head on, its chest and two front legs facing directly forward is a formidable target because the bones of the chest have a high likelihood of deflecting the arrow outside the chest, and even if the arrow somehow slips through, the chance of an exit wound or decent blood trail is minuscule. My bows are not up to this challenge, but my friend when faced with this opportunity, not on a little whitetail but rather a bull moose three or four yards distant, used his compound to drive an arrow directly below its dewlap. With his powerful bow, the arrow penetrated all the way to the far end of the huge animal and the moose wheeled around but could not take a step and sank to the ground right there. His experience is included to highlight again that while I put some emphasis on broadhead type, arrow mass, and shot selection, for many hunters with modern weapons, whether they are firearms or bows, these are not extremely important details. More important is the hunter's complete understanding of his or her weapon, its capabilities and weaknesses, and of the shot placements with which it can effect a quick kill. Taking the time to make a good shot is critical. An acquaintance once described this time as, "The few seconds that save several hours!"

CHAPTER 4

Repeated Tendencies

MANY, MANY YEARS AGO, I mapped out sixty-seven routes taken by stricken deer that I had followed. I overlapped them at the spot the deer was standing when struck with the orientation in the direction the animal was facing, in hopes of finding some pattern that might predict where wounded game would head. As you can guess, there was no pattern. Deer facing west exploded to the west but also to the east, north, south, and all points of the compass between! Many deer ran a curving course. I wondered if the side of the impact would correlate with the way their trails curved, but the impacted side didn't seem to influence the trail. For example, the heart-struck doe that left the long trail was hit in the left side and curved right. The buck in the fennel you'll read about soon was hit in the right side and curved right, as did the buck the grid search discovered. The mule deer doe that went so far was hit in the right side and curved left. I'm reminded of Howard Hill's words when he said that each animal is an individual and while, with knowledge and experience, a hunter can say what an animal might do, he can't say what it will do. This is very true about escape routes. Each one is unique. A few trends show up again and again and awareness of them helps the tracker be on the lookout for the particular possibilities. Caution should be employed for too much conviction that the tracker knows what will come next can interfere with correctly piecing out the true trail.

Nearly thirty years ago, with twelve years of trailing arrowed whitetails under my belt, my experiences led me to believe when a lightly blooded trail showed many abrupt turns, reversals, and careful selection of easy pathways that the deer was not severely injured and that finding it would be unlikely. I had just enough trail time then to believe I knew more than was the actual case. My friend Don used his recurve to hit a good buck, his first heavy, mature one. It was an evening hunt, and failing to find much of a blood trail, he came back to camp and recruited several of us to help him look. With flashlights and high hopes we started out and the first few splotches of blood on vegetation protruding from the shin-deep water coupled with his description of the hit gave me confidence we would find the buck, but an hour later, with spilled blood dwindling to nearly zero and the bits we found indicating the deer had walked an incredibly tortuous route with all sorts of abrupt directional changes, pessimism snuck into my thoughts, and I voiced out loud that when deer start meandering around like that, they usually have a survivable wound and chances were against us finding him. Most of the others agreed, but with us still finding red drops on occasion, we were loath to abandon the trail. As you have probably foreseen, it was fortunate that we continued our efforts for eventually, we found the buck dead of a good chest shot. Mortally struck animals usually do not take seemingly aimless escape routes, but this trail opened my eyes to the need to avoid becoming too dogmatic. Here is another similar example:

A spot in Bull Creek was teeming with life, birds attracted by a shallow open marsh and mammals by the bordering water oaks that were dropping acorns continuously. My daughter, Breanna, and I sat there one morning (when she was twelve or thirteen) and marveled at the bird life. All around us cavorted ibises, herons, egrets, kingfishers, turkeys, red-shouldered hawks, as well as small birds like Carolina wrens and phoebes. One of my hoots brought over a barred owl that remained on a branch near us for over an hour and allowed lots of photographs. A buck and doe passed by out of range. We returned to area that afternoon with hopes soaring.

As impressed as I was with the accuracy of Breanna's shooting and the speed of her arrows, I was still a little apprehensive about penetration. The speed was accomplished through little lightweight arrows. Never had I seen a thirty-five-pound bow take big game. True, Breanna's arrows flew as fast or faster than mine, but mine weighed well over seven hundred grains and were hard to stop. We would need a perfect shot. As I began to ascend our ladder stand, Breanna tapped my leg and stalked forward five or seven yards. A nice boar hog was feeding at the edge of the marsh. No mammal in Florida requires more penetrating force than an adult boar. My arrows at times had bounced off of boars because of their shields, and I had heard the same from many hunters. Cleaned hogs often revealed buckshot or small rifle slugs in their shields. Breanna slipped forward another three or four yards, closing the distance to near fourteen yards. I was visualizing the precise point for perfect arrow placement when she released and the arrow struck the exact spot my eyes were riveted upon. The boar rushed west, and I was happy to see that not only was the placement right but the penetration looked good as well, at least completely through the chest, although the exit wound was doubtful.

The afternoon hunt had only just started, and we climbed up and sat a while. After thirty minutes, worries assailed me. I hated the idea of tainting the region upwind of the stand with scent but at the same time did not want to risk losing Breanna's first game with a bow. Without an exit wound, even great shots can leave poor blood trails, and without a trail, black hogs are very hard to find at night in the swamp with its black earth and black shadows. I decided to wait no longer.

Blood splatters with bubbles started right where he had stood. The trailing was easy, in fact exceptionally easy considering the lack of an exit wound. At times, I had to cast here and there before rediscovering the trail, but that was primarily due to large sections of exposed black soil that obscured the blood and were stamped everywhere with tracks of all sizes and directions. The hog never continued straight ahead, veering and half circling one direction and then another. Surprisingly, he made it over two hundred yards as the crow flies, more like three hundred the crazy route he took. I had spread a lot of scent around, and my exertion to drag him out of the swamp was far from quiet so the fact that no more game came by us that afternoon was not altogether unexpected. Nonetheless, we were elated with Breanna's success and with getting good meat. (By the way, she shot a doe with the same bow the next weekend and it did not make it forty yards!)

Another deer gave proof that quickly mortal wounds can still result in erratic trails. The morning was giving way to midday, and I slipped along, bow in hand, sweat trickling down my forehead and cheeks, with little hope of finding game. The sun glared off the palmetto sprawl, rendering the fronds more yellowish than green. Above this rose the dark grey-green of two dome-shaped live oaks. These trees could be dropping acorns, so I started to them to investigate only to discover two does. The larger, and closer, one spotted my movement and was staring from twenty yards. Unimpeded progress was only possible along interconnecting aisles between the multitude of palmetto clumps, and the narrow pathway I had chosen to reach the oaks was partially screened from the doe by several fronds that bent over the trail. She had no clear view of me, and meanwhile, the other doe fed unconcernedly. At that moment, two other deer, possibly, but not definitely, does as well, stepped out and began chasing each other around. The nearby doe became distracted and apparently forgot about me. My ability to see was no clearer than the doe's with the interfering fronds and oak limbs. The deer were all within thirty yards. Then another doe stepped out of the thick, and a spike emerged and chased her east. The other deer filtered in that direction as well, so I backed out a bit and then followed. The palmettos made the stalk easy at first, but then between two thick patches, a channel of view opened to the more barren area under the umbrella-like canopies of the two adjacent oaks. In this open area, two does were heading back west very slowly and feeding yet looking around a lot. Once again, the low oak branches and palmettos contrived to shelter me from their eyes, yet I dared not move. Patience is undeniably a virtue when hunting, but there was cause for unease. The wind was from the west. The deer—I was unsure exactly how many, but at least six—were south of me, but to the east was a dike with a dense thicket bordering it. The deer that headed east would very likely be steered north by the angled dike, and fifteen or twenty yards north would position them directly downwind. One alarmed deer would "give wings" to the entire group. Nonetheless, I was pinned and could only wait and hope. Eventually, the smaller doe fed far enough west that the palmettos offered cover. It looked as though the larger one had followed her, so I took a cautious step southeastward only to realize the larger doe had actually bedded quartering toward me. My motion, although slow and furtive, had caught her eye. Her distance was in the neighborhood of twenty-eight yards. Her head was up and her eyes attentive, but after a couple of minutes, she relaxed and resumed chewing her cud although her eyes and ears did not abandon their examination of my still form. My plan had been to continue east to intercept the other deer, but now, major movement was out of the question. After a minute or so of chewing, she would swallow the lump of cud and immediately produce another. It was unlikely she would be moving soon. I thought she might turn her head right or left, but even though her attention to her cud indicated a lack of alarm, she was content to face my way.

I had placed an arrow on Daddy's string as soon as the deer were encountered. One dangling oak bough could interfere with a shot depending upon the trajectory, so I squatted in increments until I was low enough to remove that concern. When I'm not actually shooting and aim at something, a certainty comes to me that if I did release, the arrow would drive home. I drew Daddy and waited for that feeling as I concentrated on the right side of the bedded doe's throat. The shot felt right, and I released. The arrow's flight was fast and through bits of light and shadows, but looked good, and the sound of the hit was right. The doe rocketed west as if catapulted from the ground itself. I went to check the sign and caused four deer to the east to bound away. They possibly had been bedded also. The arrow was embedded in the ground five yards beyond the doe's bed and was entirely red. The blood trail started within a few yards and was sprayed high and wide, marking out an easily readable trail even though it took turns one way and another and then half circles in both directions. She fell within sixty yards, but it is hard to imagine a more convoluted trail. The arrow had entered at the base of her throat on the right side of the windpipe and exited behind the lower part of the left shoulder. I later learned it cut the very top of the heart and sliced both the pulmonary artery and aorta.

Even with these episodes as reminders of the entirely unpredictable pathways stricken game may take, it is worth pointing out a few recurring tendencies: curving courses, loops, and doubling back. First, when game bulldozes through thick cover oblivious to less encumbered routes nearby, the tracker can be extremely close to certain the injury is mortal. The wound is so dire that brush, vines, branches, saplings, palmettos, or other obstacles are completely ignored in the animal's haste to flee. Often the heart has been struck so the trail may not be short, but the forced passage through the thick cover makes tracking simple with broken, bent, and displaced vegetation pointing the way. The doe mentioned in the heart shot section of Chapter 1 that busted through the heavy palmettos demonstrated this classically and here is another example:

Late in a season, an area, overgrown to the point no one looking at it would recognize that twenty-five years earlier it had been pasture, held some decent deer sign. Probably the extreme thickness of the cover explained the reason deer were using this area after months of pursuit by rifle hunters. Although the trees and shrubs were twice as tall as a man, none were strong enough to support a stand, so I set a ladder stand and guyed it off to keep it upright. I cut a few shrubs and piled them under the stand's low platform, brushing it in, so to speak, in hopes the stand's occupant would appear as an extension of the brush rather than a dark shape looming in the air. Needless to say, at this point in the season, I took especial care to limit the human scent deposited in the area to an absolute minimum.

When I tried the stand, a spike came by in the early afternoon, and two does arrived as the sun began to sink and the western sky adopted an electric salmon hue. I drew Mellifluwood with no conscious thought and let it speed an arrow into the largest doe's lower chest. She rocketed off indiscriminately through the heaviest brush and palmettos, piling up within at sixty yards. The cover was thick in many places, but several routes offered unencumbered travel yet she sped east-northeast with no regard to the extreme difficulty of this passage. The brush around the arrow, stabbed into the ground after passing through her chest, was sprayed red despite her instantaneous flight. Cleaning her confirmed a heart shot.

A very typical escape route is a curving path. This can result, if viewed from the air above the trail, in an eighth circle, quarter circle, half circle, or even full circle or anything in between. The most common ones seem to be a fifth to just under a half circle. The path may not conform to part of a perfect circle. Sometimes it is more of an oval shape, but wounded game run a course curving in one direction regularly enough it behooves the tracker to be aware of it, especially when it becomes necessary to try various routes or extrapolate the trail.

One November, after a few weekends of almost no deer sightings, I chose a stand down in the swamp bottom. Two little creek channels that deer tend to travel along pinched near one another and acorns pattered down from the water oaks. The sign there gave hope that deer were using the area regularly. However, the only activity in the early afternoon was the persistent attention of the mosquito hordes and the short, half-hearted sorties a couple timid squirrels launched from time to time. The mosquitoes made me smile because I had recently read one of Archibald Rutledge's stories, and he wrote, "Five o'clock found me and the mosquitoes at Joel's. The things do not bite him—because they are prohibitionists, he says. They ate me alive—ravenously, joyously. But when I'm deer hunting, I don't mind losing a life or two."

Under the swamp's canopy, the light is always meager, and as the sun sank toward the horizon, it dimmed even more, and this seemed to signal a start. Barred owls hooted back and forth, and a deer drifted silently northward between palmetto clumps east of the stand. Cabbage palm fronds above him hid his head, but he was unmistakably large and a buck. I readied "Daddy." Abruptly, he turned west and approached toward me with a purposeful stride, not feeding but, rather, acting like he was going somewhere. From the straight-on angle, the number of points was not determinable, but his neck was thick and wide and he was obviously mature. Next, he was six yards off, his pace undiminished. The creek channel he was splashing along passed directly in front of my stand, so I drew Daddy fully as an intervening oak trunk hid his head. He emerged between two trunks broadside at four yards. It seemed the arrow was already driven deeply into his chest the very instant I released. He raced westward, curving to north, then east, and finally south, heading back toward me when he bounced high and disappeared. My assumption was that he fell, but with thigh-high ferns and the canopy accentuated gloaming, I was not sure.

The westward portion of his run was in water, so the lack of blood was in no way surprising. From the stand, it had looked like he covered about fifty yards on this leg of his flight. I headed about that far and looked for blood or splashed water heading north and was surprised to find none. Something drew me back east, and a prominent blood trail left the creek only twenty-five yards west of the stand and curved like nearly three-quarters of a circle to the dead buck. (The first buck that fell to Nightshade also ran a circular path within my view, and the route had seemed to have a much bigger circumference to my eye from the stand than the blood trail bore out and now the same pattern repeated itself. Somehow there was an illusion of the deer running a greater distance than it actually did. Since these two incidences, I'm careful to examine a narrower curve if the trail is not located where vision predicted it to be.) As the buck had fallen, his antlers drove deeply into the black and root-filled soil. Apparently, the bounce I had seen from the stand was momentum flipping his body over his head after the antlers rammed into the ground and stuck. It required nearly Herculean effort for me to pull them free of the earth. His eight-point rack was not exceptionally large, but he was big and his meat was much darker than average. Venison is always a dark reddish color, but this was different, dark in a chocolate type of way. It smelled fine, however. His backstraps were huge. I labeled the meat when I stored it in the freezer in case the taste would be off, but the flavor proved to be exceptionally fine.

A few more accounts of curving trails will follow to demonstrate how common they are:

One afternoon, a group of twenty or more hogs were feeding in a mildly overgrown pasture. Lots of them looked to be large, so with the wind in mind, I skirted about and stalked close. The most south-eastern one was a sow, and since the wind issued from the northwest, bypassing her would let her catch my full scent. My desired target would have been one of the big boars, but if she caught my wind, she would alarm the whole group, and getting one hog was better than none. Mellifluwood sent a broadheaded shaft through her chest with a barely perceptible thump. She ran a little half circle west and then north and fell.

With her quiet demise, no other hog displayed the slightest awareness, so I was free to slip further north and adjacent to more hogs. A couple of these, two sows, moved north, allowing me to creep closer to a gigantic hog. I still was thirty-five yards shy of him when a pudgy boar hog that looked small to me came south and started to turn toward my leeward side. He was less than ten yards off and so fat even his neck bulged and his head appeared little and an integral part of his roundish overall shape. The monster hog would easily be the largest I had taken or seen taken, but it was certain again that if the small boar continued five more steps, he would be alarmed, and all my chances would vanish as well. Mellifluwood bent again and with next to no noise propelled an arrow through the boar. He made two grunts that conveyed anger rather than alarm and ran a half circle similar to the sow except the circle was somewhat larger, carrying the boar thirty-five yards before he collapsed. Boars had been grunting and squealing and chasing one another the whole time, so this one's behavior didn't even cause any nearby hogs to look his way.

I scooted further to the north and two much bigger boars (which I estimated at 160 lbs. at the time) headed south and passed less than four yards west of me on the opposite side of a small palmetto patch. These were not in a position to smell me, and the giant boar was not far now. Two sows followed the course of the two boars and then several more hogs. The huge one was only eight yards off but facing me, not a desirable shot angle for any hog and even less so for one so thick and heavy. Like the other hogs, he was on the path to the west side of the palmettos and in a few seconds would be broadside or quartering away at four yards. Palmetto fronds would hide any movement on my part. Just then, one of the southbound hogs that had paraded past me encountered my fallen sow and spooked from her blood or maybe from my scent on the arrow near her. She let loose the long, protracted grunt of alarm! The result was instantaneous, and hogs exploded from all the surrounding waist-high vegetation. The monstrous hog, like all the rest, was gone.

The fat boar I arrowed, that I guessed at maybe ninety pounds, scaled over 140, which caused me to wonder how heavy the much larger ones that I thought were maybe 160 truly were, and then really how large was the one that dwarfed the rest? That will never be answered, but the afternoon was a lot of fun and provided a lot of good eats!

On a summer morning, with bow in hand and the hope for some fresh pork in mind, my wanderings brought me to a pasture overgrown with briars and palmettos. The briar thickets were laden with blackberries, and I picked some big, black ones as I traipsed along. They were sweet and juicy and so ripe they burst just from the light pressure of the tongue. Remarkably fresh hog droppings abounded. The berries, however, countered any inclination to rush forward in search of them, so I wended my way slowly through the fronds and clumps eating the best of the fruit. Suddenly, I spied hogs in front of me and looped to keep the wind right and sheltering patches of palmettos between us. There were several hogs, at least eight, and while none were large, they were all big enough to take, the heaviest probably about 115 lbs. and black in color.

Mellifluwood drew in her silky fashion and ushered a speedy, whispering shaft to the hog's chest, only to have the arrow bounce off and sail backward nearly ten feet up and toward me. I had left my quiver where I initiated the stalk, fearing the shafts might rattle against the palmettos and alert the hogs, but had placed an extra arrow in the fingers of my bow hand. The boar I had tried for trotted east and stopped in some myrtles thirty yards away. After readying my spare arrow, I stepped to the east side of the palmettos that sheltered me. With the boar's little run, the other hogs looked about uneasily for a second or two, but resumed feeding. A good boar was nosing about six yards east of me behind some young oak scrub that permitted a decent view but would likely play complete havoc with arrow flight. He moved diagonally toward me, and I drew when his head reached the edge. When his shoulder cleared, Mellifluwood whisked the arrow toward him. It struck with a forceful *whack*, and he wheeled in a fast, short semicircle falling seven yards west of me.

His explosive flight spooked the hogs, and they all, even my original target, ran toward me, passing within a few yards, but I was arrowless. I recovered the arrow that had bounced off, but the pasture was devoid of hogs by then. Interestingly, the two bladed broadhead had a coating of thick, clearish slime but not even a tinge of blood. Obviously, the shield protected the hog, and it had fled with no evidence of even being injured. My boar's blood trail, although totally unnecessary, was notable because it started at the point of impact and looped to the fallen carcass as an unbroken painted strip, eight to twelve inches wide, vividly red even on the sparse grass, a terrain type that often renders blood trailing difficult.

A live oak that had proven through the years to produce highly sought-after acorns was dropping one archery season. Head high dog fennel had taken over most of the pasture. There was an open area west of the tree, and some scattered shallow ponds allowed a handful of brief openings north of the tree, but the only place for a stand was in the tree itself. Even that involved a lot of sawing limbs and pruning that improved the site a bit but still only provided a few avenues for unimpeded arrow flight and discovering approaching game before its arrival was far from likely. With the base of the stand only six and a half feet above the ground, movement to ready a bow undetected by a deer or turkey might border on impossible.

One grey afternoon, I mounted the stand despite its drawbacks because the sign under it was thick and tantalizing. A spitting sprinkle ensued that gradually became heavier and persistent, so I opened an umbrella only to notice white ears 350 yards to the northwest. A doe that distant had caught the motion! After eight or ten minutes, she continued along the woods' edge, stopping twice more to stare for a minute or so. Another deer followed in her wake. Both does were full-size and mature, although the lead one was larger. They entered a pond a couple hundred yards north of me and glimpses of their backs from time to time showed they were feeding. In the meantime, I managed to get the umbrella up. I had forgotten to bring rope to tie the handle to the tree, but knowing game could appear with no warning, I wanted to be free to shoot. Somehow I got it wedged between branches and hoped it would stay. The deer offered brief views over the next twenty minutes and then were lost to sight, 250 yards away and still heading east.

Time passed. I read some of *The Thin Man*. The umbrella received enough of a gust to overcome its precarious position and fell. The rain had lightened somewhat, so I collapsed it and left it at my side, only to have the rain return a few minutes later. This time, the wind rocked the limbs enough that there was no way to stabilize the umbrella, so I held it thinking the rain would slacken momentarily. Instead, the large doe stepped under a low bough on the northeast side of the tree and, from six yards, looked directly at me. With only a short hesitation, she then started searching for acorns, yet the instant I tried to lower the umbrella an inch or two, she was right back at full attention. She bounded back a jump or two and that placed the bough between us. The other deer was now twenty yards to the north and scanning to see what was happening, so I still had to be careful with my movements, but at last the umbrella was collapsed and set aside and Elanever was ready in my hand.

The second doe was still coming toward me, but moving legs gave evidence that the first doe was skirting the low oak branches in an effort to get to the southwest, downwind. When she was west-north-west, there was a gap between oak limbs and as her head disappeared behind some fennel, I drew, focused, and released. Elanever, unerringly and nearly silently, sped an arrow into her chest. She ran north for thirty yards, slowed to a trot as her course veered more easterly, and fell. That was all, no kick or struggle. The other deer looked at her and resumed feeding. Each once in a while, she would raise her head and again give the fallen doe a look before feeding more. Over time, the second doe began staring more and feeding less until she was not feeding at all. Cleaning the doe was going to be an ordeal because the mosquitoes were exceptionally fierce, so despite my interest in the second doe's behavior, I got out of the tree and spooked her. My arrow had passed through and was still painted richly red regardless of the steady rain. Darkness was a good hour and a half away, but with the rain, the mosquitoes were not waiting until then. My truck was black with them, and they had completely covered the doe when I drove back over to her. The mosquitoes were overwhelming and relentless as I dressed her, so while I extracted the jaw, I didn't take the time to evaluate it. The biologist aged her at four and a half.

As further examples, the four deer trails chronicled in the section on heart-struck game all ran curving trails as well as the buck with the tine with two right angles and the buck I shot when I had lost the binocular eyecup and many, many more. Of all patterns I have encountered, it is the most prevalent.

Another recurring tendency is an animal looping just before it collapses, adding difficulty to the trail at the point it is almost solved. This can occur with curved trails or any trail. This loop, run in the last second of life, is fairly short, seldom exceeding thirty yards and varies from circular to oblong, sometimes so oblong the animal doubles back on its own track. When a trail seems to end all at once, it is worthwhile to consider a loop to either side or directly back. Again, there are no hard and fast rules with wounded game, but discounting gutshot animals, when a relatively small loop is encountered, most of the time, the animal has fallen nearby.

Four of us were trailing a bull elk one night and found great blood sign that corroborated the archer's description of the hit. The bull had run basically south, somewhat uphill and then slightly down. The trail was not puzzling in the least until it ended in a fifteen-yard loop of prominent blood. We could find nothing more. With experience hinting that the elk must be close, I ventured straight down the incline below the loop. Sure enough, twenty-five yards down the slope lay the bull. Apparently, he leaped at the end of the loop and tumbled over a little precipice and rolled or slid the rest of the way.

One January morning, my friend and I entered a management area without difficulty. The number of people that lined up in the predawn mornings had dwindled after the modern firearms season had been going on a couple months and the deer sightings concomitantly became scarce. The first few weeks anyone not at the check station two and a half hours before dawn had little chance of admission because the number of hunters was restricted to three hundred. This particular morning, the wind was relentless and gusty, and as I swayed in a cabbage palm, not even squirrels or birds were moving. Seldom, if ever, had I sat in the swampwoods and seen so little activity. Peculiarly, even though the morning had shown nothing the least bit promising and I had been restless earlier, when my watch read eleven o'clock, I was reluctant to abandon the stand and decided to remain at least another fifteen minutes. There was a slight skipping sound that may have been a blown leaf. It also possibly could have come from a young buck that suddenly appeared under the cabbage palm fronds bending down east of my stand. He was walking quickly and determinedly to the north, but less than fifteen yards from my stand and my arrow found his shoulder. He dashed north, and the thick swampwoods enveloped him nearly at once. The shot looked perfect, and my examination of the place the arrow caught him revealed a heavy trail that started immediately. The lush growth of lizard tail, one of the best vegetations for highlighting blood sign, held a thick, vividly red trail that was simple to follow. The trouble was that after sixty yards, it ended. Despite my earnest efforts, I could not progress even a foot further. Happily, something made me backtrack, and after five or six yards, I encountered a log to the right of the trail marked with a small smear of blood. With all the blood on the lizard tail, I had strode blissfully past with my eyes on the trail ahead. This little buck had looped so tightly that the trails merged and had then flopped over the log as he died. This was one of my first few deer taken with a bow during rifle season on heavily hunted public land, and I remember being very proud of him at the time.

Once, a well-struck doe rushed into a shallow pond right before she died, but looped back out of the pond on the same trail and threw herself well up under a low blanket of briars and greenbrier. My ears had registered the splashing in the pond, so there was no surprise when the trail led to the spot. The baffling problem was that no amount of searching resulted in even one promising lead as to where she went from there. I traced out every possible route and searched throughout the entire pond (that really wasn't deep enough anywhere to hide a deer) without uncovering the slightest cause for hope. After who knows how many times of returning to where the doe entered the pond, I happened to observe that leaves were blooded on both sides. Finally, the clue was there to help me discover that she doubled back and then thrown herself off the trail. A little more careful observation along the trail that I had thought predictable from her sounds and seemed easy from the copious blood would have saved me an hour or more of searching and the anguish of fearing I would not find this deer.

A buck I arrowed near a cypress head left a short, flamboyant trail that likewise ended unexpectedly. Once again, a loop was discovered and the buck was found under a low oak branch not more than fifteen yards back from where the trail evaporated.

Just this past season, I hunted from the low limb of an oak in a fairly open pasture cluttered with thick regions of dog fennel. In the early morning, four deer fed under oaks a hundred and fifty yards west of me and turkeys came near me without initially offering a shot. A bit later, I moved at the wrong time and a hen "pucked" at me. She walked off and other turkeys including some nice jakes, not previously in the open, milled around, and slowly followed her. None offered an un-interfered with shot until they were beyond thirty yards. I had only chastisement for myself for moving when I did, for had I not, the turkeys would have stepped out at four or five yards. The turkeys were not truly spooked and fed under some oaks not terribly far away, jumping up to pluck acorns from the boughs above reminding me of my musings the day before about how seldom I see deer reach up into oaks to eat acorns before they are dropped. Turkeys, jays, crows, squirrels, and raccoons all eat the acorns directly from the limbs, but deer and hogs often wait until they fall.

Two deer approached from the south but loitered under an oak there. The larger doe ate several acorns directly from the lower branches. Having just considered how infrequent that feeding behavior appeared to be, I couldn't help but to chuckle. So often when I think I know about deer, one reminds me how little I really know. This turned my thoughts to oranges, for while deer check out the orange trees regularly for fallen fruit, none have eaten one from the tree itself in my presence. Maybe they do this more than I think as well, or maybe the fallen ones are riper and sweeter. My thoughts were cut short as the pair resumed their course toward my tree.

The wind was coming from the north-northwest, and the deer were due south. The feathers tied to Daddy's ends were pointing barely east of their approach, and the slightest variance in the breeze could alarm them. The smaller one stopped twice, maybe with unease. The big doe was further west and came briskly to the oak. When she was broadside at four or five yards, I drew Daddy making sure the broadhead was near my index finger, paused long enough to imagine the arrow's flight, and released. The arrow leapt into her chest exactly where I had envisioned even while the bow's nearly inaudible thump sounded. Red blood shot up and out in a bright explosion. The doe bucked upward with all four feet in the air, coming down to jet westward, curving north and then northeast, and finally tightly looping back to the southwest, probably traveling eighty yards all told on the curving and circuitous course but falling within fifty-five yards of where she had been struck and in view the whole time. Anyone who has witnessed the speed of a running deer can realize just how few seconds she lived, no more than five and maybe half that.

The arrow drove through the chest, cutting the giant arteries right at the heart, exiting the bottom of the chest, and piercing through the left foreleg, tremendous penetration for a little longbow! Even on the grassy terrain, the blood trail was an unbroken ribbon. The doe's loop brought her back to collapse directly on top of her blood trail.

These loops occur so regularly that it behooves a tracker to bear them in mind.

Florida is pretty flat, so the bulk of my tracking has not allowed me to study the effect of slopes on flight patterns, but I have repeatedly heard and read that wounded game goes downhill. My experiences in Colorado, blood trailing for myself and friends (limited to no more than ninety trails), confirmed that some mortally wounded animals do go downhill, but the proportion could not even be 50 percent. Most trails included some uphill and some downhill portions, and several went entirely uphill. These trails were all during bow season, so I have absolutely no knowledge of what is typical for rifle shot game, but it seems likely that the individual nature of the animal, the location and extent of the wound, the cover and terrain, and the whereabouts of other animals of the same species (elk for elk and mule deer for mule deer) all factor into how a game animal will flee. Also, when the hunter is detected before or at the time of the shot, his or her presence can influence the flight's direction and duration. Here are a few accounts of wounded game going uphill:

Elk bugles from some aspens below sent me hurrying down some fairly barren slopes. A tremendous six-by-six worked slowly up a ravine. His eye guard tines were so long they loomed way out in front of him. He stopped and thrashed some gnarly brush, screaming and bellowing repeatedly. Other bulls were calling from across the canyon, and the air was filled with their wondrous and primal music. Every fiber of my being wanted to rush down the slope, but care was required because there was no cover and cows were scattered about and might easily spot me, even from across the canyon. If I could get down ahead of him as he worked up at an angle toward me, the wind would be in my favor. From sixty yards above him, I marveled at the photographic opportunities as he bellowed and twisted his antlers viciously to raze shrubs to splinters, but even a minute's hesitation to get the camera out and set might hinder my efforts to arrive in time to cut him off, and indeed, even without stopping, I got down thirty yards behind him. My cow call elicited an answer but did not lure him back. Elk cover ground quickly even when they walk in an unhurried manner, and although I climbed as fast as I quietly could, his bugles indicated he was gaining distance on me. Hastening upward with less emphasis on stealth only resulted in my spooking some elk in the aspens south of the ravine, and their crashing retreat spooked him as well. I ran down the ravine, hoping to intercept him on the other side of a little ridge for the cows hadn't spooked badly, and he was already bugling again. To keep the wind right, it was necessary to stay below them.

That draw spilled into the main canyon, and as I reached the bottom, bugles erupted from both sides, engulfing me in a world of ringing screams and answers and echoes. The deepest and most continuous issued from the west side, and they lured me up an aspen draw. The musical bugles and coarse grunts and chuckles urged me on, and I moved upward quietly, shifting directions wherever the moving chorus led, always with the feeling that the bulls were just over the next little crease. One screamed a hoarse, throaty cry that vibrated my chest, and an antler tip floated along the ridge top no more than twenty yards above me. As I crept upward toward this bull, a five-by-five filtered through the aspens twenty-five yards below. He paused broadside, but the undergrowth thwarted any chance for a shot. Spooking him would spook the other bull, so I waited and watched him go and then resumed my uphill stalk slowly and incrementally with the expectation that the larger and louder bull would drop down in front of me any second, but a fresh round of piercing whistles further up the ridge gave evidence that I was too late. I crept forward into an area of aspens incredibly choked with serviceberries and chokecherries. Through the tangle of branches, elk were visible twenty-five or thirty yards away, but it was difficult to see them clearly, just drifting shapes of brown ghosting between the trunks and shrubs. The elk were now on three sides of me, and when one would crash off, at first I assumed my presence or scent was responsible, but it became apparent that more dominant bulls were chasing one or two cows and lesser bulls. There were at least six bulls in my immediate vicinity and most were nice six-by-sixes. The sounds were unbelievable and breathtaking for both their power and strength and their primal beauty. Arising from so close, the ringing bugles echoed in my head (and re-echoed the remainder of the day like music even accompanying me to sleep that night). In addition, there were deep, raspy grunts and roars, repeated sounds like loud and intense "clucking," and barks similar to alarm barks, but deeper, shorter, and hoarser, and some mewing sounds, like a soft undulating cow call. Standing amid this awe-inspiring concert and breathing in the power and urgency it conveyed, I was nonetheless nervous that any second the fickle winds that swirl through aspen hollows would betray my presence. Giant bulls strode by repeatedly within what seemed like easy bow range, but the incredibly intertwined branches disallowed even a thought of a shot. A small cow hastened westward, passing at twelve or so yards. As she vanished, I mewed softly.

Immediately, fast steps sounded among the leaves, and through the tangle of branches, I could make out a large bull striding toward me with neck extended and his six-pointed antlers back. He was broadside at ten yards, but there was no shot, but then at six yards, still broadside, a narrow avenue opened between the branches, offering a bit of hope. I drew Bane Too's string, feeling the power of its limbs as the broadhead touched my forefinger. The bull's chest and the tiny tunnel through the brush coalesced, and in that instant, the arrow leapt free and the big bull staggered, then hopped and trotted a few steps. The arrow's fletches were scant inches from his chest, and with that much penetration, he was destined to expire fast regardless of his massive size, long mane, and heavy antlers.

I stood quietly, contemplating the morning and its experiences and thrills. All the time, the bulls' guttural music continued filling both the ravine and my head. Another big bull passed by at twelve yards heading to the west. He stopped at twenty-two yards and stared at something. After a few minutes, he angled off and walked south. My assumption was my bull had caught his attention and it made me feel there would be no need to trail him. My watch said 8:55. I determined to make myself wait at least forty-five minutes and pulled out Cormac McCarthy's *Cities of the Plains* with hopes of making the time go by quickly. Before I could open it, a five-by-five came up from below and stood at fifteen yards. I dug my camera from the pack, wishing I had readied it earlier, but he may have smelled me for after a pause, he turned and tiptoed back into the thick brush. I was primed for a spectacular bull photograph at this point and waited anxiously. Although more bulls came near me, the undergrowth screened them, and my camera never even got to click.

With time, the cacophony and commotion moved on, and the woods about me grew silent. My forty-five-minute goal was not yet achieved, but the shot looked superb and the idea of "just looking at the trail" gained my approval. With slow and careful steps, I cast for sign and within twenty-five yards found a blaring trail of red. As heavy as it seemed, the trail led in a surprising way for it went upward and upward and continued upward even as the ground became steeper and more rugged. I followed. After a hundred and fifty yards, screaming bugles erupted to both my right and left. A bull stepped out from the right, his thick, dark antlers stretched back over his torso, but turned at the sight of me, disappearing over the crest but not running. I pulled my camera from the pack again and stalked to the left. The next bugle was further away, so I returned to the blood trail. Scarcely fifteen yards farther up the steep trail was a dead bull. I was flabbergasted! Was this my bull? His left antler was broken off just above the first eye guard! Could it have been like that when I shot him? If it had broken off on his death run, why hadn't it fallen on the trail? With all these giant bulls around, how had I found one with a broken rack on the side away from me?

The antler showed signs of the break not being especially recent (although I did check the trail three more times!) His good antler was fairly massive and heavy and sported six thick points. By luck, he had come by me with his best side showing! As I skinned and quartered him, bulls treated me to a symphony of bugles from all directions.

Another Colorado adventure likewise involved two uphill flights, one for me and one for Mack. After taking the bull the magpies helped me find the year of my illness and infected hand, there were still a couple hunting days remaining, so as my strength rebounded a bit, I returned to the area along Milk Creek and nestled once more into the tall, blonde grass of the dry waterway where most of the mule deer had passed by during my last hunt there. I could only see my surroundings by rising on my knees at intervals.

For a while, nothing showed even though it was later in the afternoon than when so many deer were feeding a few days before, but then, as I rose up to peer, two bucks were feeding fifteen or so yards into the open grass. Both were broadside and most accurately described as being on the large side of small 4 × 4s. The lead one was slightly larger. Raising Bane Too rustled the dry grass slightly. The smaller buck picked up on the noise, staring in my direction with ears flared wide and straining. With his neck outstretched, he advanced a couple steps, raising and lowering his head, his muscles tensed and his graceful body poised for instant flight. The other buck was now alert. Movement to draw the bow would spook them for certain, but my lack of movement did not succeed in calming them, and they bounded away.

This was discouraging for the rustling was miniscule and there really was no way to pick up or maneuver the bow more silently. I sat and thought how best to revise my ambush for a few minutes and again rose cautiously to survey the area. Shockingly, there were two larger bucks in almost the same position the younger bucks had occupied! Where the smaller buck had stood was a buck in velvet with very tall antlers. In the other one's spot was a hard-antlered deer that seemed larger. I was afraid to study them too long for the opportunity could evaporate in a hurry and decided on the hard-antlered 4 × 4. He was slightly more distant but more broadside and they were both very close. The small noises as I picked up and readied Bane Too elicited no increased alertness in either deer. With my forced peculiar two fingered draw, I pulled back, reminding myself to come to full draw and to imagine the shot before truly releasing. I could sense the power of the flexed limbs. The release was quiet and smooth, and the arrow drove perfectly into the lower third of the buck's chest. The hit looked ideal and my view of the protruding fletchings as he raced uphill into the sage covered slopes; the other buck with him, like his shadow, corroborated the impression. Fifty yards up, he stopped and looked back. The velvet antlered buck did likewise. With binoculars, I studied them. The posture of the hard-antlered buck also suggested a fatal wound. The velvet buck's antlers were taller but narrower and sported only three tines per side. My buck was a wide, symmetrical 4 × 4 that also had small brow tines. He took a step back downhill and sank into the sage. The velvet buck ran as I stood. Belatedly, I wished I had photographed him. Even though my buck had carried the arrow with him, there was an exit wound and the trail was prominent in the sage.

That evening, the news reported Hurricane Francis's predicted route would likely be close to a direct hit on our homes. Being away from there and unable to secure and ready our properties weighed heavily on all of us. Of our group, two were insurance agents, and they probably had even more worries as a hit would place professional urgencies upon them as well as personal ones. Our flight home was, of course, cancelled.

Ozzie still had an unfilled tag, so I accompanied him the next day armed only with a camera. With good luck and a surge in the rut, bulls bugled and trashed trees and responded to our calls. On several occasions, it seemed Ozzie would get an opportunity, but something interfered each time. The excitement and close calls continued all day, and in the end, it was hard to believe he had not even had a chance to launch an arrow. My head swam with ringing bugles and roars and echoes and chirps as sleep enveloped me that night.

The next morning, I returned to the hospital and had more surgery on my finger as the swelling had become alarmingly worse. This time, a deep cone of tissue was removed to allow drainage, and the antibiotic changed. The relief was nearly immediate, and the touchiness of my hand was gone. The hurricane was moving unbelievably slowly, but it looked inevitable that central Florida was in its path. My wife and daughter had evacuated, and Breanna had broken her arm. Flights were still cancelled. Mack had driven out that year while the other hunters in his group were flying. Obviously, they were unable to get out of Florida, but Mack arrived. He was pretty sick (and Billy from our group was very sick and weak). Mack rested and recuperated the next day but asked me to hunt with him the following afternoon in the Little Creek canyons. We had finally booked air passage to Florida for the next morning, a flight that entailed packing and leaving the ranch by 3:30 a.m. Hunting Little Creek would get us back to the ranch two hours or more after dark if we got nothing and really late if we had luck. Since Mack's group comes out before or after my group every year, I had never gotten to hunt out west with him and wanted to do so badly. I talked him into hunting east of the ranch up toward the White River National Forest, much closer and faster.

We set out and quite soon could hear bugles and caught sight of two good bulls with a big group of cows on a slide south of us and a couple thousand yards away. The stalk would be difficult with the wind direction and with all those eyes, ears, and noses. There were likely to be elk down in a ravine much nearer to us if we could circle enough to get the wind right. I conveyed my thoughts to Mack, and he agreed. There would still be a chance to hustle up to the other elk afterward if the thickly wooded canyon proved barren. We slipped as quietly as we could along the ever branching and turning trails that tunneled beneath the forest of twisted, gnarled, and stunted oaks, heading first up and then over to stay in harmony with the wind. The narrow trails caused us to diverge slightly; Mack somehow diverted into a pathway leading east. At the edge of the canyon, I peered around the last scraggly oak brush. The canyon appeared empty, but then motion just below me caught my eye. A giant bull's head was protruding from a wallow where he was soaking. Always before the bulls I saw in wallows were active, frolicking and rolling and splashing and kicking, but this monster bull was very sedate. I eased back to Mack and told him of the bull, urging him to hurry because of the memory of the rapid exit of a bull from a wallow on Little Creek six days earlier still haunted my mind. I waited at the bush-like oak, while Mack belly-crawled down closer yet. Soon, he was in position and waiting. The bull's body was hidden down in the wallow. While reclining, the bull threw his head back and issued an incredibly loud, shrieking bugle. This occurred in the pre-digital (for me) age, and I had clicked two frames with my camera and reached the end of the roll of film. As I hurriedly tried to load another roll, the bull stood up and lingered motionless for a minute, mostly broadside, but slightly angled away. Kneeling, Mack drew his Habou longbow and slipped a silent arrow through the massive chest. The bull lunged down the canyon and then circled back, curving first toward the aspens and then away. He already looked very sick as he passed back by us, and although he continued ascending the canyon, we knew the trail would be short.

Sure enough, blood was splashed about heavily, and we walked up to him within fifty yards. He was a phenomenally long, heavy, and symmetrical six by six, the biggest we knew of ever being taken in the area. Caping and quartering was hard but enjoyable work with our happy frames of mind, the worries of how our homes fared in the storm at least temporarily pushed aside.

The beginning of this chapter points out that I could find no constant in a fleeing animal's course. I must point out that is based on my experiences and on a limited number of different species. John Taylor, who killed probably over fifteen hundred elephant and therefore must be considered somewhat of an authority, declares, "An elephant shot through the heart or lungs will always clear off after his trunk—that is, in the direction in which he is facing. He may slew round a mite and head directly away from one after running a short distance, but I have never known a bull to charge on receiving such a shot." He does go on to add that a cow elephant may whip around instantly on feeling the shot and make a determined charge. The significance is that other game may have tendencies that differ from what I have witnessed.

Mack's bull from the wallow initially started off
downhill only to loop back and run uphill.

CHAPTER 5

Special Terrains

CERTAIN SURFACES AND VEGETATIONS CAN add an extra layer of difficulty to blood trailing. These are sure to vary from region to region. In fact, there are likely several even more troubling terrains than the ones listed on the following pages. This chapter merely describes some that I have encountered.

Florida's hunting lands are often laced with creeks, ponds, glades, and cypress heads, so it is not unusual in the least for fleeing animals to enter or pass through water. As a novice bow hunter, I bemoaned my first arrowed hog entering a wide expanse of shallow water. Time has taught me that this is not as much bad luck as a normal circumstance. Water nearly instantly dilutes the blood sign and, except for certain circumstances, hides tracks as well so the two most readily followed parts of the trail are destroyed, minimized, or sequestered.

If the hunter is not far behind the animal, bubbles can reveal its course. In stagnant water, this evidence can persist several hours. Old bubbles may blow or drift. Even so, they should show the general direction of flight. In flowing waters, the bubbles are more ephemeral, but banks and vegetation may trap and preserve them several minutes or more. Of course, Florida is flat and our creeks do not flow exceptionally fast. The bubbles arise from two causes. Some are results of splashes from the plunging animal's feet, legs, and body. Rapid flights generate more of these bubbles, slower retreats, less.

160

These bubbles are of a variety of sizes, some as big in diameter as a quarter. Other bubbles form from gasses produced by accumulated debris or living vegetation on the bottom being released by pressure from the animal's hooves. Typically, released gasses form clusters of tiny bubbles. The speed the animal is traveling is not the cause of these bubbles. In fact, since the stride length is shorter with decreased speed, slower moving animals leave a more continuous trail when gases are trapped below the soft bottom.

Short of bubbles, the tracker must rely upon sign on the vegetation that extends above the surface or extrapolate the possible courses and subsequently investigate the water's edge in those directions. Protruding vegetation may display sprays or drops of water or of blood. A racing deer or hog splashes dramatically. A walking one disrupts the water much less. It is worthwhile to inspect any protruding leaf or stem with care. The greater the distance through water with little or no emergent plants, the greater the chances for variation in the game animal's course, which equates to the greater number of possible exit points to be evaluated. At exit points, splashed water or blood on the ground or leaves can evince the animal's passage. Also, the damp or muddy ground of the water's edge is often soft enough to register hoof prints. If the water is deep enough, blood on the animal's body may be washed away, so once the trail leads again to dry ground, a gap may exist before the actual blood trail resumes. Therefore, where tracks or splashed water give evidence game left the water, a lack of blood should not be construed to mean that the trail was necessarily made by a different animal. If the animal is still bleeding, confirmation should show up within a fairly short interval.

On several occasions, deer or hogs I've tracked to water died in the water, so that possibility must be born in mind. Sometimes they are readily visible, but surprisingly often, their mostly submerged bodies are tricky to discern. *Bows, Swamps, and Whitetails* includes a very great example of a trail through water and the doe dying in the pond. Here is a case that involved a lengthy portion of the trail through the swamp:

Hollowed, empty rinds on an orange tree let me know raccoons were feeding on them, and therefore, deer would also likely be coming to the tree, so I set a stand and waited one afternoon. A big doe appeared sixty yards to the east about four o'clock, browsing industriously but, despite her zigzag pattern, moving all the time toward the orange tree. At fifteen yards, her browsing behavior caused her to turn broadside on each side as she faced alternately north and south while staying nearly anchored devouring some greenish-white shoots. I drew Daddy and practiced, achieving that feeling that if I were to release, the shot would be perfect a few times with no intent to actually let an arrow fly. The doe was obviously coming even closer, but then I considered my confidence with each mock draw and that the nearer she got, the more penetration would be required for an exit wound and also the greater the chance an errant wind eddy, no unusual thing in the swamp, could alarm her. The next time she was broadside, I drew Daddy and, when everything felt as good as before, let the arrow go. The streaking flight looked good, but my eyes weren't fast enough to record exactly what happened. As the doe bolted, the bright fletchings showed above the front leg, but whether the arrow had hit low in the chest or only high in the leg was not certain. The frantically racing deer spoke of a lethal hit, and then the doe fell after about thirty yards, flipped around, got up running fast, but without a whitetail's normal grace of motion. Loud splashes came through the woods after the deer had disappeared from view.

Blood was sprayed at the impact site, so it was unlikely to be only a leg wound. More sprayed blood made the trail easy, and after twelve yards, the broken arrow lay, the pieces forming a "V" with the broken ends close together and pointing the way she ran. Continued blood led to the site of the fall, and the ground was torn from the skid and the struggle to rise. I looked ahead, expecting to see the prone form of the deer, but saw nothing of the sort and continued following the obvious blood trail until it entered water. Now I remembered how much trouble it had been to reach the stand without going over the top of my eighteen-inch boots because the water was up. Much of the swamp was completely submerged. Not only would tracking be harder, but even finding the fallen deer might prove frustratingly difficult if she were mostly submerged.

Splashes of water on plants and tree trunks were my only clues, and the course was more erratic than at first. Every time I became confused and went back to reevaluate, splashes made by my passage confused things more. After fifty yards with no blood to confirm the trail, other doubts loomed. Hog sign was ubiquitous, so perhaps these were only splashes from a hog spooked by me or by the deer. The water had reached well over the tops of my boots several times and could easily have hidden the still body of the doe. It didn't seem like she could have made it far. After I lost any splashes or indications of a trail, these doubts took me back to where the doe first entered the water. I found no body and no other sign to offer any explanation or hope. Darkness, which settles in quickly in the swampwoods, began to make everything shadowy. With the aid of a flashlight, I searched and searched.

In the general direction of the continuation of the splash trail, a couple hundred yards distant, was some higher ground with pines and palmettos. It seemed impossible a well-struck deer could make it that far. Had my arrow caught only the leg after all? If so, why all that blood? I waded to the pines and searched along the edge looking for any sign of an animal's emergence. My flashlight beam caught glistening spots on the pine needles. Had dew already fallen? No, they were limited to a narrow width! Aiming the beam ahead allowed me to see the shiny wetness of the trail. I followed. Soon dribbles of blood verified they were the tracks of the doe. Within fifteen or twenty yards, the trail became prominent again and led to the fallen doe.

The arrow pierced through the lower front of the chest and exited at the same spot on the other side, accounting for the sprayed blood. Peculiarly, both front legs were cut on the forward sides. The cut removed a rectangle of flesh and skin five-eighths of an inch by one and one quarter of an inch. Like the chest wounds, these were very symmetrical. They occurred three to four inches below the level of the chest. I could not manipulate the legs to make the hole line up with the ones in the chest, but since then, I've puzzled over it and now wonder if the doe heard the bow and starting to spring raised her forelegs up and forward, but with the hooves and lower part of the legs pointing rearward. It is also possible the protruding arrow could have twisted back and injured the legs, but the symmetry of the wounds makes the chances of that infinitesimal. Regardless, I was lucky to have found her after she entered such a large expanse of water-covered terrain. This episode demonstrated many of the features of tracking through watery terrain; water splashed on exposed trunks and vegetation, extrapolation of the course these splashes suggested, looking for tracks and wet places at possible exit points from the water, and the delay before blood began showing again on the trail.

It seems strange that grass should prove a challenging tracking surface, but the narrowness of the blades results in smaller, and more difficult to see, traces of blood. At the same time, hoof prints in grassy areas are seldom obvious and mostly border on the edge of imperceptibility. Fortunately, taller grasses bend in the direction of the animal's movement and can display the route taken. The bent grasses reflect light differently, and sometimes by standing back and observing the whole expanse of taller grasses, the trail can be traced visually for a long way without taking any steps. If it is not obvious, try looking from different sides of the trail as the angle of the sunlight affects this phenomenon. Granted, there are times the blood is sprayed so thickly that grass poses no impediment, but if the droplets become scanty, grass magnifies the difficulty. When I review my journals, grass has frequently been involved in troublesome trails:

Back in '88, I placed a stand in an interesting place. A cypress head and a thick strand of low vegetation coalesced into a narrow pathway between the palmetto flats. This pathway, maybe twenty yards wide contained soft, low grasses and a smattering of pines, and it, in turn, led to a big, flat, sedge filled pond. Most of the pines were young, but one was fair sized and had at some earlier time had its main trunk broken about twelve feet from the ground. Other branches grew upward to compensate, and they formed a cup-shaped basket about the main stem. My stand was at the top of the broken trunk, and the newer branches shielded it from view although they also imposed limitations on where an arrow was free to travel. With no extension of the tree above, there was no shade in the morning or midday, but pines to the west blocked most of the glare and heat in the evening, so on the afternoon of the second day of modern firearms season, I gave the stand its first try. As the sun sank low, a doe and her grown fawn fed from the cypress and down my corridor. Sometimes things seem to meld perfectly with the planning that suggested the stand placement, but as I rejoiced in this thought, the pair veered from the pines into the palmettos. They passed my tree and were heading further. The doe paused broadside with her head down at twenty-two yards. This was at a time when I usually limited myself to a maximum of fifteen yards. She stood long enough that I was able to draw Deer Bane, take my time, feel the shot, and release an arrow that zipped precisely through her chest! I was ecstatic! She spun and ran a loop directly under my stand, speeding into the cypress head. The smaller deer looked around and trotted off uncertainly.

The previous morning, I made a shot that did not look all that good but resulted in a superb and short blood trail. This evening presented the exact opposite case. The shot's placement appeared perfect, the arrow was globbed with blood, yet there was no evidence of a blood trail even though I knew precisely the doe's route. I continued searching. Either she wasn't bleeding or the grassy terrain absorbed it. Darkness fell as my frustration rose and I had to batter my way through the palmetto flats to my truck and retrieve a flashlight. Its illumination was no more helpful than the earlier twilight in finding blood. Where she vanished into the cypress, there were five main avenues she could have taken without exposing herself to my view east or west of the head. They were grass-lined, and I scoured each one for forty-plus yards, stooped over and searching meticulously. No blood was to be seen. On the fifth trail, at the point of stopping, I stood to ease my back. My light, mounted on a headband, flashed over something white as I did so. There, thirty yards ahead, was my doe. Even near her, no blood showed although no more than typical was held in her chest when I later cleaned her. She had fallen about ninety yards from the broken pine. I skinned out the bones of the lower portions of her legs and tied the skins right front to left rear and vice versa and made her into a pack. The palmettos were an ordeal to push through unburdened, and her hundred-plus pounds did nothing to make the half mile seem shorter!

A different year, I hunted in Tyson Creek and witnessed egrets, hogs, turkeys, raccoons, squirrels, owls, hawks, anhingas, woodpeckers, great crested flycatchers, and more. A flying squirrel popped out on a nearby tree and squeaked repeatedly at me. However, no deer came within sight. A change was indicated, so I opted for a stand near some orange trees in Antler Branch. I felt my way through the strand the next morning in the dark, trying to approach the oranges from directly downwind. My desired target was a cabbage palm near the southeastern-most orange tree. The idea of maybe spreading my scent anywhere else except downwind was extremely troubling to me, so halfway through the creek bottom, I regretted not waiting for first light or bringing a flashlight, but then the darker shape of an orange tree loomed ahead, and luck was with me as I had crossed the swamp directly to the exact palm that would be ideal for this wind.

I climbed and readied my gear. Light broke, and the woods came alive with birds and squirrels flitting and bouncing through the limbs and trees. Before long, motion to the east attracted my eye. A doe was ghosting through the fronds of the swamp. While the squirrels and birds shook the branches aloft and rustled leaves when they were on the ground, no noise accompanied her dainty movements. Bane Too was already in my hand. The swamp in the area was exceedingly lush, and visibility was therefore quite limited. Soon the deer were very close and there were at least four, but despite their nearness, only parts of deer were discernable. The nearest one, no more than seven yards from the tree, was a mature doe and nearly broadside, slightly quartering away. Another step took her out from under a drooping frond. I drew Bane Too, and before I was aware of releasing, the arrow darted through her chest. With the impact, she exploded into flight and ran as fast as deer can possibly run! She was facing northeast and took off that way despite all the palmettos. The shot looked textbook perfect. There was crashing in the palmettos that may have been her falling, but it was impossible to say because the other three deer fled with her.

Persistent bubbles can reveal an animal's passage even
hours later in stagnant water.

These two photos come from an extremely heavy blood trail. It
is worth noting that while blood is very much in evidence on the
blackberry leaves, the same amount had fallen on the grasses and
dried fennel, yet it is much harder to distinguish. By the way, the flies
in the photo with arrow will be mentioned more later in the text.

It is easier to wait when the trail promises to be simple and short, and I managed to let an hour and a half slip past before clambering down. She had carried the arrow only a yard or two past where she was stricken, and it was richly coated with blood, the fletchings so saturated that all three were now the same sanguine shade. The blood trail started there and could be followed with an upright posture, the only hesitations or stops were to negotiate the palmetto thickets. Blood was sprayed and could be seen high off the ground, in fact, in some places at eye level for me, but it was not certain whether it was sprayed that high or if the fronds were pushed over and lower as she raced through them and then sprang back up, or if she was leaping over them and spraying blood down. Regardless, this much blood at the speed she was going was a great sign, and I started expecting to see her body after sixty yards. The trail continued in a straight line despite clearer pathways right next to the way she took. An extension of her course would lead to the woods' edge, but it was about eighty yards further, and she had already covered a hundred and twenty yards. It seemed there was no way she could make it that far, but she did reach the pasture, and there, the tracking became drastically harder. The spray caused only tiny specks on the low grass, and it took me longer to track fifteen yards on the grass than the whole trail had up to that point. The fifteen yards had, however, still been a perfect extension of her path as she left the woods, so I laid my bow down to mark the last blood and walked an extrapolation of the course. Sure enough, she lay seventy yards ahead. The arrow had entered the middle of the rib cage on the left and pierced through the lower front of her right shoulder. It had double lunged her and partially severed the vessels connected to the heart. She weighed a hundred and twelve pounds and had a lot of fat stored (for our deer). This episode not only demonstrates the trickiness of grass as a substrate but it also reinforces the information on heart struck deer often covering more ground and the "bulldozer" tendency of hard-hit game.

One year, a live oak near the Airplane Head (so named because a plane on a training mission crashed there during WWII, but was not found in the thick cypress swamp until hunters stumbled upon it in the seventies) was dropping an abundance of acorns. I had sat in the same tree the year before and sawed limbs and pruned the tree to where it was possible to get shots, so I climbed up, assuming the oak was ready as a stand site. The view was clear for fifteen to twenty yards on two sides, for five yards downwind, and for sixty yards to the northeast. I was content and comfortable after a strenuous day of scouting. The east breeze was pleasant.

The trouble was that there were almost no paths an arrow could take, particularly on the southern half of the tree. Great traces of Spanish moss had regenerated and hung in thick, long beards. Also, new oak growth sprouted profusely from limbs I trimmed last year. I made these discoveries only with the arrival of a large doe from the south. The oak was unapproachable from the southwest by a man (even a deer might find it far from easy) from the tangle of overhead briars. It could be accomplished with a machete and utmost travail, but with temperatures in the mid-nineties and humidity near 100 percent, my scent level would be heightened, so with a northeast wind, I had approached the stand from the south and the doe had obviously caught my scent trail. She came in nervously and repeatedly retreated. She stood still behind a leafy branch of the oak near where the thick growth began. Five minutes or more passed, and I began to suspect she had melted into the thick jungle. Eventually, she made a small movement and I could "discover" her again. With time, she came to the tree and fed on acorns nervously, staying along the perimeter made by the lowest branches on the south side and never under the oak itself. The full realization of just how few channels there were for arrow flight dawned on me, but I wasn't too worried for it seemed that sooner or later, she must stop somewhere open. After a half hour of having a deer within six to nine yards without a single opportunity, worries assailed me. My palm was sweaty with both heat and nervousness. My arm was tired of holding the bow ready. My legs were tired from their uneven positions on the limbs (I had placed no stand). Would the wind waver and betray me? Would she ever step into an opening in a broadside orientation? Would I be able to make the shot after all this time to become nervous? It was like her nervousness had rubbed off on me.

I was not free to move much because most of the time, her head and feet were near the ground and in plain sight even though boughs screened her body. The few instances when her body was visible, she was facing in my direction. With feeding here for so long, it seemed likely she would leave soon. Her nervousness had not dissipated, and she skitted away several times only to creep back. Other times, she picked up her head and walked away but then returned. One time, she headed away, even though she was much more distant, probably sixteen yards, and moving; she crossed a window I could shoot through, and I drew Elanever and immediately let fly. The flight looked good, but her anxiousness had primed her reactions, and she ducked and sprang southward. The window framed my arrow perfectly, and as the chest had been in the middle of a volleyball-sized opening when I released and now the arrow was imbedded in the ground exactly centered, it left no doubt she had jumped the string.

She returned again and searched out acorns but even more nervously, and with time, she drew closer and closer to where the arrow extended from the ground. One whiff of the human scent it was sure to hold would probably be enough to put her in high gear, so with Elanever ready, I searched for any tunnel an arrow could slip through. A tennis ball-sized gap aligned with her chest. Elanever's limbs bent, and the arrow flew. Most of my longbows are quiet, and Elanever is the quietest of the lot, but the doe dodged even quicker this time. The arrow had scraped some twigs and looked to have been deflected up a few inches also. The doe's swiftness in reacting and the light, bouncy way she bounded east made me believe she was unhit, but the arrow was not visible down the little tunnel, and it was important to be sure, so I moved around for a different vantage point. From another branch, the second arrow could be seen, and binoculars showed it was clean and dry. I stepped back to my branch. To my surprise and consternation, the doe had circled back and returned again to the tree while I was surveying the arrow, and my abrupt motion back to the branch alarmed her and sent her bounding and snorting away.

I was none too pleased with myself for it was evident she was really inclined to feed under the oak, and if I had remained unruffled and patient, a close, easy shot would have presented. I mentally logged each and every beard of moss and branch of the tree that should be removed. The urge was to trim them at the very minute, but prudence suggested waiting and pruning them after sunset. I read more of *Mr. Sponge's Sporting Tour*, and the humor in the book definitely improved my humor. It is hard to be upset with myself when I'm laughing! The sun neared the horizon, and the western sky shone beautifully. Coupled with my admiration of the scene was my thankfulness for hunting and fishing for over the years, these sports had given me the chance to see so many breathtaking skies, sunrises, and sunsets. A redstart and a Carolina wren flitted between limbs. With the book back in my pack, I watched them and thought what a talkative little being and cheery company the Carolina wren was in the evenings. I replotted the oak limbs that needed removal.

Daylight was dwindling and some light would be necessary to prune effectively, so I stretched my legs and prepared to climb down, but a strong urine-like odor filled my nostrils. A boar hog was the likeliest explanation, and I scanned east of the tree. Movement very close and under the fringe of the thick just a few yards north caught my eye, and I tried to resolve the brownish shape into a hog only to see antlers and realized with a shock that a big, mature buck was right next to me. Again, Elanever was in my hand with an arrow on its string! The buck slipped from under the shelter of the brush. I waited as he fed on acorns. The north side of the oak offered far fewer encumbrances to arrow flight, and within a minute or two, he was in the clear, head down, and broadside at five yards. Everything came about so quickly there was no time to get nervous. I pulled back the string, my focus narrowed to a spot on his chest, and the arrow leapt forward. The shot looked perfect! The buck was immediately in flight to the east then curving north and was lost to view. Crashing in the palmettos reached my ears.

The arrow was firmly imbedded in the earth. My heart sank with its appearance for although the shaft was slick with blood, the fletchings showed only a trace along their outer edges. Normally, feathers are saturated with a chest pass through. Could the arrow have slid between the skin and ribs and not entered the chest? A few speckles of blood confirmed his route, but really, rather than them showing where he had run, it was only knowledge of his route that allowed me to find them. The largest, a drop the size of the nail on my little finger, harbored bubbles. The sparse grass showed nothing, and an hour and a half of further searching failed to extend the trail even a foot. I resorted to examining every possible route north, northeast, or northwest from the last blood. Another hour passed. I extended the search now, hoping to see his fallen form more than blood, but found neither. My flashlight, which I had pulled from my pack after the first fifteen minutes, grew dim. The lack of blood was discouraging, but the dryness of the fletchings was even more so. I brought the truck to the last blood and searched more with the aid of its bright lights. Forlorn, I drove around the pasture where the myrtle and palmettos allowed hoping to happen upon him, but it was too thick to cover much that way, and I gave up.

By the morning, after mulling the evidence all night, I was even more convinced that I had only wounded the buck but felt compelled to look regardless. As soon as the sun cleared the horizon, I resumed the search. The blood, kept moist by the dew and mists, still looked bright. A bit of blood containing bubbles was on a frond north of where I had lost the trail. This hopeful evidence did not buoy me for long for another hour of scouring the terrain went by with no more sign. My feet took me southeast of the last blood even though reason argued against that direction. Astoundingly, there was blood on a palmetto! Isles of palmettos interrupted the short grass of the pasture, and continuing east, each clump was sprayed mightily with blood. The fact that the buck had not chosen the open pathways in concert with the big splashes of blood now made me sure the hit was lethal. I gained thirty yards in less than a minute! Then the palmettos stopped. Sparse, thin grass hides blood sign in the most confounding manner. Even between any of the blood-splattered palmetto clumps, where it was apparent the buck must have traversed, the grass was barren of sign. Now beyond the last wall of saw palmettos, I was totally stumped again. Once more, it became necessary to try potential routes. The buck lay not too much further ahead. The shot was a textbook-perfect double lung pass through that should have provided an ideal trail. Happily, the meat smelled fine and later proved delicious even though it had remained overnight during some hot weather. The rack was wide and had seven points.

Grass providing less than an ideal surface for highlighting blood sign is not restricted to Florida. While it is difficult to predict the exact whereabouts of animals with certainty, as a rule in the region of Colorado where we hunt, the elk are found in the elevated aspen draws, oak brush, and green mountainsides. Mule deer also inhabit these places and may be encountered, but the very barren-looking, arid regions of Thornberg and Stinking Gulch and the wetter terrain down along Milk Creek offer the most congested populations. Yearly, I purchase a tag for each species, but somehow elk always take precedence because pursuing them over the ridges and across canyons, lured on by distant sightings or bugles, fueled with the belief a chance is almost at hand, is exciting and almost addictive. Deer hunting is fun also, but whenever a morning or afternoon is set aside to spend in their typical haunts, a little feeling of regret or maybe even guilt accompanies the time because of thoughts of elk action up on the mountainsides. For our first several years, the hunts had been for ten-day periods. Now they were restricted to six and a half days, and those days seemed to evaporate faster than most.

On one morning dedicated to trying for a mule deer among some raw, desolate, juniper speckled ridges, I discovered at least six nice bucks and nine does feeding in the draw below me. The south wind was blowing up the draw into my face, and boulders, scant oak brush, and junipers allowed me, with careful footwork and a little crawling, to get within forty yards of the largest two bucks. A small gully wound toward them and offered a sheltered pathway to close the distance down to maybe twenty-two yards. Before I could ease into it, a doe below them started acting nervous and staring further downhill. Then all the deer directed their attention downhill. This was puzzling because I was above them and the wind was coming from them to me. I couldn't puzzle very long, however, because in the next instant the entire group raced up the ridge opposite me and disappeared. I scurried that way as well but only in time to see the deer continue their flight over several more ridges and beyond. The year before, I had hunted this ridge on a morning that started with a torrential downpour and found fresh mountain lion tracks. Several times, I had seen coyotes along the ridge fingers. The deer may have caught scent of another predator or maybe some trick of the air brought my scent up the mountain face and then circled it back down. No sign of any other animal showed, but predators know how to keep hidden when they wish.

With enough time, this vicinage should provide a chance at a good buck, but how much time should I spare? Eleven o'clock arrived with no more action and with it came my decision not to give up more days from elk hunting. With that in mind, I threaded my way down to Milk Creek to patrol its grasslands, willows, and cottonwoods in hopes of any mature mule deer. In the fall, the creek is shallow, but its lining cliffs and notched-out channels give testimony to the carving force of the rushing waters from the snowmelt in the spring. I paused to photograph a vertical, eroded chute that descended thirty-five feet to the creek as almost a circular chimney, framing the sparkling ripples of the water below it. In the background was something brown in the shadow of a green bush overhanging the opposite bank. The stream curved radically at the spot. The day was phenomenally windy, and a big doe had bedded sheltered from the gusts by the bank above her. The overhanging brush prevented any predator's approach from above her, and she was keeping a watchful vigil along the creek as the curve allowed her to scan both directions for a long ways. The bank on my side was very high and steep. I backed from the cliff edge and eased thirty yards toward her and then cautiously raised up and photographed her. The sun shone on her, and the shadow of her nose demarcated an ideal aiming point on her chest for an arrow. I bent, placed the camera down, and picked up Mellifluwood. My furtive movement must have been discovered for when I rose back up, she was standing and gazing in my direction. Horizontally, she was only fifteen yards distant, but the bluff ran so high above the stream level that the view was like from a ridiculously high tree stand. The arrow that left Mellifluwood flew true and disappeared into her chest with just a scant ruffling of her short brown hair.

She ran as if uninjured. She came to a curved, fallen cottonwood where a shrub on my side of the creek blocked further view of her. I started wondering if my eyes had followed the arrow flight correctly, but my arrow was colored brightly red, however, confirming a good hit. The blood trail was obvious along the creek, but she entered some lush, nearly knee-high grass that prevailed the rest of her route, and mystifyingly, blood only showed in two places. Happily, she had fallen at the curved cottonwood log and was not hard to find. She was very large, and I quartered her on the spot. I would not have been surprised if she scaled over 165 lbs.

Dog fennel grows in dense stands nearly head high and sometimes covering several acres or more. Fennel is a ruderal species and one of the earliest colonizers when a pasture is cleared or where hogs have rooted extensively. They trouble the tracker in a few ways. Their denseness alone blocks nearly all vision, growing within inches of each other. Their stems spring back after an animal's passage, so unlike with tall grass, no visual evidence remains behind. They also wipe and scour the fleeing animal's side, removing the blood without it reaching the ground and the greenery that performs this task hides the blood remarkably well, spreading it over lots of tiny leaves that end up jammed back against those of the neighboring plants. Each clump must be parted by hand and examined for any smear. If the game slipped between the upright stems just eight inches distant, the search will offer no clue, so the effort becomes painstaking and time consuming. The tracker can only hope the deer maintains a more or less straight course.

One of the pastures of maybe five hundred acres had been chopped and partially cleared two years before. Little clumps of live oaks had been spared, and they created small islands rising from the flat terrain. I set up one afternoon in a very scraggly clump of only four trees that must have grown among a lot of competition for light for they sported no horizontal branches, only a few fingers reaching skyward. They did have long, black acorns, and it was early enough in the season that, other than scrub oaks, few oaks were dropping. The view from the stand looked nearly limitless encompassing hundreds of yards in nearly all directions. A north-south fence line brushed up within forty yards of the clump to the west. On the opposite side of it, the pasture had been planted with hermathia that was tall enough to possibly hide a hog but would not protect a deer from view. In all other directions, however, shoulder-to-head-high dog fennel had overrun the entire pasture, and except for little openings here and there, deer could slip through unseen.

I had just sawed a few limbs to create shooting clearance so it was startling, as I began to situate my bow and gear, to notice a doe through a gap in the fennel about forty yards away. She was in the mode Van Dyke termed staging, feeding a bit but not industriously and not moving, spending more time just standing. She passed forty minutes without leaving the opening that was only a few yards wide. Finally, she disappeared, but she may only have ventured a yard or two. That drove home the realization that a deer could arrive at the oaks with no prior notice and kept my vigilance high. A small buck provided a glimpse at three hundred yards but likewise disappeared and was gone for the evening.

A common yellowthroat flitted through the underbrush. It was near five o'clock, with dark coming at about 7:30 to 7:40 p.m., when a doe and yearling appeared at an oak copse in the hermathia four hundred or more yards to the northwest. The wind had died, and what little remained issued from the east-northeast. The palmettos under the oaks swallowed them, and minutes went by with no fresh view. Suddenly, a buck was striding along the edge of the same clump. It seemed likely he would rout out the does, but he too disappeared into the palmettos. Then bouncing white tails manifested the does fleeing southwest of my stand. Just south of the oaks was a skinny pond, and they must have been working its edge in the higher growth until they were downwind enough to scent me. Some of my oak's branches happened to align with the pond's edge and helped to hide their movements. The buck hadn't noticed their flight nor did it appear he was scent-trailing them.

I rattled the big antlers Mack had brought me back from one of his Texas trips, two loud and aggressive sequences. The buck stepped out to the copse's edge and stood with his tail out and hindquarters slightly down for a minute, urinating on his tarsals. He then proceeded toward my oaks. His neck was thick and left his chest at its very bottom, so I concluded he was mature. Eighty yards northwest of me, he crossed the fence and was instantly lost in the sea of fennel. The wait was not long. The fennels stopped just short of the oaks, and he stepped out at twelve yards. Since the wind had been predicted to be from the southwest, I had come to the stand from the northeast. The buck was broadside but walking at a businesslike pace and was no more than two yards from my approach route which, with the high temperature, was sure to reek of my passage. I drew Daddy fully and let an arrow fly. The flight looked perfect and drove into his chest. Two things were not perfect, however—the sound of a muffled *crick* and half or more of the shaft protruding from the entry side of his chest. He bounded away in the direction he had been facing. It seemed likely the broadhead struck the opposite shoulder, limiting penetration and preventing an exit wound. There was no time to worry now as I strove to visually note his progress hampered by the leafy branches of my surrounding oaks and the endless head-high dog fennel. At sixty yards, his speed increased like he had kicked in his after-burners and raced onward like a blur. My view was limited to tiny open patches and leaps that cleared the top of the fennel. My last glimpse was maybe 150 to 175 yards away. I picked a distant oak to line up the exact spot he was lost to view. My recollection of his run was that his tail was low but not clamped tightly down. The earnest burst of tremendous speed seemed to speak of a quickly mortal wound.

Pastures are troublesome for blood trailing in general and thick stands of fennel in particular, so my inability to turn up any trace of blood was not unexpected. I zigzagged over the course he appeared to have taken without discovering the tiniest hint, no blood, no track, no arrow, and no dead buck. Reason suggested he could not go far, but years had taught me that is not always the case. Time passed fruitlessly, and I extended the search area. It was my first season without Jody, our lab, and I had been missing her terribly. The cabin was desolate and dreary without her, and sadness flooded me whenever I sat in any of the stands where she had waited so quietly right under me, sharing so many adventures. Now I was again struck with a pang, missing not only the ease with which she could find this deer but, even more, missing the joy and excitement the trail would give her.

I started over a couple more times with no better luck. Fortunately, there was a lot of daylight left. Despite my belief my shot was good, the utter lack of a trail left me worried that buzzards would later show me where I should have looked. My gut feeling was that since he had originally run southeast and then south, he may have curved southwest. However, had he crossed the fence, he should have come into view, so he either did not live that long or curve that far. I combed the fennel southwest of my last glimpse of him and stumbled upon him within sixty yards. I had actually passed by him twice earlier from the east side. West of him, the fennel was thick but not to the extreme of the fennel east of him, and from this direction, his white belly could be barely seen. Under his body, blood was pooled, refiring my determination to solve the trail, but despite knowing the beginning, end, and some points between, I was never able to find any evidence of how he got to where he fell. He was a beautiful eight point. He only weighed 118 lbs. but was aged at four and a half years old by jaw estimate (two independent biologists) and confirmed later with cementum ring evaluation.

Snow is a tracking medium that should also be mentioned here. With little experience with snow, my impression was that it must provide the easiest terrain on which to track, blood showing up brightly against the stark white and tracks recorded prominently as well. Larry Koller's book echoed my early thoughts: "Few badly wounded deer need ever escape to die a lingering death with snow covering the ground. Any hunter with even a slight degree of woods skill can follow and find his wounded deer on the snow." Since then, my friends have explained to me that there are many kinds of snow surfaces depending upon the type of snow, the length of time it has persisted, the temperatures it has endured and more. I have been told that on some snow surfaces, the hot blood melts through, leaving only a small hole with no color, and trailing can be mystifying when several sets of tracks join. My experiences have not included that problem, but I did learn snow can be more troublesome than I first imagined. One problem is continued snowfall can quickly obscure blood and bury tracks. I saw this firsthand looking for a friend's elk one afternoon several hours after his shot. Another way snow affects the trail is that it can melt. As it does so, the blood is diluted and soaks into the wet ground, leaving no visible trace. I have had only two trails with snow, but they opened my eyes to how tricky a substrate it can be, so I'm convinced anyone with lots of trails under his or her belt would have much more information to share.

One other terrain here in Florida can at times bedevil a tracker. Many of the Florida scrubs and xerophytic areas are home to lichens, sand spike moss, and British Soldier Moss. This last mentioned "moss" is actually a lichen of a dullish green color with vivid crimson highlights. When a wounded deer's course enters an expanse of British Soldier Moss, the bright red spots on the moss mimic blood and can lead the tracker astray, or conversely, blood droplets on the moss can wrongly be assumed to part of the plant and ignored by the tracker.

Deer legs can be skinned and deboned to make a downed deer packable. The right rear is tied to the left front and vice versa. Leave the dew claws on to keep the simple, overhand knots from slipping.

British Soldier Moss adds an extra layer of difficulty to a blood trail.

The infection in the floor of Ozzie's orbit
drained through a fistula in his cheek.

CHAPTER 6

When to Follow

ONE OF THE FOREMOST QUESTIONS is when to take up the blood trail. Howard Hill wrote, "One mistake is made by most archers, regardless of how much experience they have had in hunting. Once an animal is hit, the normal impulse is to follow the creature at once and try to get another shot. However, this procedure is a grave mistake. I realize it is all but impossible to be calm and collected after having been lucky enough to get an arrow into a buck deer, a bear, or some other big-game animal. But the hunter's chances of eventually bagging the prey will be much better if he waits at least three-quarters of an hour before following a wounded animal." Writers about firearm hunting offer very similar advice. In *The Still Hunter*, Van Dyke says, "Excited by the sight of blood and signs of stumbling, burning with anxiety to retrieve the game, and impatient of any delay, one is almost certain at first to rush ahead after a crippled deer. But you must remember that (except heading, etc.) all means of pursuit, the trail, the blood, etc., if any, will generally be just as available in four to six hours, perhaps even the next day, as they are right after shooting. By waiting you generally lose nothing. By not waiting you may lose all." Larry Koller in *Shots at Whitetails* offered suggestions not terribly different, "to sit 30 minutes and smoke a few pipes of tobacco before taking up the trail, allowing the deer to lie down and stiffen up. In a wilderness country or when bow-hunting, no better advice could be given," but then explained it was not a good idea to do so where he hunted because other hunters would steal the deer, so he concluded it was best to immediately take up the trail. Happily, today few of us have to worry about our game being stolen by humans, so that is one less concern, but the truth is that there are many factors that affect the ideal time to begin blood trailing.

The shorter the trail, the greater the chances are of locating the downed game. With a short trail, the area to be searched is relatively small. As the trail lengthens, the area to be searched becomes increasingly larger. Therefore, it is not desirable for the tracker to push the wounded animal in the least. If there is a possibility of a gutshot, the hunter is well advised to wait. As stated earlier, there is no exact amount of time that can be applied to all gut wounds because the wounds vary in severity, and each animal is an individual as well. Typically, six to twelve hours are allowed.

One afternoon in early October 1994, I sat in a ladder stand in a big patch of oak scrub that was thick enough to restrict vision radically all around the stand, but it ended thirty-five yards to the east, where a pasture laced with myrtle and palmettos replaced it. My interest was on game moving through the scrub in search of the multitude of ripe acorns, but I must have glanced to the east for I noted a deer running through the open pasture to a small cypress head near the beginnings of the scrub but more than a hundred yards from my stand. Five minutes or so later, a doe bounded out of the head and ran in my direction, entering the scrub forty or so yards away. Of course, she was instantly lost to vision. Her manner indicated a buck was likely following her. If I could slip down and get near but downwind of her path, my chances could be great! Yet where should I go? The trouble was that she may have turned north or south or even be heading toward the stand. With the scrub enveloping and hiding her, there was no way to tell or even to guess.

At this point, an eight-point buck came across the pasture in quick bounds, grunting all the way! His G-2s were long and arched forward, crab clawlike, and both they and the main beams themselves wrapped forward and inward almost to the point of touching in the front imparting to the rack a graceful, crown-like appearance. He was beautiful and large and the antlers magnificent and amber-colored. He entered the scrub at the same place as the doe and was likewise lost to sight. My eyes were frantically searching all around! Then she walked through an opening forty yards to the northeast, revealing he would not come close to my stand. By now, there was no time to climb down and sneak through the oaks, especially with two sets of ears and eyes and, concurrently, a need for my haste, so I grunted a few times. Surprisingly, he actually deviated my way in the thickness of the low oaks and may have continued, except he entered a more open area where I could see him and he could see the doe now fifty yards ahead. He turned toward her, and I drew Whispering Magic. The arrow it launched flew swiftly and straight, but the buck was already moving, and he leapt forward with the sound. The arrow may have struck further back than the chest or possibly completely missed. The buck crashed through the palmettos and scrub in the direction of the doe, disappearing behind some higher scrub oaks. The sound of his exodus stopped there as well. The doe ran all the way back to the thick little cypress head. Silence then prevailed.

For twenty minutes, I replayed the shot in my mind but was still unsure of the hit or even if he really was hit. Many trails of white sugar sand laced through the scrub. The last sound could have indicated the buck had stopped. Conversely, it could mean he continued on a quieter path. Also, maybe the crashing had been further east than I thought and he had gained the open and quiet pasture to continue his flight. Doubts assailed me. Light might last another fifteen or twenty minutes, so if I wanted to examine my arrow for signs of a hit and his tracks for blood, it would mean starting now. My thoughts were in a jumble, and I will confess that if the same thing happened today, I would sneak out of there as silently as possible, but instead, at the time, I eased down the ladder and softly made my way to the site. He crashed off again! I sprinted back to the ladder and scampered up it to get a view. He launched himself over the fence and stopped and looked about. Even with binoculars, I could see no arrow and no wound, but he did not look right. He loped a few steps and stopped and then loped a few more. In this fashion, he reached the cypress head. The doe blew a few times.

I went to the spot from which he had spooked and found his tracks but absolutely no blood even though he had stood there for a minimum of twenty-five minutes. This was discouraging. The light began to fade, and I searched for the arrow, finding it only with difficulty. My fingers told me it was wet, and my nose declared the shot was too far back. I felt incredibly bad.

I left the area. On the drive back to camp, a jet-black skunk without even a hint of white on it ambled into my headlight beams. I followed it, at first unsure of its identity for the color wasn't what would be expected of a skunk. It led me to two more. One was all white except for a single blotch of black between its shoulders and the other a dirtier, blonder white with a faint black stripe down its back. At camp, I learned Billy had arrowed a buck and went to congratulate him. It was a nice eight-point, and the chest wound showed the bright, frothy blood that spoke of a clean and fast death. It was beautiful in a way hard to describe. I was happy for Billy but felt even worse about my shot.

My friend Don and I looked the next morning, and Don found the buck nearly immediately at the edge of the little cypress where he had headed after I spooked him the evening before. If the buck had continued, however, finding him would have been accomplished only with great good fortune for we could find absolutely no sign between the scrub and the head. He was a wonderful and beautiful buck, my best ever at that time. Had I done nothing but slipped out of the area after my shot, chances were great that he would have succumbed where he stood and been easily found the next morning for the buck had no awareness of danger and did not know what had hit him. Once again, the greater distance a deer flees, the greater the opportunity of losing it. This is exceptionally true with gutshot game. I was lucky after a serious blunder, lucky that he stopped where I last saw him and lucky that I was able to get a view of his broken flight. Had he run into the scrub or the pines north of them, there would be little clue as to the direction he fled or the distance he covered.

The size of the game also affects the amount of time a hunter waits before tracking. Although this book has included accounts of a few bull elk and one bull moose dying in seconds after being stuck, the larger the animal, the smaller the wound in proportion to its size whether inflicted by bullet or broadhead and the greater the creature's blood volume as well. Therefore, it would not be unexpected for the animal to survive slightly longer. The story of my first elk, a cow, elucidates how my assumption the timeline would be similar to the small whitetails of Florida caused me a much more difficult trail:

It began the morning of the last day of our first trip to Colorado more than twenty-five years ago. We had all had exciting times and experienced close encounters with bulls but let no arrows fly and were now hopeful to take an elk of either sex. The previous day from a distant ridge, I had noticed a large group of elk cross a beaver dam bordering a steep drop, so it seemed a good place to try an ambush. The cool air was still sliding down the canyon, ruling out the convenient places to hide among the fallen aspen above the pond. I sat beneath a couple young box elders that stuck out of the sheer side, reasonably well hidden and right below the dam itself. The wait was not long.

The elk came in silently. Suddenly, their brown forms drifted into the cleared areas the beavers had created. In the prior days, there were occasions when the cracking of timber would announce their presence well in advance, but other times, as on this occasion, the elk were ghosts that abruptly materialized. The closest ones were maybe eighteen yards from me when I first saw them. Deer Bane was quickly in my hand and ready. Blood was pulsing through my head as the big animals continued to arrive. A large cow, by luck the largest I had seen the entire trip, and her two calves walked along the dam above me, all three within four yards. It seemed certain one must see me any second. Eight cows were within twenty yards. Knowing how fleeting chances can be, I drew Deer Bane. The big cow, scant feet above me, caught the motion, wheeled along the narrow dam, and started to hightail away. She was probably eight yards off when my arrow caught up to her, piercing the back part of her shoulder but not penetrating fully. The other elk looked around in bewilderment, offering stationary targets and my mind raced, wondering if the penetration was adequate and acknowledging if it was only a flesh wound, I might later regret not shooting again, but regardless,

I couldn't persuade myself to let another arrow fly, so I set the bow down and tried to pull out my camera. My efforts were too slow, and the nervous elk disappeared into the oak brush to the north.

I resolved to sit for a long interval before taking up the trail, but after twenty minutes, my memories of the length of the arrow extending from the side of the cow caused uneasiness in my mind. How much of my last day of hunting did I want to give up if she was not mortally struck? Maybe the sign could help indicate if the wound was significant. At the place she disappeared from view, decent blood dotted the grass and tree trunks. The direction she had run intersected a fence-line a hundred yards to the west, and I checked it to see where she crossed but found no blood nor even any fresh tracks. I returned to the blood, and after a few broken spots where it was initially hard to follow, the trail metamorphosed into a prominent red ribbon that, with my limited experience with animals larger than deer or hogs, instilled confidence that she would be found without trouble. She had doubled back immediately after the first splatters of blood and had headed east, sticking to a heavily trodden path. My eyes were absorbed on scanning for blood and failed to see the cow and one of her calves bedded a few yards above the trail until they bolted. The other calf may have been wandering nearby or maybe had continued on with the herd. By the way, both calves were big for calves and beyond any need for nursing. (Also, it should be pointed out that this was another classic example of lack of forward awareness—too much concentration on the blood sign and too little on the big view. The value of forward awareness cannot be overemphasized.)

I returned to the pond and resumed my seat below it, irritated at myself for not waiting longer initially and determined now to wait at least another hour. I kept my camera on ready to give me a sense of purpose and to make the time pass faster. No birds or mammals presented. At ten o'clock, I resumed the trail. It was more difficult for the cow must have clotted some during her first rest, and also the blood was no longer glossy because the desiccated leaves and soil absorbed it and the dry air sucked out the moisture, leaving what blood there was dull and hard to discern. After four hundred yards, the trail petered out entirely. I followed one game trail after another until a portion with soft earth and no fresh tracks or some other indication would cause me to abandon it and try another. The trails zigged and zagged and intersected each other so frequently it seemed the possibilities were endless. Then finally, about three hundred yards from the last sign, a bit of blood showed on some grass next to a weathered-looking sage. What a stroke of luck! I ran down the trail but saw no more sign and, needing to meet Woody at the truck, gave it up for the time being. I was somewhat buoyed by the last sign indicating the elk had traveled on a fairly constant heading.

All three of us came back after a quick lunch. Ozzie asked me to guide him to the last blood. We were in the general area, and as I searched for it, we must have wandered apart. After a few minutes, I recognized the sage that marked the last sign and yelled to Ozzie that I had located it. He yelled back that he had found the cow! The bottom line, once again, is that more patience at the onset would have left me an easy trail and reduced the risk of possibly losing the game.

Other factors besides the nature of the wound influence when tracking should commence. Impending rain would skew the scales toward tracking earlier for fear of losing blood sign. Even so, with a gutshot or a nearly nonexistent trail, it might be better to wait. Melting snow is another consideration as it can erase both blood sign and prints rapidly. Terrain that lends itself to the probability of a hunter getting a follow up shot before spooking the game also argues for less delay before tracking. While circumstances could align for any hunter to prosper in this endeavor, typically firearm hunters in more open areas are apt to employ the technique. Coyotes, mountain lions, bobcats, and bears are drawn to downed or wounded game, and sometimes the expected interval before other predators find the game determines how safe it is to postpone the trail. I lost a good portion of a doe to a bear once and an entire doe to coyotes. The first mentioned doe I did leave overnight, but the second was arrowed at about 7:45 a.m., and despite the appearance of the shot being perfect, I waited until 10:45 to begin my investigation of its trail because of lots of other animal activity. In that interval, the coyotes stripped the carcass to almost nothing.

While waiting often is the most prudent thing to do, at times, the early assumption of the trail is beneficial. As mentioned before, in Florida with water covering large expanses, sometimes fleeting air bubbles are the only evidence of an animal's passage, and finding them before they disappear or spread out is immensely helpful. *Bows, Swamps, Whitetails* includes a detailed description of a trail where a doe crossed a pond northward, circled, reentered it, headed south, turned east in the middle and deepest part of the pond, and died against a forked cypress. If I hadn't been in the pond trailing at the time, I cannot imagine any way, through skill or luck, of finding that deer. There was no hint of a trail. The deer's head was nearly level with the water and hidden between the twin trunks of the tree. In addition, the trail through the shallower and more vegetated part of the pond led well past the death site to the north. I would have looked long and hard but nowhere near the right place. In the same book, was an account of a doe I tracked immediately that was carried downstream by the current in a creek channel. It was an exasperating trail as it was, but more time would have let the body travel further and lessened the chance of finding it.

Trails deteriorate and an understanding of the processes that cause the changes helps the tracker who tackles a less than fresh trail. The delay may be intentional because of uncertainty about the wound or the result of needing more light or even because of the recruitment of a tracker after the hunter's initial search proved unsuccessful. The drying of blood renders it much less visible because the color fades with moisture loss, and concomitantly, the rusty remnants have none of the glossiness that can reflect light and sparkle in an eye-catching way. Dry earth can soak in blood to where it is barely perceivable. The rate of change in the appearance of blood varies tremendously with climate and terrain. In Florida, blood left for hours out of the direct sunlight or even overnight may retain much of the color and liquid nature or if it dries some will usually still hold a sheen and red color. This is especially true down in the swampwoods. In the sunlight and in the scrub, it dries more quickly but often is fairly visible as brownish-red smears even a day later. In Colorado, on an arid, rock-covered ridge smattered with a couple cedars and occasional sage clumps, I first experienced just how quickly blood can dry:

One September morning, once again many decades ago, I sat among the boulders and a couple cedars in a shallow bowl on the ridge top. Two mule deer bucks in velvet topped the ridge adjacent to the one I was on and fed, eventually bedding in the sage at the ridge's base. One had good spread and sported four or five tines on the right antler. The other antler was only a single main beam and a brow tine. His companion was small. Next two large, hard antlered bucks fed in the sage flats below hundreds of yards away. My site was chosen because earlier in the week, many bucks crossed this ridge after leaving the lowlands on their way to bedding places. Now it seemed their pattern had changed. Twenty-one does come by, one as close as ten yards. Many of these had bedded by 8:30, so I was less optimistic, but determined to wait longer for as nice as it would be to secure a mule deer, it was the last morning of the few remaining days of our trip that I was willing to forsake elk hunting.

At 9:45, two bucks clattered down the adjacent ridge and trotted to the ravine below heading in my direction. They were both large and hard antlered. One's antlers were red, and velvet strips dangled from them. He may have been a five-by-five. The other was definitely a five-by-five with a remarkably large, tall rack. The steep side of my ridge hid them from sight once they reached it base. With bow ready and heart pounding, I waited. And waited. Then movement sixty yards to the southeast manifested a buck bedded below a cedar.

A stalk would be necessary. The dry, rocky slope made silent movement unobtainable. Even the smallest pebbles, once dislodged, rattled noisily as they bounced or trickled downward. Complicating things further, while one buck was accounted for, another set of eyes and ears were somewhere else nearby, and if they detected me, the stalk would end prematurely and unfavorably. I inched along and finally was about thirty yards from the cedar. The tree blocked any view below it. I eased gradually to my feet. All was still, and neither buck was visible. I surveyed the next few possible steps and saw no promising routes. Thirty yards would be a long shot for me, but I considered chunking a small rock into the cedar to see if the buck might rise to look about. The cedar's foliage was too dense to see through, much less to allow an arrow to pass. With luck, and not what at the time I considered good luck, at this very second, a velvety two-by-two buck crested the ridge down from me and worked past about ten yards below me. This presented even more of a complication. Continuing on his way, he would likely scent me within another twenty yards and alarm every deer nearby. I was close to big bucks, but even without the small buck, the stalk was going to difficult. The chance of getting a shot at a stationary target at a reasonable distance was not at all likely. So often in hunting, the archer's mind whirls with choices without much time to truly ponder. A large buck would be special, but a small buck would be nicer than a view of rapidly departing deer and an unshot arrow on the string.

I pulled Simplicity's string; the limbs bent and then sprang forward. The arrow whisked ahead and drove though the buck's chest and landed lightly on some sage a few yards below. The two-by-two jumped, then bounced fifty yards downhill and stood still. A big, velvet covered 4 × 4 bounded out from under the cedar and ran over the opposite ridge. He was wide and impressive, but not one of the two bucks I believed I was stalking. Even though they were the impetus for my stalk, they must have never lingered earlier.

The 2 × 2 jumped again, this time behind a cedar. I waited to see the direction he would take. It seemed in this arid, open country of brown, tan, and orangish rocks, at least a glimpse would be visible of his fleeing form, but he had disappeared. The hard, desiccated soil absorbed and changed the appearance of blood so much that at first, I could find none. Upon realizing the dry-looking dark patches of ground were actually sites where large splashes of blood had fallen, I discovered the buck was bleeding profusely. The blood trail showed no sign of wetness two minutes after the shot! How exasperating would a trail be with scant blood or if hours had passed? Thankfully, I did not have to experience that, for the buck lay five yards beyond the cedar where he was last in view. I dragged him out by his velvet-covered rack and was surprised to discover the extreme oiliness of the velvet.

Wind degrades the trail. Not only does wind increase the drying rate, but it moves sand, dust particles, and leaves and such to alter blood and prints and can move grass and other vegetations back to a normal position, erasing that type of evidence of an animal's passage. Even gravity itself works to reduce tracks over time. Rain and dew can wash away or, at least, dilute blood. Rain and dripping dew disturb prints as well. Melting snow can also play havoc with trails very quickly. Obviously, accumulating snow can bury a trail. I've witnessed insects impact trails in a few ways. Their trails and diggings can erode prints, but that is usually negligible. Several times, dung beetles have removed fecal droppings that were part of a stricken animal's trail. The times I've discovered their activity, other droppings were still present, but it brought to mind the possibility of cases when no evidence would remain. Earlier in this chapter, the trail of the cow elk was described including the mention of the last blood near some sage. The sage had a distinctive shape that made it easy to recognize fortunately, for when I returned later, ants had found the blood and had removed much of it. These ants, medium-sized and reddish-brown in color, were still industriously engaged eating or packing off the little flaky bits that remained. How common these ants are and how often they destroy blood trails are questions beyond my knowledge. Flies are at times beneficial to a tracker as their buzzing and presence can attract attention to fecal material, gut contents, or blood, but they do consume these parts of the trail as well. Exactly how quickly they may remove this evidence is impossible to say, but it could possibly have significance. One year, Ozzie came out to Colorado with a draining infection below his eye. Years before, he had been in an auto accident that crushed part of the floor of his right orbit, the part of the skull that supports the eyeball. It had been replaced with a synthetic graph that had now failed. Surgery was scheduled, but Ozzie didn't want to miss the Colorado hunt in the meantime. Eating was a bit difficult across the table from him as, when he chewed, pus spewed from the fistula, but climbing mountains all day can build one's hunger to the point that niceties can be overlooked. One afternoon, Oz decided to sit near a beaver pond or a wallow (I can't remember which), and enough pus was protruding that it bothered his vision, and using a leaf, he wiped about a half a teaspoon of it from his face. Flies swarmed to the discarded leaf, and within twenty minutes, all the pus was gone. At that rate, when blood sign is very scant, flies could conceivably diminish a trail.

As this chapter shows, the question of when to assume a blood trail has no simple or universal answer. The variables are staggering. Keen observation of the wound and the game animal's reactions, bundled together with knowledge of the animal, knowledge of the terrain and climate, and reasonable prognosticating of the weather and other interferences can, applied in concert, guide the hunter toward the wisest choice.

The question of when to follow can be taken in a totally different sense, and this answer is simple—always, unless you are absolutely, positively sure the animal was not hit. Archers here have a little advantage because it is easier to see evidence of a wound both from the relatively slow speed of the projectile and from being able to recover and examine the projectile. Over the years, I have found a few dead deer that rifle hunters shot at and believed they missed. I'm sure they sincerely did believe it because they were my friends and I knew them to be blatantly honest.

I read of two studies in the eighties that demonstrated the same tendency. Their findings in no way should be construed as undermining the integrity of firearm hunters but rather as a defense of bowhunting's efficacy. Both studies involved special hunts open to a limited number of hunters in very large but fenced-in areas. I believe they may have both been military bases. Two hunts were allowed on each site, one for archers and one for firearm hunters. Hunters were interviewed after the hunt, and as expected, bowhunters reported a substantially greater number of wounded animals. However, a search was conducted after each hunt, and the number of unrecovered deer that died was tallied. In both cases, the firearm hunts resulted in more dead but unrecovered deer. The explanation is twofold. First, the speed of the bullet can make it terribly difficult to see a hit, and a deer that runs off looking unhurt can lead a hunter to think it was a clean miss. Secondly, flesh wounds from broadheads are relatively clean wounds and less likely to cause infection. If these samples are representative of hunting as a whole, bowhunters are no more likely to cause wounding losses than hunters in general.

The story of Ozzie's arrow striking well below the chest of a spike yet still killing it has already been mentioned, but a few more episodes may be worthwhile to illustrate the importance of following up every shot:

On the opening day of modern firearms season, one year in the eighties on some very heavily hunted property, I sat in a stand amid some slanting live oaks and palmettos. The shiny surface of water west of me was disrupted by undulations large enough to rule out a frog or snake as the cause, and sure enough, soon the slender legs of deer could be seen pushing through the shallows. Two deer approached pretty quickly. I readied Deer Bane. As they neared, their course became more southerly, skirting the edge of the palmettos yet allowing them to remain in the shade of the swampwoods and keeping them within nine or ten yards of my tree. With their quick pace, I led the largest doe a bit and released. My lead was more than necessary, and the arrow struck her ahead of her chest. She bolted away and was swallowed by the lush growth, so I tried to picture her course with my ears. The next few hours passed with agonizing slowness as my eye kept straying the short distance to where she had been and where my arrow was now stabbed in the ground. Although the shot happened at 7:00, I forced myself to stay on the stand until 10:30, not to let the deer have time to die because it was obviously no gutshot but rather because it seemed there was no chance the arrow seriously hurt the deer and searching early would only spread my scent around. When I finally did clamber down, despondent from a blown opportunity, it was to a pleasant surprise. A heavy blood trail started at the arrow and led directly to the doe. The arrow had zipped through the junction of the chest and neck and happily cut a major blood vessel.

A buck once strode briskly by my stand and was eighteen yards off and about to disappear behind some palmettos by the time I had Bane Too drawn and ready. Without thought, I led the moving deer and let the arrow loose. The scant initial image of the hit looked good, but a crisp, quick *shrick* sound of a broadhead striking bone seemed at odds with the mental picture. Instantly, the buck vanished behind the palmettos. Was the shot good? Or had I been deceived in the blur of the instant?

When I climbed down and investigated, torn grass and strewn sand testified as to the exact location he was stricken, and a diligent but unsuccessful search for the arrow assured me the arrow did not pass through. The arrow was, however, lying on the route the buck fled maybe twenty yards further along. Finding it let my hopes plummet for it was broken four inches from the broadhead. Both pieces were side by side, and the broadhead end of the one piece and the nock end of the other both pointed back toward the stand. The blood on each piece was scant and dry and extended only halfway to the fletchings on the longer portion. The only interpretation that came to my mind was that the hit was low, striking a leg and only driving through the four inches, and then, as the buck ran, the other front leg applied pressure that snapped the shaft off. The pieces fell as described. This explanation was in harmony with the sound of the hit, the absolute lack of blood on the trail, the thin smears on the arrow, and the peculiar position of the broken pieces, so I accepted that the buck was wounded in the leg but not fatally. I resigned myself to disappointment and only continued the trail out of respect for the buck and out of a compulsion to trail game as far as possible. Bent grass blades and sprays of sand let me advance thirty more yards. Then he had entered a miniature forest of myrtle, and the only recourse was to follow each possible route for a ways, hoping for some confirmation or refutation. On one pathway, a tiny speck of blood decorated a leaf. On my hands and knees because of the low boughs, I looked forward from the spot and spied his sprawled form! He had only made it sixty or seventy yards! He was a beautiful eight point. There was no blood on his coat nor on the ground around him.

The shot had been perfect, double-lunging him and severing one of the great vessels of the heart. The sound of struck bone came from the opposite shoulder, which had stopped the broadhead and prevented a pass through, rendering the trail blood poor. Blood gushed copiously from his chest later when he was hoisted on a scale. He weighed 142 lbs. The only explanations I could think of to explain the exiguous blood on the arrow and the alignment of the broken pieces were that skin and hair wiped the arrow fairly clean as it worked out whole from the wound and that as it fell, a hind hoof landed on it, snapping it and kicking the broken ends forward so the other ends ended up facing rearward. This trail has stuck in my memory because of how easily I convinced myself the wound wasn't lethal.

On a December morning, I waited on a stand in the Bull Creek swamp. Oaks and cabbage palms provided a dense canopy. Two creek fingers merged toward one another, and a cypress pond lay to the south. A doe threaded along the edge of the pond about thirty-five yards from my tree, too far for a shot. I had hoped the falling acorns would lure her closer, but she seemed not to be feeding and disappeared behind a screen of young cabbage palms. I bleated with my mouth a few times, waited a few seconds, and bleated again. Plashy steps heralded her approach and guided my eyes to bits of slender running legs beneath the fronds. She stepped into the clear twenty-two yards from me, broadside, but with two more steps, she would be hidden once more by fronds and end up downwind before emerging again. I was ready and drew Mellifluwood at once. The arrow's flight looked good in the air, but the doe wheeled with the sound. The arrow may have caught the front edge of her chest or neck or may have missed entirely. She bounded off and was lost to sight after the first jump, although a glimpse at forty yards showed her still running with her tail down.

Binoculars revealed the arrow, apparently stuck vertically in the swamp earth, buried nearly to the fletchings with no visible blood. The mud can be soft, and therefore, it was conceivable that the arrow could drive in that deeply, but the upright orientation made no sense at all. If it had ricocheted off the deer, why would it penetrate so deeply? The only explanation that seemed to answer the evidence was that the arrow missed and the fleeing doe kicked it upright, but that seemed incongruous with the thickness of the mud. It may have let an arrow penetrate deeply, but wouldn't it be too dense and laced with roots to subsequently allow the arrow to be moved nearly ninety degrees? I reasoned that there must be an explanation, but regardless, it was unlikely the doe was injured and so remained on the stand, hopeful of more action.

Woodpeckers and Percival's *A Game Ranger's Note Book* entertained me, and hours passed. I threw my spears for practice and scooted down. It turned out that the arrow had driven into a tree and the fletching end had broken off and fallen upright on the ground. A little blood adorned the feathers, but major blood sprayed the vegetation! The broadhead was removed from the trunk with difficulty. The blood trail was unbelievable and easy to follow. Blood was everywhere, leaves totally coated, and tree trunks sprayed up to a height of four feet. Every green thing along the pathway was crested with crimson. She had fallen after a hundred yards. The arrow had slipped through her throat and cut something major. A broad area of red foam lay about her nose. I made a backpack of her with cabbage palm stems as stops between the tendons of her fore and hind legs. Anyone who has spent much time in our swampwoods knows of the travail of walking though the water and soft mud, over fallen trees, trammeled by cypress knees hidden by ferns, challenged by constant obstacles and struggling to keep balanced. Add an awkward and heavy load, and the difficulty increases markedly. It is probably only another sign of years accumulating on me, for I found the tote out very taxing and was shocked to learn she only weighed 103 lbs. The main point is, of course, to check all possible wounds. This one only cut through about two inches of flesh.

Hollow cypresses had no value to loggers in the thirties, so they left a few giants standing. These trees are so big three people joining hands could not reach around them. I placed a stand near where a few of them reigned over Bull Creek. The wood is close to impervious, and even fallen ones from the lumbering days remain, nearly ninety years later, moss-covered slumbering remnants of earlier grandeur. It is a beautiful spot with shallow tea-colored creeks and the lush greenery of ferns and lizard tail. Otters and raccoons worked along the creek, and as I was photographing one, slender brown legs appeared and pushed round ripples up the creek. A few more steps brought a buck in view from under the fronds. He moved quickly and steadily toward me, not feeding, and suddenly was under me, forward progress arrested, sniffing the ferns at my tree's base. Obviously, he discovered my scent for he became at once cautious and remained still for more than a minute. By luck, he was positioned so my stand's tree sheltered him from a shot. I waited as he waited and studied his surroundings. Finally, he turned and tiptoed upwind. As soon as he was three yards off, there was room to draw, and I pulled Deer Bane's limbs back and let an arrow fly. He was walking directly away, and the arrow struck him in the middle of his back but did not seem to penetrate at all. He jumped and skitted twenty yards and then turned and walked away. The arrow protruded from his back nearly vertically. After nonchalantly traipsing along the creek channel for sixty or more yards, he was lost to sight. The extreme length of the shaft extending above him coupled with his unexcited behavior convinced me totally that he had suffered no serious injury. I did pick out a distinctive tree trunk where the swamp had swallowed his retreating form, but I had no doubt he would survive. It was 7:40 a.m. Woody and Billy were hunting north of the edges of Bull Creek, and since the buck had headed in that general direction, I wondered if they would see him with a bright orange arrow with pink fletchings protruding from him like an antenna. They would have no doubt about the culprit's identity.

Later, when I left the stand, I checked out the last place he was visible and was surprised to find an obvious but not heavy blood trail. Any trail without an exit wound is unusual, and this one was from a wound high on the back and with little penetration. The buck left the creek and followed a well-worn deer trail that held many fresh tracks in its black earth. The trail crossed a couple shallow sloughs and then angled for the wood's edge. After fifty yards, however, the blood vanished. Since the tracks looked so fresh, I stayed with the trail, but as it left the swamp, it squeezed under a large number of young cabbage palms with low fronds. There seemed to be no way an animal with a wound on his back could push through them without leaving a trace of blood. After a search of about ten minutes, prudence dictated returning to the last blood. The trail just seemed to stop. I happened to glance back up the creek and saw his half-submerged body. He had jumped off the trail and looped back in his last second of life. In total, he probably made it a hundred yards from the stand. The arrow had penetrated much more than I had thought. Somehow, the shaft wasn't bent. With the site being all the way across the Bull Creek swampwoods, the drag out was, of course, effortful, but the elation of getting a buck I had already cataloged as a missed opportunity made it easier!

The mindset to follow up any shot lends itself to another trait a tracker should cultivate, persistence. Trails can be very discouraging, and all sorts of doubts bombard the tracker in such cases. So often, when sign dwindles, game is found primarily through sheer pertinacity:

In the grey and misty light of an early morning, I carried my bow and stand toward a small cypress dome surrounded by a rough and overgrown pasture. I traipsed through the briars, grapevines, myrtle, and oaks, selecting a meandering route that allowed the least encumbrances and yet maintained a pathway into the wind. I rounded a myrtle and eyed a broadside buck twenty yards ahead, sporting heavy antlers out past his ears. He was eying me as well. I nocked an arrow and eased Bane Too to full draw, expecting the buck to bolt at any second, but he held. The arrow flew and struck with the sharp crack of bone. The buck exploded off to the south!

The trail showed a splatter of blood thirty yards from where the buck had stood. A tiny droplet speckled a frond twenty-five yards further. This was disturbing and disappointing because the buck had obviously busted through the palmetto hedge at that point yet had deposited not even the tiniest trace of blood. I followed possible routes and turned up nothing. Returning to the beginning, I slipped the stand from my back and reexamined the trail painstakingly. Finding nothing new, I extrapolated potential courses and searched and searched, all the time dwelling on the crack of the striking arrow and my glimpse of the fleeing buck with a lot of the fletching end of the shaft extending from his side. The going arrow had looked good, but the buck lunged into action before my brain could register precisely what truly occurred. Over the years, many alert deer, with the sound of the bow, had completely dodged my arrows, so it was quite within reason that he moved enough for the arrow to have struck far from its intended target. I pushed out at least four hundred yards on all the routes extending from the last blood, knowing the further I went, the less likely the chances of stumbling upon him or blood.

Tired, disheartened, and starting to more firmly believe the wound could not have been fatal, I gave up, returned to the truck, dumped my vest and long-sleeved shirt, and resumed my trek to the cypress head, picking up the stand where the buck had stood. I sat late into the morning having started the hunt late. The entire time, the evidence bounced around in my head, convincing me more and more that not only had the buck not bled but had not died either. At the end of the hunt, I carried my gear to the truck and loaded up. Despite my intentions, something compelled me to search again. I tromped everywhere and turned up nothing new. Several times, I headed toward the truck, intending to quit, only to be drawn back to the mystery of that trail. Finally, to the northwest, more than sixty yards from the last sign and not at all in line with his southward course, a "splot" of blood showed on a dead frond. Twenty yards further was a smear on a long grass stem, and ten yards beyond, it the palmettos held a decent speckling of blood. Then the trail became blank again. Routes west and northwest out to forty yards offered no clues. The only choice seemed to be to look further along those routes, and sure enough, on one of them, a hundred yards from the new last blood, was the dead buck. The arrow had driven through the near shoulder and the head imbedded in the far one. Both lungs were pierced. The shaft looked long in my glimpse of the buck because it had broken, and I had actually seen it as it was cast out. I later found the piece upright deep in the palmetto patch he crashed through. Doggedness (maybe stubbornness) can be credited with recovering this buck.

One September afternoon in Colorado, I waited at a pond in the Little Creek canyon. I had got there pretty early, an accomplishment in itself as the drive from the ranch house was close to an hour, and then there were still a few miles of mountain trails to traverse on foot. The evening before, the canyon had been full of elk, and I saw nineteen cows on my way to the pond. I crafted a blind, hastily remembering elk had visited the pond well before four o'clock the previous day, but 4:00 came and then 5:00 without any game arriving. My confidence was high regardless. Time ticked by. From down the valley came the alarm bark of a coyote. It seemed far away, but possibly it caught my scent as the thermals were drifting that way. More time passed. Two mule deer does and a fawn came to the pond from below, passing within eight yards of my blind and obviously getting enough of a whiff to become nervous but continued to the pond's edge. There they were hesitant to drink and ended up snorting and bouncing away.

Darkness would fall at about 8:00. At 7:15, the buff hides of a couple cows flashed intermittently as they passed though little openings in the brush on the opposite ridge side. At first, they appeared to be heading to the pond, but instead headed south. At 7:30, I decide to go look for elk. The shot would have been simple from the blind, but the chance of them coming now seemed bleak. I slipped up the valley into the wind.

Not far above the pond was a wallow up against a sheer bank of four or five feet. A cow elk trotted from this vicinity nervously but not with rapidity or alarm. She may have caught some of my movement without getting much of a view. Another canyon emptied into Little Creek there, and she moved up it. A bull was in the wallow, and her departure caused him to run up to the small knoll that made the upper bank. Seeing nothing, after a minute or so, he ran back into the wallow. I hurriedly scooted up to what I judged was about twenty yards from the wallow. Either another cow was there or the first one had come back down, and again, my movement sent her trotting away. I hunkered behind some brush, and the bull rushed back to his vantage point. I bugled, and an unseen bull, not far above where the cow disappeared, bellowed an answer. I used (abused) my longbow to rake the limbs of a bush and shrieked back a shrill reply. The bull near me stalked along a trail toward yet above me and scanned my locale from twelve yards. I eased forward of the brush a bit to allow me to draw, and the movement unsettled him enough to send him back to the knoll above the wallow where he stood broadside, looking my way. I drew Mellifluwood and, when everything felt perfect, released. Moments like this one can be hard to sort out, and even today, I'm not sure if the bull turned just after I had sent my fingers the command to release, but before they had time to obey or if he did so after my release. I suspect the latter for I did not jerk the bow, which could have happened if I had tried to correct for his motion. Anyway, he actually turned back toward me and started down the knoll probably to investigate me again. The arrow, directed at his right chest and flying true, caught him in the right side of the front of his chest or the base of his neck as he turned, and it nearly vanished. The penetration looked surprisingly good, for I would not dream normally of trying that shot with my 54# longbow on a deer facing me, and an elk's skeleton is much more formidable than a deer's. He ran up the valley and was lost to sight and hearing within three bounds. My concerns were, first, the arrow could have slid between the bull's shoulder and ribs remaining outside the chest cavity. No matter how much penetration, it would not kill the elk. Secondly, even if the arrow had driven into the chest, the chance of having a blood trail with no exit wound was slim.

Not unexpectedly, no blood was to be found, and my rummaging turned up no other sign or clue. Darkness was not far off. Happily, the temperature was cold and getting colder. With Ozzie and Billy waiting for me, it seemed best to sprint to the truck and sort the trail out in the morning. It was quite late when we stumbled into the cabin, and any hunter can imagine my thoughts, hopes, and fears as I tried to sleep that night.

Billy and I drove along Milk Creek to the middle ridge before light. He planned to hunt that area, and I intended to climb up and over the high wall to Jensen and down into Little Creek. On my way up, a clatter of hooves on loose rock warned me of the presence of elk. Soon, some of them drifted through the seviceberries as close as fifteen yards. Believe me, I did pause to consider things. It was an easy downhill tote to the truck. My shot of the evening before left a lot of doubt as to whether the bull died or could be found. Despite my thoughts, I never seriously considered a shot or even put an arrow on the string. I hadn't put much effort into looking for the bull after the shot, and the bull deserved more and so did I. Nonetheless, I knew if my efforts were not successful, the memories of these unsuspecting elk would come to mind.

After letting the elk feed far enough north that I could continue up without spooking them, I topped the ridge and angled down toward the canyon bottom, keeping high enough to note any lump or patch of color or unusual contour that could be a dead elk. These were scanned with binoculars, and each one that had the remotest chance of being the bull was recorded in my memory to investigate when I was down there searching. I would move along the ridge and glass again as meticulously as possible, even memorizing things I was 99 percent sure were rocks or stumps. A cow was at the wallow. I was reluctant to spook her and impatient to start my search at the same time. After waiting a minute, I walked unhurriedly, but openly out into the less brushy bottom. She left with a trot but didn't bolt and did not bark. I studied the site and then paced the shot distance. It turned out a little longer than I thought, twenty-four yards. No blood was visible. A couple running tracks large enough to be from a bull indented the hardened mud, but the next set could not be discovered in the low, coarse, hardy vegetation.

After exhausting my hopes of piecing out a trail, I examined all the possible spots I had glassed. Then I climbed the west side of Little Creek canyon and glassed the east side. I found no dead bulls and no leads. Elk on the east side of the canyon up toward the rim revealed themselves fleetingly as they passed openings in the brush. Since the bull had started up the canyon, I searched a tacking course that way for more than a thousand yards and then worked back down. Midmorning had passed and discouragement weighed on my shoulders as I faced the enormity of the task of stumbling on a bull with no trail in all the vast and densely covered terrain. I again thought about the group of elk so close to me earlier in the morning.

I returned to the wallow and resumed my position at the time of the shot. The bull had bounded up, but the little knoll blocked any view of him after that. The main canyon went up, but so did three other smaller draws. I had searched two of these earlier. The third was incredibly brush choked, and it staggered my imagination to think of the bull busting through all that without creating a loud racket. I decided to try it regardless and then drift back down through some aspens that stood along a ridge finger and the canyon side. Entering the draw required twisting and ducking and pushing, but after eighty yards, it opened a bit into a shallow ravine studded with aspens, and now things could be seen fifteen or maybe even twenty yards away. Not far up it lay the bull. My luck to find it in such a spot was immense. My happiness was immense too! The bull was a nice 4 × 5. The arrow had driven into his chest so deeply that only the fletchings were visible near the base of his throat on the right side. His death run was probably three hundred yards, a distance he could cover in twenty or thirty seconds at most.

Fortunately, he fell in the draw, and even though the sun was only an hour and a half from its zenith, its rays had not touched him yet. He was still plenty cold, but I felt urgency to be sure the meat stayed good. I quartered him and boned the quarters and hung them, the tenderloins, and backstraps in shady spots. Loading a ham and shoulder into my pack and carrying Mellifluwood in hand, I pushed through the thick back down into the Little Creek canyon and then climbed the steep east side to the crest. From there it was downhill to the sage flat on the top of the middle ridge, where I found Billy. An oak offered a shady spot to hang the meat and leave my bow. All my hunting friends are hard workers, but no one totes out a heavier load of elk than Billy and I was thankful he was with me.

Billy and I hoofed it back up and over the crest and then down to the carcass. I had no saw, so we had to cut off the whole head. Billy toted the other ham and backstraps and tenderloins, a gigantic load as anyone who has tried it can attest. I carried the remaining shoulder and head with the antlers, planning on leaving the head on the sage flat where I could collect it another day and thereby avoid repeating the steepest and hardest part of the walk. We strained up to the crest and then carried our loads down to our bows. It was still a long way to the truck, but it was almost all downhill, and except for the first part that twisted through the sage (plants that almost seemed designed to clutch at a laded hunter and trip his legs) and a couple rocky, steep declines, the going was good. Billy said he could carry both bows, so I added the other shoulder to my pack and slung the cheesecloth bag that held the ham over my shoulder, picked up the head, and trudged on. It was a respectable load and caused concern about my back, but the extra weight would make the route no longer and it would save a whole long trip. Eventually, we made it to the truck to the relief of our tired legs and aching shoulders and the delight of our mouths and throats for we knew there was water in it. It was after four in the afternoon before we made it back to the ranch house. Billy left almost immediately to hunt elk. Ozzie and I hung the meat in the cooler and then I set out for a mule deer hunt. That evening, Woody arrowed a cow. I was not feeling too spry and I doubted Billy was either, but we both cheerfully and excitedly abandoned any ambition we harbored for an early rendezvous with our beds. We clambered up Box Elder canyon and had a pretty easy go of it quartering and toting the meat out as there were four of us, and the way was short and downhill.

CHAPTER 7

Tracking with Dogs

ONE FALL MORNING, I SAT on a stepladder in an area of low scrub. The running oaks held acorns, and the bigger oaks hadn't started dropping yet. I rattled. The dense fog made the gnashing grinds seem hollow, dead, and close at hand. Ten minutes later, a small eight-point appeared and wandered off to the southwest, feeding little if at all and tarrying nowhere. A half hour passed, and I rattled again. Within less than eight minutes, out from the mists and the myrtle and palmettos, strode a bigger buck. Despite the humidity and heavy dew that silvered all the vegetation, his legs and dun-colored pelage appeared dry, but his antlers glistened. They were a rich bronze in color but shiny and reflective with a wet glossiness. The sight was breathtaking; the lacquered antlers were wide and curved inward and their ends were flattened vertically, like twin daggers pointing at one another, the buck himself was the picture of grace, and as if to frame it perfectly and, concomitantly, add the mysteriousness associated with special bucks, the mist-shrouded, sparkling and dripping background haloed him.

His pathway closely followed that of the earlier smaller buck that had passed south of my stand until, at about twenty yards from me, he turned to the north. Oaks and palmettos shielded him until he was east-northeast of the stand, angling away and really not offering much of a shot. My stepladder stands are light, portable, and useful for stand hunting where there is no place for a stand. I fashion bow holders into them, but when placed into the thick vegetation that renders the stand and hunter less noticeable, the bow holder becomes nonfunctional. That was the case in this thicket of myrtle, greenbrier, and grapevine. Before I picked it up and nocked an arrow, Bane Too had been resting on a bed of tangled grapevines. As the buck angled north, it seemed a couple tickles of the antlers would pull him directly back, but to accomplish it, the arrow would have to be unnocked, the bow placed down, and the antlers picked up. It likely could be done, but if the buck responded, then the antlers would need to be set down, the bow lifted, and an arrow readied all with him looking and heading toward the stand that held me only six and half feet above ground level.

As a consequence of my rapid consideration of these factors, I elected to keep the bow in hand and grunt with my mouth. In hindsight, I later wished I had merely let him continue further and then rattle, but minds don't always think of all options when rushed. At least, my mind doesn't and definitely did not in this instance. The grunt did stop him, and he came back around, but this time circled further south so that he was twenty-five yards distant when it was apparent that he would get a nose full of me after just another step or two. I seemed to be calmer than typical when a buck is involved and drew completely without hesitation. Bane Too sprang back, propelling the arrow towards its mark with a noise that almost sounded like a fast and snappy *think*! The flight looked good, but the hit had too hollow of a sound. After a few bounds, the fog enveloped the buck, and everything was still.

I made myself stay on the stand for a couple hours. Then the haunting memory of the "ploopy" sound of the hit gave me another thought. If the buck were gutshot, I would have to drive to Indian Harbour to get our lab, Jody. Mack was out at his club with Skylar, a beagle with a lot of experience with difficult trails, but on days with work obligations, he seldom stayed later than 9:30. If I caught him before he left, hours of time would be saved. Plus, Jody had only one easy trail to her credit. I hustled down and checked my arrow. The sign was good and bad. The broadhead half was coated with blood, but the fletching half showed gut contents. I scouted in the direction the buck fled a short distance to see how promising the trail was, but the absence of blood prompted me to quickstep to the truck and call Mack who was happy to help.

Skylar led us east but then seemed unsure. We started her over, and she led us back by a slightly different route. There was a shrub there that had been thrashed severely that morning. The leaves from the fallen branches were still fresh, green, and uncurled. Apparently, Skylar followed both the buck's approach route and his escape route that were basically parallel and side by side. The buck probably had terrorized the bush in response to my rattling, a behavioral tendency I have seen enacted many times.

The buck had been bedded quite close for Skylar's attitude and excitement changed with the fresher sign. Our noise must have spooked him from his bed, and now Skylar was trailing hard with confidence and earnestness. Even with the rapid pace that Skylar set, Mack and I couldn't help but notice all the blood along the trail. Before we jumped the buck, only two small smears along the original trail could be located. Typically, less blood is visible after a deer has bedded, but my assumption is that the lack of blood on the initial part of the trail and also the fainter scent for Skylar were both due to the phenomenally heavy dew and its subsequent drying. The buck led us out of the scrub, through thick, unruly tangles of growth, down into the Right Creek bottom, across it, out, and then through a rough, overgrown pasture, and finally, into the Tyson Creek bottom. The blood trail was copious enough that it seemed the buck must be out of the stuff, but a third of a mile north on Tyson, we jumped him again, and he plunged through the chest deep creek channel to the west. The buck didn't look strong, and we thought it most prudent to leave him unmolested another couple of hours even though Skylar was straining with eagerness. Mack had a meeting with a customer but left Skylar with me.

I showered and changed into clothes for wading and put a second set of clothes in the truck and settled down to wait impatiently. Then something unexpected happened. It rained. Then it poured to the point water was flowing in the pastures. Finally, it stopped only to rain again. (Rain can help dogs track as will be discussed in a bit, but this was so extreme I feared the entire trail would be washed away.) In the swamp, Skylar picked up the trail with confidence even though she was swimming through the flowing, chest-deep creek. She followed it to the edge, but at that point, an acre or two of hog rootings left only soupy, raw earth that swallowed the scent. We spent time circling about, for the rainwater flowing across this open ground must have carried tiny particles of scent here and there. We covered miles but all in a little, tight area. Eventually, I gave up and took Skylar back, frustrated by the timing of the weather. I was in no mood to hunt and instead was drawn back to look again. I followed the bearing of the buck's trail as it left the creek, all at once realizing it pointed toward a gap between two cypress heads. The buck had expired and fallen just beyond the gap. All in all, Skylar had tracked it over two miles and pointed the way for the last couple hundred yards. She would have been happy and proud to have been in on the find, and I fervently wished I would have had the knowledge at the time to carry her over the hog rootings and let her cast about on the far side to re-pick up the scent trail.

No matter how much practice and effort I put into tracking, dogs have a way of making me feel slow and bumbling. The dogs I have watched are fast and primarily decisive. Now and then, they get bogged for a time, but undeterred, they return unerringly to the last scent and sort the trail out. A good dog makes finding wounded game simple. Because of their speed and efficiency, the person accompanying them may not have time to study the minutia of the trail and therefore not improve his or her own tracking skills, but the tendencies of wounded game will be made quite plain and the tracker can learn a lot from that. Please keep in mind that states set their own laws for hunting regulations and tracking wounded game with dogs may not be legal in all states. Also, even in states where it is allowed, there may be differences as to whether the dog must be on a leash or not. It is imperative for any hunter to familiarize himself or herself with applicable regulations.

Humans miss out on so much information and communications that animals receive through olfactory evidence. Dogs are privy to much of it and can become great assets to hunters and trackers.

Tracking is a joy to a dog, and their excitement and pride are quite obvious while they are performing. There is lot of fun for the dog's handler as well, and I savor the times one of my dogs solve a difficult trail and help a hunter recover a game animal that could easily have been lost.

The first step is to pick a dog. My experience is limited primarily to Labrador retrievers and beagles, but many other breeds are quite capable. I have heard of black mouth curs, leopard curs, dachshunds, bloodhounds, Jack Russells, Brittanies, and poodles all being good trackers, and no doubt there are others. John Jeanneney has written a fine and fairly comprehensive book on tracking dogs, and it is well worth reading. My training differs slightly from his, but no doubt, he is more expert for I have only trained two tracking dogs personally and he has trained many.

My family was set upon a Labrador retriever, a very versatile hunting breed, so a good bit of the selection process was already accomplished. When examining five-week-old puppies, we subjected them to a couple tests. We banged a wooden spoon on a pot and looked for a puppy that would notice it but without alarm. We dragged a bit of meat through the grass for twenty-five yards with one right angle turn. The dog we chose, Jody, followed the trail to the end without getting distracted and was interested in the pot without fear. These may not be conclusive tests, and I have heard puppies at a young age may not show their true traits, but they helped us find a suitable and wonderful dog.

On a trail, dogs can be subdivided into two categories, air sniffers and ground sniffers. No dog is purely one or the other. Both types do some of the other sniffing, but ground sniffers primarily keep their noses to the scent on the ground and move slower and more methodically while air sniffers keep their noses more elevated and tack back and forth over the scent. They lose the scent more often, but have an uncanny way of rediscovering it. Typically, they race around a lot more to cover the same length of trail. Most often, bird dogs are air sniffers and hound-type breeds like beagles, dachshunds, and Basset hounds are ground sniffers. If the handler is keeping the dog on a leash, air sniffers can be extra work as they zip around brush and trees and race back and forth. The handler may still need to thread through thick brush or narrow places with a ground sniffer, but usually only to the extent the game animal did.

While labs are undeniably air sniffers, they do have an advantage in that as a whole they are easy to train. Pleasing their masters seems very important to them. Their other advantages are that they are great companions and helpers for other hunting activities like duck hunting, snipe hunting, and quail hunting. That said, I will admit when I watch an experienced thirteen-inch beagle sniff her way slowly along a trail at a pace I can equal without great effort and without having the shirt stripped from my back, I do feel a little envy! I have gotten to know and watch four tracking beagles, and three of them are very methodical. The fourth is still young and may slow down with age and experience. I have taken pains to train my newest lab to go slower when tracking, and so far, it seems to be working. The ideal setting for labs is where tracking dogs are not required to be on a leash. Then they can be ebullient and cover the ground and either bark when they have found the game or come back to lead the handler to it. In Florida, it is a little worrisome for the dog to be out of the handler's sight, for many of the trails they follow do involve water, and gators can pose a real and terrifying threat.

On the subject of the leash, two points should be mentioned. Smaller dogs are much easier for the handler where leashes are required. A harness that involves the shoulders and chest is best so that the strain of the excited pulling of the dog is distributed over a large area rather than have it concentrated it on the throat as would a collar. Chest protectors function as harnesses yet act as a protective barrier for sharp sticks that the excited dog may rush against. If a collar alone is employed for the attachment of a leash, clipping on to it so the leash runs down between the dog's legs causes less choking of the airway when the dog strains forward.

I mentioned alligators as a danger for a tracking dog. Snakes are not as worrisome as the gators but should be considered as well. Pit vipers typically coil rather than try to move away from dogs. The trouble arises in that dogs are often curious and sniff and nose the coiled snake. This can result in a strike, and if it does, the dog's face, head, or neck is often the target so the results can be severe. Whenever a nonpoisonous snake is encountered, I take my dog within two or three feet of it and then pull the dog away urgently saying, "Careful!" This hopefully plants the association of snakes with danger.

Training sessions for tracking were initiated pretty early for our puppies, the first at about ten weeks of age. Again, please remember, I am no expert, and there may be advantages to waiting. My luck has been good with the two dogs I've trained. Also, many people advocate collecting blood and using it to lay the trail, even though it involves substantial effort to keep the blood from clotting in the dispenser. My technique is to cut strips of skin from a freshly killed deer (it could be any game animal the dog is being trained to follow). The strips have bits of meat attached and usually a little blood. The size is not critical, but one by four inches is typical for mine. These are stored in a freezer in independent bags or wrappers and can be available anytime. The strip is tied to a line that in turn is attached to a pole so the strip can be dragged away from the exact track the handler leaves. It is important that the young dog doesn't learn just to track the handler's scent. The first trails are simple, and the dog is rewarded with praise or a treat upon accomplishing it. A specific spot should be selected to start the trail, and the strip should be repeatedly dragged over this place so that the strip's scent stands out strongly at the beginning of the track where other scents may be present. It is possible another dog had been at the spot or a bird or squirrel. It is important that the puppy knows which scent he or she is to track. Over several sessions, the difficulty is increased by making more abrupt turns and leaving longer sections where the strip doesn't touch the ground or vegetation and by extending the length of the trail. It is amazing how when the puppy loses the scent, it instinctively goes back and finds the last scent and sooner or later solves the puzzle. The dog obviously learns for, after the first few such puzzles are solved, there is less time involved in sorting the trail out. As these mock trails become more complex, the trainer may need to map their exact course to remember the turns and breaks. Care must be taken, however, not to give the trail away to the puppy for dogs learn quickly to pick up subtle cues from their handlers, and on real trails, the handler will know no more than the dog, in fact, usually less. Some trainers engage another person to lay more advanced challenges, so both the dog and the handler have no knowledge of the trail's configuration.

Some of my friends advised me against using deer skin strips to lay the mock trails for they thought blood was required in order for the dog to know not to trail unwounded deer. This never seemed to be a problem, although I do now lay an artificial trail over where a deer has recently traveled as one of the advanced tracking sessions. I did see Jody once confuse the trails of two deer, one wounded and one not, but she did correct herself with time, and once she found that arrowed deer did not make that error again on her many subsequent trails. (A description of that trail follows shortly.) The strips may be no better for training than sprayed blood, but they are easier. In truth also, the cases a dog is needed most are the times when the game animal is leaking little to no blood. By the way, although I use strips from deer skin, the dogs I have trained had no hesitation extrapolating the idea to the trail of a hog or turkey. I even put Jody once on the trail of a lost dog.

I also believe it is helpful in making the conversion from mock trails to the real recovery of game for the first trail or two to be easy. The problem is most people don't want to waste time when they can find the game themselves and only call when it is a difficult case. If the first case results in a found animal, the dog can put the whole idea of tracking together.

Jody's first trail on a real deer was not difficult in the least, but it was a learning experience for her, and I'll include it here with a smile for her initial reaction was amusing. She was young and later demonstrated remarkable courage many, many times.

My stand was in a cypress that was part of a tiny cypress head just south of an extensive cypress strand. Around the head were expanses of palmetto flats. Between the palmettos and the large cypress strand was an alleyway, maybe forty yards wide, of belly-button high, wavy brown grasses stretching hundreds of yards. The tall stalks of the grasses bent over in such a way to precisely mimic the contour of the back of a feeding deer, and with the movement induced by the wind, it would be easy to imagine a deer where there was none and yet not see deer that were present. Hours passed, and I began to regret my choice to hunt this area. I had scouted earlier and found three places that harbored a lot of fresh deer sign. It was now late for changing stands, so I reminded myself that while scraggly cypress and overgrown pastures do not offer as much action as the scrub or the swampwoods, the majority of sightings of really big bucks stem from this type terrain. Also, a line of freshly rubbed cypress saplings ran right under my stand.

An hour and fifteen minutes before dark, a doe was standing in an open spot a hundred yards east of my tree. A doe would be great to give Jody a real trail, so I mentally urged her in my direction as, at the same time, I wondered how she reached that spot without my awareness. The grass was the answer, but a discouraging answer nonetheless for I thought I was surveying it with extra diligence. The doe angled my way but too far to the south and eventually disappeared behind the reaches of the little cypress head.

The wind, predicted to be from the north and conforming to that forecast thus far, made a ninety-degree change and issued from the east. This made it less likely the doe would smell me, but it wasn't at all likely she would come back regardless. The worrisome aspect was the rub-line ran east-west. The wind change removed the approach that held the highest chance for a buck.

A half an hour passed. Although the doe hadn't come within archery range of my stand, she buoyed my spirits, being undeniable evidence that deer were using the area and that game was afoot. I ventured a blind rattling sequence. Ten minutes passed and nothing showed, or maybe it did, for my eye thought something changed in the grass north of me. Maybe *suspected* is a more accurate term than *thought* because I was not conscious of seeing movement, and further scrutiny revealed nothing. Binoculars, however, found a big buck crossing through the grassy stems and striding purposefully near the edge of the big cypress seventy yards away. Unfortunately, his westward heading would increase that distance. My earlier rattles may or may not have brought him near, but it seemed worth the effort to tickle the tines again in hopes of turning him before he got downwind. In response, he immediately headed southeast and blustered standward, but at twelve yards turned further to the south to check the scent. This turn positioned him broadside, but within a pace, or three at most, he would have my wind. His coat was greyish brown and his rack walnut.

I stretched the tight bowstring and bent Bane Too's limbs deeply. Instinct aimed the arrow subconsciously, and it leapt from the bow! The buck leapt as well, but I thought I saw the arrow vanish into his chest. After a couple of bounds to the west, he walked north-west never looking back, and as the tall grass enveloped him more and more, I felt like he sank below it, but it may only have been the grass swallowing his retreating form. The shot replayed in my mind, and despite the buck's peculiar post-wound behavior, signs pointed to a quickly lethal wound. I climbed down. The arrow had passed through and was thoroughly doused with blood. I packed the stand and gear and hustled to the truck to get Jody!

Jody sniffed the arrow and wanted to play with it. She normally would fetch arrows for me when I would stump shoot. As soon as I said, "Track it, Jody!" she got the idea and took off immediately. At first, her pace wasn't hard for me to keep up with, but when she got about twenty yards ahead, I called her back and then asked her to track again. Shortly, she was out of view in the long grass once more but came racing back on her own, and her posture conveyed some uncertainty. This was near where the buck seemed to evaporate, so I assumed she sniffed her way right to him and was shocked by her find. I strode to the spot and she followed me cautiously. She nosed the eight-point buck timidly but became more excited as I praised her, and in a minute, she was dashing around, sniffing all parts of the buck and acting happy and proud. It was a simple trail, but it helped Jody put all aspects of tracking together and realize the desired outcome.

Just before the beginning of the above account, mention was made of confusing the trail of the targeted game with an unwounded animal. The following episode is of Jody's first experience with this difficulty. In the end, she discovered her mistake and, in the years that came after, was not deceived in that fashion again.

Labradors make good tracking dogs and are easy to train.
They are versatile as well and can participate in duck, quail,
snipe, and pheasant hunts and even find shed antlers.

Often Jody would accompany me on hunts, and I would command her to "stay" next to the tree trunk under my stand. One evening, a four-point buck walked directly under my ladder stand and did not detect Jody attentively eyeing him from a few feet away. The next morning, I tried another ladder stand nearby and turkeys started yelping just before 8:00 a.m. I stood and called a few times in hopes of encouraging them to fly down near me when I noticed a doe eighty yards to the north. She appeared to be alone although my views of her were brief and mostly only partial. The turkeys must have flown down elsewhere for their yelps diminished. Fifteen minutes later, the doe stepped out about twelve yards from the stand's base. She seemed to be heading closer but actually walked to the far side of the oak that was dropping near my stand. It had a broad dome so that while its nearer branches were only nine yards from me, the far side was more like twenty-two. Twice during the next twenty minutes, she fed to the near side but stayed under the shelter of the low boughs. It was now 8:35. At first, it seemed the lack of shooting opportunities was good because she would provide confidence for other deer and maybe even lure in a buck, plus it allowed time to be sure she had no young dependent fawn. She was obviously alone, and now there was the worry she would be sated and depart from the far side, so I was glad when she stepped from under the limbs on my side and stood broadside as she sniffed for fallen acorns. I drew Mellifluwood. She turned a bit, quartering away, but I was imbued with confidence and let the arrow drive forward. The shaft penetrated at least two-thirds of its length, and the doe hurtled away with her tail down.

Jody and I waited an hour and then started the trail. Jody traced the doe's course initially but turned at a right angle from where I assumed the doe had headed. Having a definite spot of blood or saturated arrow as a starting point for the dog is helpful to ensure the dog knows exactly what trail to follow. Without one, as in this case, the dog can believe the handler is putting them on a totally different animal's trail, so I had a bit of doubt Jody was leading me correctly. At the same time, dogs have taught me to trust their abilities and at least consider the route they point out, and this time, giving Jody the benefit of doubt was rewarded. A bit of blood on a leaf we passed was proof enough. We entered a cypress head and plunged through the water and, despite the greenbriers that clutched and gouged us and tore my clothing, made it out the far side. Here, Jody led me through a rough pasture in a very meandering manner. No blood was obvious, but wherever sand or mud was exposed, fresh deer tracks were present. These tracks wandered more like a feeding deer, crossing and re-crossing paths and not showing signs of haste or distress. We had traveled more than seven hundred yards at this point, and even through the thickest vegetation, not a smear of blood had been found. It seemed if my arrow found the doe's mediastinum, she wouldn't have made it this far, and if it was only a gutshot, she should have laid down long ago. We had found no bed, and if we had unknowingly jumped her, there should be running tracks. Jody was content to keep tracking, and it was obvious she was true to a trail, but I pulled her off and restarted her at the blood we had seen early on. She led me back through the tangled cypress head the same way, and as we emerged, I noted a spot of blood on a small leaf. She continued on the same way as before, but this time, seventy yards further along, she left the trail with the fresh deer tracks and headed through some thick, low brush back toward the cypress. There, twenty yards in, was the doe. The arrow had pierced both lungs but did not make it through the opposite shoulder and therefore provided no exit wound. I wanted the trail for Jody's training, but truthfully, this would have been a ridiculously hard deer to find without her help. Since then, if she confused another deer with the one she was tracking, she realized it and rectified it before I was aware.

By luck, Jody had another trail waiting for her that day. In fact, Craig dressed my doe so we could help Morgan look for a buck he shot with a 7 mm rifle. The buck dropped with the shot but got up and charged into a barbed-wire fence so hard one antler broke between the base and the brow tine yet still managed to run off. Jody and I followed him over 1,300 yards through unbelievably jumbled vegetation including a bay head with its devilishly intertwined and nearly solid understory. Even Jody was getting hung up miserably, and she usually could find ways through very tight areas. I disentangled her four times. I bled all over and my shirt was shredded down to nearly nothing. We jumped the buck twice in the thickest stuff, but after the second time, he seemed determined to leave pursuit way behind, and we never saw him again.

The foregoing account brings up two points worth expanding upon. The first is the desirability of having a precise and unmistakable starting place for the dog. Sometimes hunters pick up the arrow or track a game animal far enough they are unsure of the exact site of impact. It is understandable because likely the possibility of needing a dog to help find the game seemed remote at first. Game is usually encountered at the food sources or travel routes that animals frequent. Therefore, it would not be unusual to have the scent of many animals present in that area. Just turning a dog loose in such a location and commanding her to "Track it!" could send her off on any trail. The more specific the scent the dog is to track, the greater the chance for success.

The other point is to trust the dog. A learning dog may lead you astray a few times, but it has been surprising to me how often dogs are right when my brain was telling me, "Wait, this can't be the way it went!"

The scent track is composed of millions of small skin particles and the bacteria and oils they hold. This track disappears over time. Wind disperses the particles and thereby dilutes the scent. Heat, at first, increases the scent by making it rise but contributes to evaporation as well, and prolonged exposure to heat degrades the scent. Rain and dew are very interesting. The oil component of the scent track spreads out on the surface of any water like a drop of gasoline would on a lake. It makes a thin layer phenomenally wider than the original particle and, in that way, increases its area of contact with the air. This, in turn, allows more scent molecules to escape up into the air, and therefore, the scent is more readily detected. Hence, the old saying, "Rain freshens the scent." Obviously, too much rain can wash scent particles away. Also, since the scent is spread further but thinner, after the moisture has again evaporated, the scent is less strong and more subject to erosion. By the way, heat and moisture aid noses, animal or human, in detecting odors and cold, dry conditions render noses less able. This is true for game animals sifting for traces of hunters and also true for the dogs we enlist to help track game. Besides heat, wind, and water, scent is also destroyed by some bacteria, which break down the oils and the particles. Raw earth is full of soil bacteria that can deteriorate the scent track quickly, so dogs encounter difficulty tracking over newly plowed fields or fire-brakes or hog rootings (like where Skylar was stymied tracking the misty morning buck at the beginning of this chapter).

The older and more degraded the scent track, the more difficult it becomes for a dog to follow. Older trails are termed cold trails. There are dogs that can track even more than three days after the trail was left when conditions aren't too unfavorable, and most dogs have little trouble with a day or day-and-a-half-old trail. To test this, on a long and tricky trail that she solved, I started Jody again the following day, and she led me to the same place. It might be possible she memorized the route, but that seems unlikely, and she certainly showed the signs of running and sniffing as she progressed along the trail.

By the way, when mock trails are laid out by dragging deer skin pieces or sprayed blood, as the puppy gets surer of itself, the trails are aged for longer periods before starting the dog. Aging drag trails, including distractions like the trails of other animals, placing gaps and sharp angle turns on training trails help prepare the pup for the transition to real life tracking.

As far as gear for the handler, the area will dictate that for the most part. I have learned if there is a chance the game is still alive, it is best to bring a weapon capable of dispatching it. Don't count on the hunter's weapon because sometimes the hunter may not be nearby when the game is discovered. Carrying water is important for when a dog gets hot and thirsty, its sense of smell dwindles dramatically. In the sun, hats can help the tracker; in the thick brush, they can be a nuisance. Rubber boots are good for shallow water but fill up and weigh a lot after crossing deep water. I've never worn gloves, but they may have saved my knuckles all the times Jody pulled me through saw palmettos or greenbriers. A good flashlight is important and a compass or, if you prefer, a GPS unit or phone.

The next section will chronicle some dog tracking episodes that illustrate some of the information mentioned:

Two consecutive years, Ozzie shot bucks north of Deep Crossing that gave Jody fun and fulfilling trails and me exercise to boot! The first he shot with a muzzleloader fairly early in the morning. He found a little blood but no deer. He reached me in the late morning, and it was noon by the time Jody and I arrived. Jody took the trail with alacrity and I held her to as slow a pace as I could with her chest-protector-type harness but still was running to keep up. Primarily, the terrain in that particular area is a huge piney flatwoods with sprawling palmetto flats. For the most part, the buck had kept to the open pathways between the clumps and the going wasn't too bad. Within three hundred yards, we jumped the buck. Jody had set a difficult pace and Ozzie was not up with us, but it would not have mattered for the buck was only a brown streak over the palmetto tops for a second and then was gone. I yelled to Ozzie that we had seen the buck and kept running with Jody, encouraging her to go slow, but if I had much influence with her on that aspect, her normal pace would have made a cheetah proud! The sight of the buck or the freshness of the trail spurred her on! Over a half a mile slipped under our thudding feet. The fresh scent must have been quite evident to Jody for she mainly stayed directly on a single course with very little of the zigging she often employed to "tack" along the scent track. We jumped the buck again, and when I yelled back to Oz, I heard no reply.

After another five hundred yards, some incredibly dense growth loomed up in our path, and I felt pretty sure the buck had bedded again somewhere in its midst. I had no weapon, so I called and whistled for Ozzie again without response. After three or more minutes of yelling, I elected to resume the trail. The going was nearly impossible, and I had to crawl, squirm, wiggle, and slide through and over the dense vegetation and, of course, release Jody's rope. She jumped the buck nearly immediately! Jody would make no noise when she found fallen game but bark when she found animals that were still alive, so I knew what had occurred despite not being able to see more than a couple feet ahead. I called to her and shortcut to the last sounds, but even this was slow and difficult. Jody came to me. Although the strand was now less congested with growth, I still was unable to proceed and keep hold of her rope. She got a bit ahead in the hard going and jumped the buck within fifty yards. I called Jody back and then set her back to tracking. This time, the buck jumped within thirty yards, and I could see him get up. The terrain now was more typical creek bottom, maybe not truly typical for it was still densely understoried but not nearly as restrictive to movement, and as Jody led me forward, the buck's head was visible at fifteen yards. He was watching but did not rise. I yelled and yelled and whistled. I began to look for a sapling I could fashion into a spear as I kept calling. Then Ozzie responded from fairly close but couldn't force his way to us. He knew a way around to the north and detoured there, adding another five minutes, but it let him through. The buck had not moved despite all the commotion, and Ozzie finished him with a well-placed shot.

Ozzie and Jody with a buck he shot.

The buck had fled primarily eastward. The initial wound was only a graze to his neck. There was little blood in his first bed, and while there is no way to ever know, I have wondered if the buck may had survived if not for our fast-paced and relentless pursuit preventing the wound from clotting and keeping both his blood pressure up and oxygen requirement high. Regardless, it was an exciting trail, and Jody, Ozzie, and I all returned to camp happy and maybe a bit tired.

The next year was uncannily similar. Ozzie was in the same stand or, at least, one in the same vicinity. This buck also ran to the east. I had gotten back to camp after dark and then went to meet Ozzie at Deep Crossing. He took Jody and me across and told us he had shot the buck with his rifle at two hundred yards. When we reached the spot he believed the buck had been, there was no blood, but Jody reacted with urgent excitement and began tracking at once. Ozzie confirmed her route was the same as the buck's, and within fifty yards, my flashlight beam caught blood splatters even at the fast walking pace Jody, with my restraints, was setting. Within two hundred yards, we jumped the buck, a very large deer.

We continued on the trail and jumped him a few more times. The buck never ran more than a couple hundred yards before stopping and the last time not even half that. I held Jody back to let Ozzie get up to us, and then we tracked slowly. When we saw the reflection from the buck's eyes, Ozzie slipped ahead. The buck's body was lying pointing away from us, but his head was looking back. Ozzie shot, and the buck crumpled. After warning Ozzie, I let Jody go so she could smell the buck and feel pride in the job she did, but when she sniffed him, he launched himself up and fled with Jody right on his heels (or hooves, I should say!). I called and she returned, and I reclipped onto her harness.

Jody started tracking and soon jumped the buck again, and I could see him stop after little more than twenty yards. We held back, and the buck toppled lifeless with Oz's next shot. Jody sniffed the dead buck from every angle and looked happy and proud. Oz and I were happy as well, but our smiles faded slightly as we started toward his Jeep. Even with the two of us, the drag was hard because it was such a big-bodied buck and because of the many thick patches of palmettos. We didn't really know the shortest route, and that added to our labor as well. Jody was still grinning as she kept easy pace with us.

Skylar is a tremendous tracking beagle with
countless deer finds to her credit.

Jody works a trail (note the bloody arrow) wearing her chest protector. A leash can be attached to the chest protector. Dogs learn to associate wearing it with a coming trail and exude their excitement!

Greenbrier stems grow in tangled, sprawling clumps dense enough to resist a tracker's forward movement. They are hardy and tenacious, and their spines ensnare clothing worse than barbed wire, causing rips and tears.

On the edge of the creek bottom woods, the higher ground held a line of live oaks surrounded by dense clumps and walls of waist high briars. The tightness of the canopy blocked light and kept the shady area below growth free except for a few palmettos and a young hickory under which the earth was bowled out from repeated buck scraping. Acorns rained from the oaks. Years ago, I had a stand set against one of the oaks for my dad, but Hurricane Jeanne had split the tree and the part with the ladder stand fell. It was bent a bit but not ruined, and now, more than a decade later, I moved the same twisted stand back against the half of the trunk that hadn't fallen early one afternoon and climbed up. The platform was only seven feet from the ground, an advantage for both photography and shot angle for a longbow. The wind was light and changed direction every few minutes. The forecast called for southeasterly winds, and it did blow from that direction on occasion.

At 5:30, I rattled and a buck came in within two minutes. He looked like a small eight-point, but as he drew nearer, it became obvious he sported no brow tines and was only a six. After eyeing the area, he started feeding on acorns and allowed me plenty of photographic shots. After five or more minutes, the wind changed again, and he left nervously. I rattled twice more, once forty-five minutes after the first and then again at 7:00, the latest I planned to blind rattle for fear of a buck responding belatedly and coming in when the light was fading. The mosquitoes, persistent all afternoon in the light winds, became even more energetic and frenzied as though they were aware I would be leaving soon and "last call" was fast approaching. Their attentions made me consider abandoning the stand early although plenty of light was left even in the shadiness of the swamp.

As I started gathering my gear, I suddenly realized a tremendous buck was searching out acorns not seven yards from my stand! Behind him was a thick wall of briars, and he had silently slipped out of them. Whether my rattles ten minutes before had drawn him or if he was merely coming to the food source, there was no way of telling. When his head was down, I drew Mellifluwood, nervous of the wind betraying me at any second. He raised his head, maybe sensing something or maybe just alertly checking as deer do. I released. The sound of the hit was a sharp crack, and as the buck bolted to the east half of the arrow was visible, proclaiming limited penetration. I watched his course carefully, already doubtful of an exit wound and, therefore, of a good trail. One or both shoulders were struck. The sun started to sink below the horizon, so light would fade in about twenty-five minutes.

I gathered my gear and toted it to the truck and returned to where I last saw him, anxious to at least get a start on the trail while it was light. Bits of mud and splashes of water mapped his course through some crawlingly tight cover. The lack of blood was dismaying. A yard before the tight growth ended, the arrow had broken, and the half on the buck's trail was only lightly smeared with blood. Despite the hit being in the chest, the signs thus far were all discouraging.

Beyond the thick cover was an open strip about seventy yards wide that had been choked with unbelievably thick and high briars five months earlier but had been chopped then and chopped a second time a month ago. The technique for chopping is a gigantic tractor drags two huge and heavy cylinders armed with blades that run parallel with each cylinder. As this apparatus is pulled across the terrain, the cylinders roll, and everything is chopped into pieces from twelve to fourteen inches in length. Even trees nine inches in diameter are chopped easily. After the intervening time, the overhead briars had been reduced to flattened mass of rust-colored twigs and decaying leaves two to four inches thick all wet with the standing water tropical storm Faye had dumped upon us. Thousands and thousands of mosquitoes stirred up with every step. I worked forward, bent over, inspecting for more freshly broken stems among all the broken fragments, and the mosquitoes swarmed my face, hands, ears, and head and feasted on my back where my sweat-drenched shirt pulled tight with the stoop the search required. I could find no definitive tracks but was overjoyed to discover speckles of blood here and there. In a slow, tortuous process, I advanced the trail maybe thirty or forty yards. After that point, no further clue showed.

I went to my truck and got a flashlight and a heavy shirt to wear over my shirt for a little protection from the mosquitoes despite the heat. Mack called and, by coincidence, had hunted on the other side of the dirt road probably within three hundred yards of me. We lost signal before I could enlist his help, and my repeated calls failed to go through. I knew his beagle Skylar could solve the trail with ease, so I carried the phone with me in case the signal returned. My pockets were too squishy with sweat to trust placing the phone in one. The mosquitoes took delight in my hands being tied up with a phone in one and a flashlight in the other. No more blood was to be found. I tried jumping ahead to where the buck may have entered brush and then all the way to the swampwoods, hoping vegetation would display blood spots more readily. The cellular signal never rebounded. After spending hours with no success, I drove to Mack's camp and asked his help. He and his wife, Colynn, and Skylar volunteered, and Skylar led us to the buck quickly. There was very little blood even in the lush swampwoods. The buck dropped amid thick palmettos, and he would have been very hidden to any searches I might have tried even in daylight the next morning. The total distance was about a hundred yards but more like a hundred and forty by the route the buck took. He ran a complete circular loop five yards in diameter fifteen yards before he collapsed.

The buck was a beautiful, symmetrical eight-point with extremely long tines. He weighed 145 lbs. The arrow had double-lunged him but double-shouldered him as well. The broadhead caused a bulge that moved the skin on the far side when a leg was moved but had not cut through the skin. Just piercing the skin would have left an entirely different and more readable trail. Thank goodness for Skylar!

Skylar was the first dog to offer me firsthand evidence that hogs are not afraid of dogs or at least of a single dog. Mack was keen to get a hog with his spear, so we had covered some ground and finally located a group of them coming out of the swampwoods near Deep Crossing. Breanna, my daughter, was five or six years old, and we left her holding Skylar's leash while we stalked the hogs. Skylar is a small beagle—I believe it is termed a thirteen-inch beagle and my assumption is the measurement applies to the dog's height. (If there are eleven-inch beagles, she would be in that group!) With Mack ahead of me, we closed in carefully for there were several sets of eyes, ears, and noses. The nearest hog was probably more than thirteen yards off, a long throw anytime and senseless if a little patience and crafty stalking would yield a much closer one. The vegetation was predominately over a hog's back, rendering stalking easier but finding a clear path for a throw harder.

All of a sudden, I heard a little cry from Breanna and looked to see her on her belly being dragged by Skylar, who had scented the hogs and determined she was not going to be left out of the excitement. Soon, the leash slipped from Breanna's hands and Skylar was by us in a streak. Moments later, there was a yelpy little bark, and Skylar raced back through Mack's legs, nearly toppling him. A big sow was only a yard behind the beagle but whirled from Mack's upright form, grunted, and the whole group raced to the swamp. We didn't get any hogs that evening, but had a lot of chuckles!

Jody would fetch arrows for me. On rainy days, Mack and I would practice archery from the cabin porch, shooting into the rain at hickory nuts or palm fronds pieces, and Jody was the only one to get wet. She didn't mind in the least! Jody mastered the art of "staying" when commanded to the point even game within inches of her would not entice her to break "stay," but when she was a pup, I once, when afield with her, shot at and missed a hog in a group. Apparently, she assumed she was to fetch the arrow, and I hadn't thought ahead of time to tell her any different, so she raced the way the arrow went and, the next instant, had the whole lot of hogs running after her to me. I was yelling at her "Stay!" and was upset that she had ruined my chances on the formerly unspooked hogs, never dreaming she would lure them all the way to me, and I failed to even nock another arrow. Of course, when they got within a couple yards, the hogs lost their enthusiasm for the chase and rushed into the thick.

Mack did get a hog with a spear a different day.
In fact, we speared many over the years.

J. M. Murphy in 1891 wrote similar observations about Florida hogs: "They are never so few, however, that they are not ready to engage in battle with a dog or a pack of dogs, for they seem to hate these animals with a hatred that can only be satisfied with their annihilation. The moment they see or wind a dog they open on his line, their "music" being a series of fierce grunts and revengeful squeals." He goes on to say, "They will even attack a man accompanied by a dog," and "I have known more than one man accompanied by a hound to be sent clambering for dear life up a tree."

With the above preface, reader, you have probably foreseen a few hog tracking accounts, and the best course is to relate them in the order they occurred:

Jody and I had hunted together one February morning and encountered a group of hogs. Signaling Jody to stay, I eased forward and drew Mellifluwood, letting an arrow fly that appeared to strike soundly and accurately. I called Jody from her sitting position thirty yards back, showed her the first blood, and told her to track. She responded exuberantly but took off after the whole group of hogs. The stricken hog had veered off from the rest to the east, so I called her back and started her over, and she raced off just as fast and excitedly but this time on the correct trail and led me to the fallen boar within forty yards. She and I hunted snipe in the midday, trudging through the deep mud of the low ponds, and she retrieved all the birds I hit.

Between the long tramp of the morning hunt, the drag of the hog, pacing the miles necessary to flush snipe, and all the retrieving, both of us had legs that had gone the distance, but late afternoon, an hour before dark, found us still hunting. We were a long way from the truck, and I had just decided to start back in its direction when we found feeding hogs again. With Jody in "stay," I sneaked up to them and awaited the right opportunity. Some of the sows had piglets, but a very large grey one had none. When she turned broadside at twenty yards, I bent Mellifluwood and savored the "feel" of the shot. The bow's thump was as muffled as the arrow's light hiss. The shaft, fletchings and all, disappeared into the grey chest. Myrtles obstructed the view in many places, but my impression was that the sow ran north and the other hogs scrambled to the east.

The walk back to the truck would be long, so it would be helpful to locate the hog quickly and somehow mark it because, in the overgrown pasture, returning to it in the truck would be difficult once darkness fell. If I found the sow fast, I would be able to navigate the rough terrain while there was still light. The boar from the morning hunt had been trailed immediately and was stone dead when we got there. This shot looked equally as good.

I called Jody, put her on the spot the sow had been, and told her to "track it." She leapt off to the east in the frenzied, zigzag manner of her tracking. My perception was that the wounded hog fled north, and at the same time, I recalled how Jody initially went after the strong scent of the group of unwounded hogs that morning, so instead of trying to keep pace with her, I elected to look north for some actual blood to start her on. Suddenly, there came a ferocious series of choppy, growling grunts, and Jody was flying back toward me with a big grey block of angry hog in pursuit. Fortunately, I could see well in that direction and had time to nock an arrow. Jody passed my legs like a blonde blur, and the hog was nearly on me. I drew and aimed at the center of her approaching bulk. The arrow struck with a cracking, forceful thwack that stunned the hog enough to stop it two yards out. The broadhead had driven into her head near midline but below eye level. The sow turned and shook her head against a pine trunk, snapping the shaft off at the rear of the broadhead, the tip of which was imbedded more than an inch and a half into her upper snout. She turned further and trotted around a myrtle.

I nocked another arrow and strode hurriedly around the myrtle, hoping to get a shot as she retreated before she got into the thick. The biggest problem with my plan was that she had not retreated. She had only waited and charged again as I came into view. Unexpectedly, she was suddenly near my legs! I attempted to draw and shoot, but my arrow missed the entire 140 lbs. of her even though she was only a few feet distant. With Mellifluwood, I tried to hold her off, but she was determined and angry and weighed nearly as much as me. As hard and desperately as I struggled, she drove forward and was wrenching her head about within eight inches of my legs. The rear of the broadhead in her face was carving and scraping against the lower limb of the bow. I tried to move backward and, at the same time, maintain force on the bow, but my foot hit a tuft or ridge of grass and I felt myself starting to tip. Flashes of this furious hog's onslaught once I was helpless and on the ground flicked through my mind. At that instant, Jody dashed around the sow and latched onto her rump. The hog spun around and went for Jody, who agilely darted back. With the hog's attention diverted and my balance restored, I nocked another arrow (my last tipped with a broadhead). Happily, luck and necessity merged, and Mellifluwood propelled it through the sow's ribs. She rushed a yard or two toward Jody then halted and seemed to jump over on her side, kick, and was still.

I have read of hogs in Europe and India being among the most stalwart and courageous of animals, but seldom had I seen it first-hand. In fact, I had seen sows trample their own young in their haste to be first away from a perceived enemy. This sow demonstrated dramatically a tendency toward fearlessness and the resolve to sell her life as dearly as possible. I should add that I was wholeheartedly grateful to Jody and her dauntlessness for I am convinced I would have suffered substantial injuries if she had not intervened.

My first arrow had hit the sow's chest but deflected back, slicing only one lung and then entering the abdomen. My second arrow hit below eye level and penetrated the skull but only into her nasal passages and sinuses. The third arrow double-lunged her. When I lamented to Mack about the scrapes gouged into my bow by the protruding rear portion of the broadhead or maybe by the sow's teeth—in an effort to cheer me up, I suppose—he advised me not to think of them as scratches but, rather, as a scar!

One chilly day after deer season was closed, I accompanied Mack on his quest for a hog. I was armed only with a camera and hung back, hoping for decent photos. Skylar was very used to tromping about with Mack by this date and stayed near him. We were lucky enough to find two large boars on the edge of a cypress strand and crept through the trees to close the distance. The trunks of the cypress presented photographic difficulties. I could get pictures of Mack and partial pictures of the boars but no one frame that would show them simultaneously. With his longbow, Mack arrowed one of the boars. The shot looked good, and we pursued him immediately with Skylar showing us the way. The course crossed a pasture and then down into a cove formed by U-shaped cypress head. Some black could be seen through the vegetation ahead and, standing behind Mack, I readied the camera still eager to get Mack and the hog in a single frame. As I worked to get the focus correct and maximize the depth of field, several grunts disrupted the still air. Skylar, with an angry hog right behind her, had raced to Mack and Mack had run south. Through the viewfinder, I saw Mack's blue sweatshirt disappear but didn't see the hog until I lowered the camera. Happily, the boar had come to a stop still six yards from me, and then he casually turned and walked back north. Why he stopped is hard to guess. Maybe he was only interested in Skylar. Maybe he felt he had routed his foes when Mack and Skylar fled. Mack had only retreated a few steps and nocked an arrow. He quietly stalked up to the walking hog and drew again. The second arrow finished the boar quickly. In fact, the first arrow was lethally placed, and the hog had to be on his last legs at the time. Mack knew of some of the charges hogs had perpetrated upon me over the years and was quick to point out, since hogs never responded to him in such a fashion, I must have somehow been to blame for this aggression.

Jody and I waded the Bull Creek swamp bottom with my bow and a couple arrows. The water had risen drastically with the heavy rains of Tuesday and Tuesday night. We came upon some hogs, and leading Jody up to some slightly higher ground, I gave her the sign for "stay." The three nearest were sows, but deeper in the swamp was a boar. The sows fed toward me and to the downwind side, so I retreated ahead of them although they were from six to twenty yards from me. Eventually, one got a faint whiff of me either from a gust forcing air west or from scent blowing off of where I had just been. She raised her nose and started trotting. Either less tainted air reassured her or the reluctance of her companions to accompany her changed her mind. She resumed feeding forty yards to the east. The other sows continued rooting, but their overall movement was toward her, so after a few minutes, I was able to slip to the northeast, closing to within seven yards of the boar. A big oak trunk sheltered my approach, and I readied Mellifluwood, drawing as he stepped out at a quartering away angle. Mellifluwood was nearly silent, and the heavy arrow drove unerringly into the boar's chest. He rushed to the east, then south, and then west, passing by Jody at less than three yards, apparently not noticing her still form. She noticed him however as the strained intensity of her sitting posture and her steady gaze in the direction he had run made manifest.

The swamp floor was all water and trodden black mud, and if any blood fell, it was not to be seen. The arrow had penetrated very deeply, so I let Jody track it as soon as I got to her. These accounts make it seem that I should know better by now, but to defend myself, it is fair to add that between these instances, scores of hogs Jody tracked right after the shot were dead when we reached them. Jody was not on a leash and tracked at her typical running pace but did return to me repeatedly without getting too far ahead. Then her bark sounded from thirty yards accompanied by the short, repeated grunts of a charging hog! She evaded him and came to me, urgently encouraging me to hurry. I was close enough to see him when he charged her again and whisked my other arrow into him. He was quartering to me, and the arrow hit well but failed to penetrate much at all. Nonetheless, he abandoned his charge.

He ran about twenty yards and stopped in a tangle of vines that sprang from a mound of higher ground, although it too was underwater now. The poor penetration of the second arrow allowed the vines to pull it free. I eased to within six yards of him. The water was knee high and the swamp bottom so muddy that when my feet pushed in, it became difficult to move them, and extracting one only drove the other in more deeply. Unseen logs, roots, and cypress knees added to the treacherousness of the footing and quick movement was not easy. The top of the little mound, two feet in diameter, was even with the water level, and on this tiny island, the boar stood, then swayed and fell over.

He was still breathing, but it seemed he must expire any second. Instead, he lifted his head and watched Jody. I broke off a palm frond stem and used it in an attempt to retrieve my second arrow in order that I might hasten his end. The vines that had pulled the arrow from the hog thwarted my attempts, fouling it each time it was coming my way. The hog seemed done in, and my attention was on the vines that frustrated my efforts to get the arrow. I may even have scooted a foot closer. For some reason, the hog exploded into a charge, clacking his teeth and issuing short, mean grunts. I tried hopping back a few steps, but the mud held me firmly. I went down and the boar closed on my face. My hands went out to hold him back and somehow managed to grab each side of his head without getting my fingers in his mouth although, in truth, I didn't aim but rather just reached out protectively. All the while, he was making short, aggressive grunts and grinding and clacking his teeth less than a foot from my face. He couldn't get good footing in the water, but it was still a struggle to hold him off. Jody barked and bit his butt and barked and bit again. He wrenched free of me and turned to pursue her. I got to my feet and stumbled away drenched but feeling fortunate. My belt pack was closed, and I pulled out the new camera. It was wet, but that was all. The pack was pretty remarkable for it had been submerged for what seemed to me close to a minute (but probably much less), and the outside of the pack was thoroughly soaked. Another stroke of luck!

Jody lunged through the water back to me and turned and we watched the hog. He lay back down, this time in the water. His head sank, and bubbles trickled up. He raised his head with an effort, inhaled quickly as his head sank again. This time bubbles rose, but the head did not come up again. Another minute's patience may have saved me a drenching and near injury, but possibly, the boar's extreme efforts to attack his tormentor may have hastened his end. My first arrow had hit liver and lung and the broadhead lodge into the left shoulder. When I cleaned the hog, I discovered a mass of congealed, jellylike blood bigger than an orange but smaller than a grapefruit around the broadhead. He went no more than 150 yards, in fact, probably not even a hundred from where he was shot, but that does not include the running involved in the charges. After the shot, only minutes passed before he died, but with the severity of the wound, it is hard to fathom him lasting anywhere near that long. The second arrow did not penetrate the chest cavity and did not contribute to his death. He weighed only 110 lbs.

You may have heard an old saying, "Do as I say, not as I do!" and it is reasonable advice to suggest a waiting period before putting a dog on a trail of a freshly shot game animal. These hog trails are convincing testimony. Although I have had no such mishaps, I have also heard of wounded bucks attacking tracking dogs.

Earlier, I mentioned how dogs do not seem to find it difficult to transfer the concept of tracking to different species. This account is of the very first time Jody was ever put on a turkey trail: One December morning in the swampwoods, I climbed a palm near some wild oranges. In the misty grey, a coyote trotted directly toward me, pausing twice to reconnoiter the area with both his nose and intelligent-looking eyes. His trot was interesting to behold. His head and body seemed uninvolved, just floating along above the fast steps of the feet, and the gait covered ground quickly without sound or excessive motion. He hopped onto the long trunk of a fallen cabbage palm and walked along it rather than the ground. Bobcats do this regularly, but this was the first time I saw a coyote perform the feat. He scanned for fallen oranges but then found my scent below me and was gone.

A short while later, three jakes approached but one descried me just when it seemed I would get a shot. They headed west slowly, "pucking" their mild alarm "puck," nervous yet unsure and unwilling to run, finally climbing a tree blown by the hurricanes down to a thirty-degree angle forty yards off. Since it was in the swamp, they were sheltered not only by the distance but also by obstacles growing up or hanging down between us. For twenty minutes or more, I was under their surveillance and therefore not at liberty to move. I was glad when they finally left. Flying squirrels are common in our woods but seldom seen for they are almost entirely nocturnal in their habits. For some reason, one scampered across the swamp floor below me and made it to a tree. The morning was still young, and I marveled at how interesting the start had been.

A group of turkeys, hens and jakes this time, probably eight or more in all, came from the northeast, and with the low cabbage palms screening me, I was able to ready Bane Too for a possible shot. The first bird to step out was a hen, but a jake was close behind her, and they were not ten yards from my palm. I aimed an arrow that missed. I consoled myself with the closeness of the miss but was far from truly happy. The targeted jake and the hen in front of him had executed a little jump and flutter with the thud of the arrow and other turkeys came out from under the fronds and joined them. The eyesight of turkeys is phenomenal and their curiosity nearly nonexistent, so I rarely get shots at them from stands, but the low fronds combined with good cover around my stand somehow kept them from discovering me, and I readied Bane Too again. A jake, maybe the original one or maybe another, was facing directly away at fifteen yards. I drew, tried to be at ease and picture the arrow's flight, and then released. The arrow disappeared into the bird's center. He skittered a few feet forward and then walked north. After a few feet, he was sheltered from view by the young cabbage palms.

The other birds milled around, heads cocked this way and that, acting puzzled and nervous. Any hunter can tell of the thoughts that race through the brain at times like these, when there are only seconds to make decisions. Had my eyes deceived me? The jake didn't act injured or really all that alarmed. Had the arrow only gone through the feathers of his big tail? Even though the pages of this book concentrate a lot of episodes and make shot opportunities seem commonplace, often many, many days or weeks of diligent effort pass between any chances. Here was still an opportunity in hand. Should I try for another while the chance was still offered?

Somehow I remained undiscovered and nocked another arrow. Two jakes were a little less than twenty yards off, but then my jake reappeared, walking northeast now at twenty-eight yards. His gait and manner were peculiar, and his plumage looked ruffled. Despite the distance, his appearance solved all my doubts, for whether it was a lethal hit or not, I now was sure he was hit and I could have no other target. I drew Bane Too a third time and for some reason felt that surety and confidence that accompanies my best shots. With a gentle and prolonged hiss, the arrow arced precisely to the turkey's wing. It appeared to be the perfect shot again!

The jake scooted forward and resumed his march to the northeast. The flock trotted to the north, and he may have turned to parallel their course, but the closeness of the swamp made it impossible to tell. The trail should not be long or tricky, but Jody was young, and every trail would add to her experience and confidence. Both arrows had blood on them, so I left the first in the ground to give Jody a definite starting point. Originally, I planned to wait a couple of hours at least so the trail would not be too easy, but then I heard some noises to the north and remembered the times raccoons tried to drag off turkeys I had arrowed, plus I had seen the coyote earlier. If something absconded with the jake, it would not help Jody's trailing knowledge, and I would lose the turkey.

Jody sensed something and was full of excitement, almost like she knew she had an important role to play. John Jeanneney suggests having a special collar or harness used only for tracking so the dog knows what is expected. I later got Jody a chest protector-type harness, which proved to unfailingly evoked her readiness and exuberance, but her enthusiasm was heightened this time just from my manner or some other cue.

She sniffed the arrow and, after the "Track it!" command, took off. Since I knew where the second arrow had been and the approximate route the turkey took to it, I was pleased to see Jody trace it quickly and accurately. She led me to the fallen bird. It had made it over a hundred yards and changed directions several times pushing through and under very tight cover. Blood confirmed the trail in a number of spots, but blood trailing would have been arduous and frustrating and may have failed to locate the bird, so I was lavish with my praise of Jody. Her pride and happiness were obvious.

The first arrow had driven down through the jake's center and barely missed the backbone. The second was not as good as I had thought, piercing the meaty part of one leg and grazing the other. It had fallen a little short and would not have been lethal although it may have contributed to the blood trail.

While on the subject of tracking turkeys, another of Jody's finds should be included. I said *find* instead of *trail* because this turkey flew. There was a low spot in the cypress strand, and the hunter told me the gobbler had flown over it with his arrow dangling. After locating cut feathers that denoted the exact spot of impact, I took a compass bearing on the flight path. In my experiences, fatally arrowed turkeys that flew often did so in a beeline. I walked around the cypress strand and discovered a thickly overgrown and tangled jungle of shrubs and vines that extended for many acres. It was hard to penetrate for a person without a machete. Nonetheless, I asked Jody to "Find it," after allowing her to sniff some of the feather pieces. She raced around awhile and led us along the cattle trail that skirted the thick for at least three hundred yards. It seemed no severely stricken bird could have made it that far. Hen tracks showed where the dirt and sand allowed, and it was likely she was following the only turkey scent she had found since she had been given no starting point. I now brought her back to the extension of the compass reading and actually waded into the thick to line up the compass reading with the low spot. She located the gobbler in very short order. The hunter was overjoyed as it was the first turkey he had taken with a bow. The vegetation was so thick and intertwined where the bird perished it is inconceivable to think it would have been found without a dog's help. In cases like this one, an air sniffing dog has a decided advantage over a ground sniffer because there was no trail. By the way, the chest protector was mentioned earlier and this search for the turkey was the impetus for purchasing it. When I reached Jody and the bird, there was a rip in Jody's skin on the forward part of her chest about an inch and three-quarters long. In the excitement of the chase, she never even yelped nor appeared to be aware of it in the least. As thick and potentially hazardous as our terrain can be, the chest protector is comforting to the handler. I ordered a blaze orange one as an extra precaution against someone mistaking a yellow lab for a light-colored deer.

Often what the hunter believes the game animal did and what the tracking dog seems to indicate are at odds. The hunter's belief can be shaped from glimpses of the fleeing game or sounds heard or just a gut feeling of what the stricken animal should do. The account of the charging sow is a perfect example where I thought the hog fled north and discounted Jody's path eastward as an error. As mentioned earlier, trusting the dog is important. Here is another lesson I underwent in learning this trust:

One afternoon, early in bow season, I sat in a stand along a tiny ditch. Jody was in "stay" across the ditch in the shade of a myrtle four yards from the base of the cypress I had climbed. The wind was fairly strong from the east, and Jody was west of me. A doe looked for palmetto berries in the flats west of the ditch south of us. She came closer, but the fronds were thick and covered most of her body until she was only thirteen yards away. Another handful of steps and she would either have my wind or be on top of Jody! I had to lean out from the tree to give the bow clearance, and she may have caught this motion for she seemed suspicious for a second but then continued ambling north. I couldn't understand how she hadn't seen Jody yet. As I drew Elanever, she stopped and stared. Shooters of the longbow know the sensation just before the shot when the body feels the energy of the bow's bent limbs and the mind envisions the path of the going arrow. I savored the instant and released. Alert deer are faster than an arrow from a longbow even at short distances, and she ducked enough that the arrow, aimed low in the chest, actually hit in her back, but she was so close that the sharp downward angle still drove it into her chest. She fled to the south again paralleling the ditch.

I was proud of Jody when she tracked her first
turkey. She was pretty proud too!

Jody and I had to penetrate this growth to search for the gobbler that
flew with the hunter's arrow. This episode precipitated my purchase
of the chest protector because Jody sustained a gash in her chest.

Jody and I began tracking after I pulled the stand and organized my gear in a pile. Jody's southward pace was fast and I hurried to keep up, but it was reassuring to see good blood on the brush along the way. Suddenly, Jody turned west into a skinny swamp finger and led me through water and terribly thick thickets. Of course, my pace came nearly to a halt, and I was dismayed to find no blood. It seemed highly unlikely a wounded animal could pass through places I had trouble crawling through without leaving some blood smears especially in light of the good splashes of blood in the more open palmetto flats. There were an abundance of hog tracks and wallows, and my fear was that Jody had diverted to one of their trails. I pulled Jody off and returned to the north-south trail. The heavy and obvious blood reassured me, but once again, Jody turned west. I stopped and searched methodically for blood and found none, so I pulled her off sooner this time and returned to the good blood determined to trail it myself rather than rely on Jody. I searched until dark without finding a continuation of the trail.

How had such a trail stopped? I decided maybe I had better follow Jody again, and this time, after quite a distance, my flashlight beam fell on a light smear of blood on a grass stem! Jody had been right all along! I plunged on along after her. Cat briars ripped my shirt and arms, hands, face, and head. My hat was stuffed into a pocket because the vines wouldn't let it stay on my head. The greenbrier vines repeatedly pulled the glasses from my face and dropped them in the water with a *sploosh*, and I would have to grub along with my hands to locate them. The greenery also clutched at Elanever and pulled arrows from my quiver. I regretted bringing the bow. It made movement through the thick more cumbersome and progress difficult because I needed a hand to move vines and branches aside, up, or down, yet one hand was tied up with the flashlight and the other with the bow. It was too thick to think of stashing the bow for worries of finding it again. All parts of me were bleeding freely, and I was soaked from sweat, from going through deep parts of the swamp and from wiggling on my belly under branches and spiky greenbrier stems in watery channels.

It was hard to move at all and impossible to keep up with Jody, who somehow managed to race through it all and leave me behind each time I called her back. I feared for her from the spiky greenbrier stems in the dark, from snakes, and especially from gators in the deeper parts. Now I regretted putting her on the trail. Had I trusted her originally, daylight would have aided in the negotiation of the tangled swamp. In desperation, I tried to force my way forward to catch back up to her but only cut myself more without making any headway. I retrieved fallen arrows fifteen or twenty times.

Suddenly, great plunging sounds from deep water emanated from ahead of me somewhere in the dark followed by silence! Nothing could have scared me more, and in a panic, I yelled loudly into the blackness for Jody to come, fearing she had been taken by a gator and that silence would be the only answer, but she splashed back to me happy and oblivious to any danger or worries. I was relieved but wanted no more scares and determined to abandon the trail. Going back the way we came was out of the question for in the past hour or so, we must have covered more than two hundred yards. A veritable wall of brush kept me from going to either side, so I continued squirming forward and just a little ways further, the swamp opened a bit into a deep cypress pond, and Jody was sniffing the fallen form of the doe.

The trouble confronting us now was that we had pierced far into a cypress swamp, it was black everywhere, I couldn't stand upright much less drag a deer, and other than to go east, it was all guesswork as to how to get out. The only choice was to leave the doe until morning. I pulled her out of the water and draped her between two trunks. It took twenty minutes to force our way twenty yards to the southeast, and I had to carry Jody through much of it, but finally, we reached part of the palmetto flats. The trudge to the stand was comparatively a breeze, although we traversed sprawls of dense palmettos. We pushed on to the truck, and even Jody looked tired. The worry now was whether I would be able to relocate the doe in the morning.

The next morning, to shortcut the arduous part of the trail, I searched for where we had left the swamp, believing my forceful exit would leave a visible trail. Unfortunately, my estimate of where we had been was not accurate, and the sun came up. Having no desire to squander more time with a deer already left overnight, I led Jody back to the start of the westward portion of the trail knowing well the travail facing us. It was not easy, but with light to see and no bow or quiver, it was less hellish than the night before. Jody had no trouble retracing the route and guided me directly to the doe.

Jody also tracked a nice buck for Pete later that weekend with no difficulty even though the buck had run over a hundred and fifty yards. I was proud of her and felt she had increased her confidence level. I know my confidence and trust in her had increased immensely.

While Jody and I were still a fairly inexperienced team, we bungled a trail—no, I should say I bungled a trail with a few poor choices and fell back upon veteran trackers. Perhaps someone can learn from and benefit from my mistakes.

Food sources dictate most of my choices of sites to sit and hope to ambush a buck. Even when bucks are on the prowl, the does they are trying to encounter are often on food sources. In early October, however, the acorns and persimmons were dropping crazily and enticed me to try around them, yet they never truly came through on their tacit promise of deer sightings. Many sits offered not a single glimpse of a deer.

The explanation may have been the tremendous bumper crop of saw palmetto berries. At this time of the year, deer droppings typically don't last long at all because of the heat, moisture, and dung beetles, but droppings with saw palmetto berry skins and pits in them seem to be less desirable to dung beetles and more resistant to heat and rain. These droppings were everywhere and proclaimed the preponderance of these fruit in their diet. Hog, coyote, and raccoon scat mirrored that of the deer. The trouble to a hunter, and even more so to a bowhunter, is the absolutely vast acreages of palmetto flats. Game can feed anywhere, and predicting the sites would be impossible. In addition, palmettos thickets in many areas achieve heights higher than a man's head and would completely hide a deer from view.

One day, I sat on acorns, and even though I saw more game than I had for a while, a three-point, a small eight-point, and a turkey, the idea settled on me to try something entirely different. I scouted hard through the midday and even into the afternoon, covering a lot of ground and even clearing some places and setting stands. I had sweated and spread scent far and wide. Already, it was time to be on a stand, but where?

Some places are pleasing to set up in just from their beauty or past memories or the small birds that make them feel busy and alive. One such spot was a tiny, hollow cypress dome in the midst of a very old and rough pasture. I went there in the late afternoon and put Jody in "Stay!" under a cypress and, with a climbing stand, worked skyward inchworm style. The view was pretty. Although there were myrtles and palmetto clumps that could screen deer easily, in places the visibility extended a hundred yards to the north and to the east. The cover was much thicker to the south, but a couple narrow shafts were open between cypress boles. Vision was limited to twenty-five yards to the west and that far only in two narrow places. It was a pretty, peaceful place with almost no understory and walled in with a thick hedge of myrtle. At times, water fills the slight depression the cypress grow from, but when it is dry, like this particular year, rich, green grass grows, and that soft, verdant floor in concert with the cool shadiness and the quiet whispers of wind in the cypress leaves render the head lovely.

The openness of the view at ground level raised the concern about how a deer would react to Jody sitting at the base of the tree. I knew Jody could be counted on to stay as she had when deer were close before, and she had also resisted a squirrel, one of her favorite creatures to chase, on the ground waving its tail within five feet of her. While my head held some doubts whether deer would notice Jody or tolerate her presence on this occasion, I soon learned wildlife often demonstrated no fear of her in "stay." Even though it diverts the reader from the account at hand, let me jump forward a couple years and relate an extreme example: I leaned a ladder stand against maple in the swamp and also attached a chain-on stand next to it. Breanna and I sat there one evening with Jody below us. A six-point, too young to shoot, angled by us at twenty-five yards. This portion of the swamp was quite open, and the buck spotted Jody as she sat beneath our tree. Jody saw the buck as well, and they watched one another. The buck circled north and then east, coming closer but staying at least ten yards distant. As he circled, Jody stayed sitting and followed him only with her head until her neck would allow no further movement. Then she would shuffle her body so she was still sitting in the same place and yet facing the six-point. This was repeated a couple of times as he made the circuit. The wind was from the southwest, and I whispered to Breanna that the buck was about to get a noseful of us and bolt, but he proved me wrong. His curiosity or belief that the smell emanated from the animal in front of him prevailed, and he circled even more until he was six yards from Jody from the southeast. At this point, amazingly, he took a step toward Jody and stretched out his neck, trying to smell her better, I suppose. I was ready to yell, for I was unsure of his intentions and his head was within a couple of feet of our lovable pet, but he did not look the least bit aggressive and, after this sniff, walked off back to the west in no hurry and ambled away. Okay, back to the evening in the hollow cypress head:

A few birds jostled about in the hedge-like fringe. Jody looked cute below me and looked upward to check on me regularly. The sun was more than a half an hour from setting and darkness more than an hour away, but a few clouds banked low in the west, so the sun-rays carried the salmon shade of molten metal and strands of Spanish moss draping down from the cypress limbs and trunks glowed gently of the color. A movement seventy yards to the south attracted my eye in time to see the rear half of a large deer disappear into the myrtles.

Jody and I had entered from the south because the wind was predicted to be from the north but now had fluctuated, issuing from the southeast. The deer had headed west and could encounter our entry trail soon. I rattled loudly. At first nothing seemed to happen, but then the buck, for it was a buck and looked like a good one, strode into an opening making his way toward us! The fringe immediately hid him, but I had Mellifluwood ready because he was close. A sawing sound started and it continued on and on! He was making a rub and, from the sound of it, doing it earnestly and unhurriedly. The screened buck was so close I was reluctant to put the bow down, yet the wind had been so fickle and could change any moment and probably would change before he finished rubbing. Additionally worrying, our approach trail was only twelve yards west from where he sounded to be. Nervously, I managed a couple light clicks of the tines and rehung the antlers. Mellifluwood was barely back in my hands when he appeared inside the head walking west. He was eight yards off, but several small cypress trees interfered with a shot. Jody watched intently and quietly. Two yards from the trail we used, two saplings that were slightly larger and therefore had fewer low branches grew two feet apart. I drew Mellifluwood and aimed midway between the trees. Because of their varying distances from me, the window was about fourteen inches in width. When the buck filled the spot, I released. The arrow flew truly and skewered the buck but, as I hadn't panned with his movement, may possibly have been further back than ideal. The buck leapt into action and ran west, then north, and then east, and it sounded like he fell.

If the wound was a gutshot, I should wait for morning. However, if the shot was good and he was down, it would be better to retrieve him now and worry less about coyotes or spoilage. Perhaps the best course would be to check the trail while the light was still good. I climbed down and praised Jody lavishly for holding still and quiet through the whole encounter, and she greeted me excitedly as though I had been a million miles away for a week rather than right above her for a couple of hours. I guess her perfect behavior through it all gave me the idea to try mixing commands, something we had never practiced and, it turned out, something I never was able to teach her. I said, "Heel and track it." She looked at me and took off on the trail with her usual enthusiasm and quick pace. With a half-yelled whisper of, "No Jody. Come," I called her back. She came and stayed near me as I investigated the trail a short ways. Then the wind carried her a fresh whiff of him, and she ran to him. The buck was right there and jumped up, and they crashed off northward until I could hear no more. My calls to Jody to come were swallowed by the empty-looking twilight. I had just spooked a wounded deer that had gone no distance at all and now might be running out of the county! On top it, and even more worrisome, would I ever find Jody?

I called and whistled and called, and there was Jody greeting me happily. She was totally unabashed about her desertion and the chase. I was too relieved to see her to reprimand her, plus it was my fault, not hers. Removing my belt, I used it as a leash, realizing belatedly I should have done so from the start. Jody tracked the buck four hundred yards, and we quit the trail at a place that would be easy to find in the morning.

I wasn't confidant enough in keeping Jody slow, and I had no tracking harness at the time, so Jody's eagerness to track equated to her pulling forward, and my restraint all focused on her collar and I hated the idea of a prolonged trail with her straining the entire time and gasping for breath, so I called Mack and asked for his and Skylar's help in the morning. Mack agreed willingly even though the next day was to be the first day of a week he had taken off to hunt. I "earlied" it to bed. Luckily, the long day of hunting and scouting and hanging stands without break or food had left me tired down to my bones, and even while my mind whirled with chastisements about not thinking to leash Jody, sleep found me.

I must have slept soundly too, for Mack woke me later in the night. He told me he had banged on the door, came in the trailer, and yelled, and concluded I could not possibly be there. He went to Craig's and they were still up but told him I had gone to bed. This time, he came to my bed and shook me awake. He also explained a storm was coming with more storms predicted to follow and that we should look for the buck now. My voice said, "Let's go," while I looked around groggily and still tried to figure out where I was. Jody was fully alert and looked crestfallen when we left her behind.

I took Mack and Skylar to where the buck had been when I shot and then started for where the arrow had fallen free fifty yards off. Skylar trailed the buck a ways then trailed it backward, then sorted it out and trailed it to the arrow ahead of me. Many theories have been advanced on how dogs (or other animals) determine the direction of the trail, and I must confess I really don't know, but I'm always amazed how quickly most dogs realize the correct direction of travel.

The moon was bright, and the storm actually now seemed to be receding. Skylar led us north-northwest and the path was nearly straight, but once we passed where Jody and I pulled off the track, it curved and meandered more, actually looping completely around at three places. In our flashlight beams, blood confirmed the trail, easily visible even at the steady pace Skylar set. However, the twists, turns, and loops would have rendered trailing without a dog difficult and tedious at best and possibly unsuccessful as the buck traveled about nine hundred yards in a straight line and obviously a much greater distance by the route the buck chose. We came upon a few beds, but they were not fresh, and Skylar's degree of enthusiasm was not heightened upon passing them as it would be where a deer was jumped up ahead of us. Soon, Skylar led us right to the buck. His eight-point rack had twenty-inch main beams, fairly long for our area. He weighed 147 lbs.

The next two accounts demonstrate the resistance of the scent trail to rain. In truth, not only does the scent resist the rain, but it often blossoms in the rain.

Some live oaks not far at all from the Bull Creek swamp edge were dropping heavily early one October. With a predicted east to southeast wind, I set up in the mid-afternoon, only to be blown at by a few deer east of me while the breeze fanned my back. I felt the all-too-common frustration that accompanies trusting the weather service, but in my defense, they do make their guesses sound so factual and unequivocal that it is easy to fall prey to the belief it must be as they say.

A spike came from the east without displaying alarm, and finally, the forecast came true. After a minute, he disappeared into the hairy indigo but emerged at an oak forty yards south of my stand. Shortly, he vanished again to reemerge a bit later under an oak seventy or more yards away and fed there for ten minutes, after which he was aggressively chased off by a large, black boar hog. As soon as the hog was satisfied the young deer was completely driven away, he set to serious acorn eating and continued to do so for a long time. The creek bottom, of course, was heavily vegetated and wooded, but the pasture had been roughly cleared and planted with hairy indigo that had now grown up thickly and was higher than a deer's back. The canopy of the dome shaped live oaks blocked most of the light, so under them the indigo had failed to thrive. Game could only be seen in low spots in the indigo and under the oaks except for occasional glimpses when deer lifted their heads high.

A white ear flashed where the spike first appeared. Eventually, two does fed out following nearly, if not exactly, the spike's route. While searching for bits of the does in the indigo, my binoculars caught a brief image of a buck coming through the swampwoods east of them, heading north. He looked good, and my pulse quickened. Although he was immediately out of sight, the repeatedly elevated heads of the does peering in his direction was assurance enough that he was still nearby. The does reached the forty-yard oak and were feeding.

The likelihood was that the buck would take the same course as the does and spike, and forty yards was a longer shot than I wanted. The wind was now behaving in accordance with the forecast and held pretty much from the south-southeast. Getting down to close the distance wasn't really an option with the does in the clear under the oak certain to see the movement. Antlers in the indigo confirmed the buck was tracing their steps. I grunted with my mouth twice. The buck looked up, strode to the nearest myrtle, and savagely thrashed it with his rack. Two more grunts caused him to abandon the myrtle and march head on toward me. The platform of my stand in the oak was no higher than seven and a half feet, so it was essential to remain motionless. Fifteen yards out, the buck halted, still facing directly toward me, and stared. After a lengthy pause, he turned south toward the does, and I drew Nightshade. His chest was partially hidden by the rank indigo, and either because of poor shooting or deflection from an intervening stem, the striking arrow looked good but further back than perfect. The sound of the hit was normal, but the buck's two bounds to the east and then slow walk with a hunched posture and frequent stops seconded the doubt my eyes first suspected. The arrow may have hit lungs as well. I studied him with the binoculars, wanting to see the exit wound, but the hairy indigo thwarted those efforts. He reached the edge of the swampwoods and stopped there. The does ended up walking nearly under me and searching for acorns under my oak and the two oaks close to it. I feared if they became alarmed, it might spook the buck and froze. When I could glass again, the buck was gone.

Prudence urged waiting until morning to trail the buck, so I was back at camp well before dark. I went to bed early but awoke to the noise of a nocturnal storm and was restless for a while, redebating whether or not I should have left the buck. Now with the rain, there would be no blood trail and game in puddles spoils faster than dry game. First light found me where I last saw the buck, nervously hoping he hadn't moved far from the spot. That was not the case, however. I followed out various possible routes that forked and forked again, working deeper and deeper into the thick woods. It was all guesswork because the rain had washed off any blood, and the puddled earth held no tracks. The woods where the buck went had been lumbered twenty-three years before and then allowed to re-forest. A lot of the trees were young and close together and the understory was thick, viney, and tangled. I could have passed quite close to the buck and been no more the wiser. Discouragement settled in. I was bathed in sweat after only an hour and a half. He had to be nearby.

I decided to go home and get Jody. It would take over a two-and-a-half-hour round trip. The vegetation was still wet with rain from last night, but by the time I returned, it would probably be dry and much of the scent trail would evaporate with it. Would enough remain for Jody to find? On my drive home, the vapor trail from a rocket launched from Cape Kennedy streaked up through the sky. It seemed remarkably incongruous that a phenomenal technological accomplishment should be happening precisely while I was struggling to solve a problem people faced thousands and thousands of years ago.

Even though the vegetation had indeed dried by my return and the rains of the previous night had been heavy and repeated, Jody took up the trail excitedly. She lost it twice but circled back to the last sure whiff. Amazingly to me, she came back by a completely different route and yet found where she lost the trail each time without casting about. In less than ten minutes, Jody led me to the dead buck. He had gone in about eighty yards through and under thick stuff. The spot we found him was not muddied or matted or thrashed, so I believe he probably expired fairly quickly there the night before. The wound also supported this belief because while it did pass through guts, it exited his left shoulder. In retrospect, maybe I could have followed him the night before. The main point is that despite the intervening eighteen hours and several heavy rains that erased all visible sign, Jody could track him with relative ease.

Before continuing with another account of a dog not being inconvenienced by rain, mention should be made of a few other tools the modern handler has for his or her use. From prior episodes, the reader has probably gathered that I don't use GPS units or phones normally. This is just because of how I enjoy doing things and certainly kind of arbitrary considering I do use modern composite arrows and I do fly on jet planes to reach my hunting grounds in Colorado, neither of which would be in keeping with being totally traditional. One of my favorite longbows has a carbon fiber component. Somehow, gadgets for woodsmanship appeal less to me, but I don't discourage or disparage their use. Tracking dogs can be fitted with GPS collars, and the dog's whereabouts can be monitored on a screen or phone with the dog's location overlaid on an aerial photo or map. Such an apparatus would have helped me the time I felt Jody might have been lost or when we found the doe deep in the cypress. Had I known where we were, I could have dragged the doe out that night without much trouble. A few of my friends believe I'm too hardheaded to change and they may be right, but in just a bit the reader will see that I do use a phone when my daughter hunts with me because staying in close touch with her adds a lot to my enjoyment.

The following account, the last of this book, was also Jody's last trail. She had developed cancer, and we were destined to soon lose her. Dogs are such wonderful and devoted companions that it is impossible not to love them wholly. If Jody was an exception, it was only that maybe we loved her even more. Although this book has only chronicled a handful or so of her trails, Jody had tracked and found many, many deer, hogs, and turkey in her career. She was always elated to fetch a snipe or quail and even more so to retrieve a duck, but she was never so proud and happy as when she found a downed deer for us. Breanna and I desperately wanted to get her one more trail while she still had the strength to enjoy it.

Once again, some live oaks were dropping near the edge of Bull Creek. I sat in a group of seven oaks and could see Breanna in a stand in one of five oaks, both of us armed with bows. Between us lay six hundred or more yards of rough but not excessively high pasture. The cattle on our hunting lands fend for themselves year round although the ranch supplies them with molasses and other feed at certain times. They are fairly flighty overall, and many of my stalks on deer, hogs, or turkey have been disrupted by the cattle's response to the sight or smell of a human.

A cow was six yards downwind of Breanna with her head up, looking mystified by the scent. A doe approached at the same time, and then a wasp landed on Breanna's neck and crawled around her shoulder. Breanna didn't want to move for concern about spooking the deer or spooking the cow that would in turn spook the deer. The wasp proceeded to crawl up her throat and the underside of her chin, of course, tickling her unmercifully the whole time! She endured, but then it wormed its way under her shirt, and she feared if it got squeezed at all, it might react by stinging her. In slow motion, she moved her hand to her neck and held her shirt open a bit. Eventually, the wasp climbed on to her hand and she was able to send it off with a gentle fling! Neither the doe nor cow noticed.

The animals did not venture to my group of oaks, but I was kept busy watching her area. Here is a little excerpt from our texts over a couple hours:

> Bre: Surrounded by deer. Other doe is back. Love you.
>
> Me: Cooool!
>
> Bre: Darn, six-point just chased her off. Still two more.
>
> Me: Yowey! You are having the excitement. I'm in suspense for you. Those darn six points!

Bre: Now another deer—he looks big! Maybe a
    buck downwind of doe in heat, so hopefully
    he'll come in!

Me: !!!!!

Bre: He is coming right to her with his nose out!
    Looks like a thick neck! Can't count antlers
    yet. He just chased her but coming to me.

Me: Get him!

Bre: Ahh he's big, but right on her trail! I used
    the bleat, but he wants her!

Me: Hope she comes your way!!!!

Bre: She is running further away :(He's so big!

Me: Maybe in the morning

Bre: Little buck still right next to me

Bre: Other two does coming in.

Me: Golly!!!

Bre: He's so nice! Definitely a shooter

Bre: Another deer right in front!

Me: !!!!

Bre: Another buck! Or the six-point again!

Me: If it is big, go for it!

Bre: Too far and running toward doe in heat

That gives a good idea of the excitement of the hunt and how communicating with Breanna tripled my fun. We resumed our respective stands the next weekend about four o'clock in the afternoon. Just after six o'clock, two gobblers came to the oak thirty yards north of me. I thought I had been watching Breanna's area closely, but she texted me that two deer were near her, one right beneath. Sure enough, my binoculars revealed the does. She texted the one within spitting distance was small. The other one did not look large to her but was definitely mature and long headed. I watched with the glasses while the other doe came near Breanna's stand and suddenly darted northward to the thick woods.

Breanna called and said the doe wasn't exceptionally large and she wouldn't have shot it except for wanting Jody to get a tracking adventure. Because of her course load at college, she could only get back to the cabin and hunt now and then. She felt the doe sprang forward with the sound of the bow quickly enough that the arrow might have punctured the abdomen. I clambered down immediately and spooked the two gobblers that were almost to my tree. In the excitement, I had forgotten all about them!

The edge of the woods was fifty yards from Breanna's tree. We only found blood between two oak trunks where the doe ran, but finding blood on grass is exasperatingly difficult. Finally, a bit more beyond the trunks corroborated the actual trail with Breanna's memory of the doe's departing flight, so I decided to proceed in a line toward the thicker vegetation that should offer easier visualization of blood sign. The tracking we undertook was not to find the deer but rather to gather evidence whether to let Jody start the trail or wait. Upon reaching the thick, I instantly found obvious blood. Almost concurrently, however, I saw the head and ears of a prostrate but alert deer staring at me from fifteen yards. I tried to retrace my tracks, but the moment the doe realized she had been discovered, she sprang up and ducked off under some low brush.

I backed out and consulted with Breanna. The blood sign was good, but the fact that the doe was still capable of fleeing twenty minutes after the shot made us decide to postpone the trail until morning. She may have already fallen, but it wasn't worth taking the chance of pushing her again. We wanted Jody to have a trail with a deer at the end, but we didn't want it so long that it would overtax our staunch friend.

During the night, the patter of rain on our tin roof woke me. It usually is such a comfortable and comforting sound, but this night, it carried the knowledge that the nice blood trail was being washed away, and now we would be entirely dependent upon Jody. No doubt Jody could do it. The concern was a long, stretched-out trail could overtire her.

The same desire not to tire Jody overmuch influenced Breanna and me to forego the chest-protector harness. Jody gets so excited and strains against it so determinedly that much of her energy is wasted. We decided she would like it best to track on her own and check in with us at times when we were unable to equal her pace. It ended up we needed to call her back eight times because the thickness of the growth prevented us from seeing her and slowed our progress more than hers. The doe made it only a hundred yards, and Jody led us straight there. In muddy places, tracks showed the multiple times Jody coursed through the spot, doubling back to us and then returning to the doe again.

Jody was incredibly happy and proud. She walked all around the deer with her head high accepting all the praise we poured on her. The greenery was so dense that a decent photo wasn't possible, so Breanna and I took turns dragging the doe to the more open terrain. Once everything was arranged for good photographs, Jody started acting like it was all "old hat" and had lost some of that exuberance and her perky, excited grin. We drove back to the camp, a contented trio. Breanna's "small" doe that caused panting on my parts of the drag turned out to weigh 109 lbs., a large doe for our area. When we hung the dressed doe in the cooler, Jody followed us in and, as was her custom, sniffed all the aging deer but ended with a prolonged investigation of the one she had tracked. Breanna and I looked at each other and then at Jody and shared a heartfelt smile.

Reader, my hope is that my experiences will have offered you some insights into finding wounded game that you can apply in your hunts and, at the same time, may also have entertained you. Sadly, Jody and Mack are no longer with us in body, but memories tie them inexorably to all my wilderness haunts, and they are with me in spirit whenever I venture into the swampwoods.

ABOUT THE AUTHOR

DR. TIM L. LEWIS HAS written of outdoor pursuits in many sporting magazines for several decades and is the author of *Bows, Swamps, Whitetails*. His bow-hunting addiction dates back nearly six decades. Scholastically, he holds a bachelor's degree in zoology and a doctorate in dental medicine. Watch for his soon to be released *Bows, Swamps, Mountains, and Game*.

CPSIA information can be obtained
at www.ICGtesting.com
Printed in the USA
LVHW022348141120
671501LV00012B/183